THE BIBLE

WHAT THE BIBLE SAYS SERIES

WHAT THE
BIBLE SAYS
ABOUT

THE BIBLE

By

Owen L. Crouch

College Press Publishing Company, Joplin, Missouri

Library of Congress Catalog Card Number: 81-65515
International Standard Book Number: 0-89900-082-7

Scripture quotations, unless otherwise noted, are from the New International Version, New York International Bible Society, 1978.

Topical Index from *Topical Index and Digest of The Bible* edited by Harold E. Monser. Reprinted 1960 by Baker Book House and used by permission.

TO

Larry and Jennie Willis
Tom and Lucy Bottorff
Ken and Pam Keller
Lucille Crouch

Six devoted friends and a dedicated wife
who for three years (1978-1980) have
resisted distractions, reserved time, and
studied together what the Bible says!

Table of Contents

Dedication   v
Preface   ix

Chapter   *Page*

Part I — THE NATURE OF THE BIBLE

One   God Has Spoken   1
Two   The Human and the Divine   7
Three   How the Authors of the New Viewed the
         Sources of the Old   15
Four   What Scripture Say *Because* of What
         Scriptures Say   27
Five   Peter on the Prophets.   45

Part II — WHAT THE NEW TESTAMENT BOOKS SAY ABOUT THEMSELVES

Six   The Synoptic Gospels   65
Seven   The Johannine Writings   91
Eight   The Pauline Epistles   116

Part III — WHAT THE OLD TESTAMENT BOOKS SAY ABOUT THEMSELVES

Nine   The Law   148
Ten   The Prophets   178
Eleven   The Writings   203

Epilogue   222
Appendix I. How We Got the Bible   224
          II. How Did the Books Become
              the Book   229
          III. The Ground of Our Faith   234

    IV. "Men Spoke From God" 243
     V. Grounds on Which We Receive the
         Bible as the Word of God, and
         the Only Rule of Faith and
         Practice 261

A Bibliography on the Inspiration and Authority
  of the Bible 305

Topical Index 315

Index of Scriptures 346

Preface

As a completed product the Bible says nothing about itself. But every book, every author, gives signs that God is speaking in them. If we allow the messages to speak for themselves the Bible books have a great deal to say about themselves. God speaks through people. He speaks in books written by the people He inspires. The divine Spirit speaking in the depths of the human spirit produced the biblical literature. The Bible authors make forthright assertions about God's speaking in them. We have examined the claims and also discovered how the message of each book speaks for itself. The message often speaks louder than any claim of the author.

One should be warned that in one limited volume there's no way to cover all sixty-six books of the Bible. We have been forced to select some books as typical of all. Especially is this true of the Old Testament in which only one sample from each of the broad divisions has been made. Genesis represents the law. Job serves as an example of the poetical books. We have noted a number of the prophets but Jeremiah is the example quoted most frequently.

Part I — The Nature of the Bible

Chapter One

GOD HAS SPOKEN

For all who are committed to the Christian faith, that God has spoken is a simple truism. When, where, how he spoke are questions that find their answers rooted in the Bible. Opinions differ as to the method in which God breathed his message. The understanding of the nature of the authority of the Bible varies with different students. But the element of inspiration and the aspect of authority are a couplet of ideas which are universal among those who profess confidence in the Bible.

Many passages in the Bible affirm inspiration. "All scripture is given by inspiration of God, and is profitable for . . ." (II Tim. 3:16 in KJV). The *New English Bible* reads, "Every inspired scripture has its use for. . . ." In either translation the idea seems to be a clear claim that the Bible is the inspired word of God. The opening verse of the Hebrew letter plainly declares that "God having spoken to the fathers in the prophets . . . has spoken in . . . [one who is] Son. . . ." Is there any statement more positive than that of II Peter 1:21? "For no prophecy ever came by the will of man: but men spake from God, being moved by the Holy Spirit." Similarly I Peter states, "Concerning which salvation the prophets sought and searched diligently, who prophesied of the grace that should come unto you: searching what time or what manner of time the Spirit of Christ which was in them did point unto, when it testified beforehand the sufferings of Christ, and the glories that should follow them" (1:10, 11).

To these New Testament references add the multiplied claims of Old Testament passages in which the authors allege that they are God's mouthpieces. Repeatedly the Pentateuch

1

states, "And the Lord spoke unto Moses, saying, . . ." (Exod. 14:1). And it becomes a mighty chorus swelling up to fill all creation to hear, "The word of the Lord came unto me, saying . . ." (Jer. 1:4). It is safe to say that these prophets of old labored under the conviction that they were the voice of God in the crises of their times. "Thus saith the Lord . . ." was their constant refrain. Furthermore, the New Testament authors shared this conviction about the Old. Matthew 2:15 may be cited as but one sample, ". . . that the word having been spoken by the Lord through the prophet might be fulfilled saying, . . ." The Lord was the primary spokesman; the prophets were his agents, his media.

Both testaments are intertwined by foreshadowing and fulfillment. Both show a consciousness of the Spirit of God in their message. Yet it was years after the time of writing before the books of the Bible were all recognized as canonical and collected into one volume.

The Bible comes to most English-speaking Christians as one volume. From childhood it has about it the halo of inspiration. It is the Holy book, sacred, infallible, authoritative. Hallowed memories of childhood, family, favorite Bible class and teacher, the presence of beloved parson at baptisms, weddings, funerals—all these emotional experiences feed the roots of belief about the Bible. As life matures and godless detractors with negative views become a part of experience the believer reacts defensively. The unity amid diversity, the universal appeal feeding the universal hungers of humanity, the undying, indestructible persistence of the Bible in the face of continuing opposition are evidences that fortify the believing mind of the presence of God in this remarkable book. It surely originates in the mind of God. Yet, since the Bible is one volume we tend to forget that it did not appear as a once-for-all finished product. It was not written by the finger of God in celestial isolation. On the contrary, the harsh human realities of history are its seedbed. It was written by men to meet men's needs in the midst of muddles made by men. Certainly God's presence in the superintending of the writing is plainly present. Yet the Bible itself says that God spoke "in the prophets" and in one who is "Son." That is to say, God spoke *in* human beings who lived in particular places and at specific times in history.

For one who believes that the Bible reports history, at least a hard core of history, it is difficult to deny that God spoke in and through Moses. And the revelation was author- itative at the moment in which God spoke. The integrity of the speech of God did not have to wait on some council's vote. The same is true of all the Old Testament prophets. During Judah's downskid into political and economic limbo in the 6th century B.C. the word of God came to Jeremiah. The revelation in the prophet was not delayed until some scholars declared Jeremiah's prophecies a part of the "canon." The inspiration is a fact independent of the councils and decisions of men.

That God's word has come in the Bible seems safe to assume in view of the claims of the individual authors. The assumption rises to certainty when we recall the history of the book as a book plus its uplifting effect on human history and civilized cultures.

God spoke through the preaching of the prophets as well as through the writing of the prophets. The opening declar- ation of Hebrews sets up a sharp contrast between the Old and New revelations. First, as to method: a variety of parts, ways and circumstances. Second, as to time: of "old time" versus "the last of these days." Third, as to agents: "in the prophets" contrasted to "in Son." Several standard English versions translate the phrase about the agents "by the prophets" and "by [his, a, the] Son." The particular term that imparts the author's idea to both "prophets" and "Son" is not *by* but *in*. This is significant! God spoke His message in persons, in their feelings, their thoughts, their actions, their motives, their personal relationships, their victories, their defeats, their joys, their sorrows, their anger and prejudices, their gentle forbearance and calm serenity. God spoke in the man Isaiah including his speech. And insofar as he wrote anything God spoke in whatever Isaiah wrote. But it ought not be overlooked that God burned in the heart of the man first before the prophet delivered the message, usually spoken to a living audience.

The prophet Amos was one of "the shepherds of Tekoa" who delivered a true message from the Lord. Repeatedly the book of Amos declares, "This is what the Lord says . . ." (1:3, 6, 9, 15; 2:1, 4, 6, etc.). He was sensitive to the fact that God was using him to deliver a divine message of warning and promise to eighth-century Israel. But in the very opening words of the book the text avows, "The words of Amos, . . . what he *saw* concerning Israel. . . ." True, God spoke *in* Amos what "he *saw* concerning Israel. . . ." He was a herdsman who saw some distorted ways that needed correcting in the nation's life. In the high view which Amos had of the moral character of God the Spirit found a ready channel in whom to speak judgment. God spoke in the thought, feelings, actions and reactions of the prophet when he went to the wool markets at Bethel. Widows dispossessed, orphans' cries, greed of court and king, priest and people was more than a pure spirit could stand. The heat and indignation of this simple-hearted herdsman gave

4

God a ready instrument for voicing judgment on that state of affairs. Amos' sermons were really outbursts of righteous wrath when confronting the selfish immoralities of a decadent, covenant-breaking people. With a flaming message in his heart Amos spoke to a living generation whose sin demanded rebuke; yet whose impending destruction needed tempering with a promise for the future.

God spoke in the man Amos! The book of Amos is the written expression of that speaking. It records what God said in the environment and circumstances in which the prophet lived.

Should one need further confirmation that God spoke in persons as well as through a written message he need only note that "God having spoken . . . spoke to us in [one who is] Son" (Heb. 1:1). Except when Jesus stooped to write in the sand we have no record that he wrote anything. God spoke in the Son. That was the necessity of the Incarnation! God speaks to persons in persons. "In the beginning was the Word . . . and the Word became flesh" (John 1:1, 14). If one is to communicate to a human he must talk in human terms. God speaks to man in person. The Hebrew letter describes the word of God as "living and active, sharper than any two-edged sword." The author reveals how utterly perceptive and penetrating this word is: "It penetrates even to dividing soul and spirit, joints and marrow; it judges the thoughts and attitudes of the heart; there is not a creature unmanifest before it, but all things are naked and have been laid bare before the eyes of him to whom for us [is] the accounting" (Heb. 4:12, 13).

The fact that God speaks through persons in no way lessens the fact that he speaks through the written message. The written word comes as a result of the activity of God in

5

the living person. The prophet speaks; those who hear listen; they repeat what they hear; they, or a friend, or the prophet himself records in writing that which has been spoken. Thus, within the limitations of human language we have an abiding record of what God revealed through the prophet.

The written word is a record, a permanent memorandum documenting precisely what God revealed through His spokesmen. These persons in their situation will never be exactly repeated even as no two snowflakes are absolutely alike. But snowflakes have enough in common that each can be recognized as snow. So history does repeat itself and each person has enough in common with all persons so that he can identify in the crises of life. The situation that the prophet faced is similar to the situation I face. There are pointed parallels between his times and my times. What God said then in him, God is now prepared to say to me in my life. When I read the written word I sense from my own feelings in my situation just what the prophet or apostle faced. I can with empathy identify with the prophet and hear the message of God to him. That becomes God's message to me today. The written record is the medium by which God's word in the prophet comes to be God's word to me.

The written word is inspired, God-breathed, because the prophet in whom he first spoke was moved by the "breath of God." But to remain living the word must not be left on the printed page. It must live in a living heart. As it lived in a living person's heart before it was written it must live in a living person's heart after it has been written down. The written word is the means of transferring it from the ancient prophet's heart to the modern reader's (or listener's) heart. Such is the place of the written word of God, inspired, authoritative, sufficient for "instruction in righteousness."

Chapter Two

THE HUMAN AND THE DIVINE

A fact of very practical significance about the Bible is its balance between its divine source in God and its human origins in man. Its inspiration by God would hardly be denied by any Christian believer at any level of scholarship. Men may differ, and do, on what comprises inspiration and the degree of authority that adheres to the Bible. Yet there is general consensus that the Spirit of God certainly was in some sense or other involved in the production of the biblical literature. It manifestly has the breath of God in it. How it could ever have been written, assembled and survived without a superintending providence would be a harder problem for faith than to credit God with its shaping.

But after giving full recognition to its divine composition the human situations that drew forth the assorted biblical books are of equal import. He who would read the Bible aright must transport himself into the skin of the author, walk in his shoes, absorb his feelings and think his thoughts in terms of his culture. No individual book within the Bible came into existence by magical art. Nor was any part of the divine library artificially created suspended halfway between earth and heaven. Though the book be supernatural in its ultimate origin the flesh and blood, on-this-earth method of human production is quite natural and normal. Not even divine initiative generated any portion of the Bible apart from a human instrument. And included is not just a human being as the penman of God's writing but also included is the human tragedy, crisis, problem or need to which the human author speaks. He who reads the exact words of the Bible yet ignores the transient, earthy background will never get the eternal divine message. The Bible was not written by the finger of God in the ivory palaces of a heaven disentangled or unrelated to mortal dilemmas. Each book of the Bible was written by some human being for some human being about some human being in his needs. As the centuries unrolled through a period of a millennium and a half it would be quite inevitable that later books would draw on, refer to, build on, explain and interpret some of the experiences recorded in the earlier books. So, in that sense the books of the Bible are like other books which depend on previous writings. The fact that God's book is inspired in no way eliminates man's normal needs for research, learning, investigating. This fact that men, as they produced their own part of the sacred scriptures, researched other documents ought offer no surprise. We note that most of the literature they referred to or quoted was itself hammered out under the "breathing of God." That is, it too was inspired!

This principle of using sources is especially notable in the writing prophets. Isaiah and Micah were both eighth-century spokesmen who lived through the troubled days when the Assyrian juggernaut was gaining its deadly foothold in the affairs of the southern kingdom, Judah. Culturally these two prophets were poles apart socially. Isaiah was of noble blood, possibly even kin to the king. Micah was of the common people. He lived in the small rural village of Moresheth a few miles west of the capital. It was a town of small farmers whose parcels of land were gradually being gobbled up by greedy absentee landlords. Social inequalities between the rich who were getting richer and the poor who were getting poorer was aggravated by increasing corruption in high places. Violent crime also was stretching its savage barbarism out from city to countryside. The cry of the suffering peasant found a voice in the rebukes of Micah, a man close to the soil.

By contrast Isaiah was literally a prince among prophets, whose royal blood and cultured intellect felt comfortable in the refinements of the city. He had access to the ear of king, noble and priest. He was privy to the hardened hearts of many of those greedy absentee landlords whose grasping hands had foreclosed on the struggling farmers of Moresheth. He faced daily the warped evils of organized crime that reached even into the sacred temple to find cover and blessing for its brute force. He too felt the rising surge within of righteous anger at the social imbalances of the age.

The message of judgment was as much a part of Isaiah's word to a faithless court, as Micah's was to a countryside of wondering doubt. Their's was a "word of the Lord" straight from the covenant God of Israel. Yet from a literary, human point of view they may have made use of one another's works as guided by the Spirit. This is particularly true of their words of hope and promise. Only a few variations exist between Micah 4:1-5 and Isaiah 2:1-5. And these variations find adequate explanation in the differing personalities and circumstances of the two men. They both faced the same sorry national predicament, they both based their appeal on the same covenant, they both pointed to the same coming judgment, and they both looked toward the same hope founded on the same promise of God. Thus each could say,

> In the last days the mountain of the Lord's temple will be established as chief among the mountains; it will be raised among the hills, and all nations will stream into it.
>
> Many peoples will come and say, "Come let us go up to the mountain of the Lord, to the house of the God of Jacob. He will teach us his ways, so that we may walk in his paths." The law will go out of Zion, the word of the Lord from Jerusalem. He will judge between nations and will beat their

swords into plowshares and their spears into pruning hooks. Nations will not take up sword against nations, nor will they train for war any more.

Nowhere has the longing and hope of mankind been expressed in a more classic form. But the substance and meaning of this stirring passage is not our present concern so much as the fact of the literary relationship between the two prophets. Micah and Isaiah were contemporaries. It is not unreasonable to believe that they met and talked together to encourage and exchange views. On the other hand, that is not a necessary conclusion. They may have only heard of the ministry of one another and sought to hear or read some prophetic utterance of the other. Or they may have drawn on older literature of prophetic proclamation. But the chief point of our concern here is that God's inspiration of each of these eighth century prophets did not prevent their occasional use of other sources. Whether they made direct quotations from the other or from older prophets who preceded them or simply just borrowed ideas, vocabulary and style, they did use sources.

Paul in preaching to intellectual pagans on Mars Hill, referred to "one of your poets." As he was pressing home the real immanence of God as He dwells in human beings the apostle quoted verbatim the Greek poet Aratus of Soli in Cilicia, "We are his offspring." It would seem that if the biblical author sought to teach a truth by citing a heathen gentile it surely is to be expected that biblical writers would draw upon and quote other biblical writers.

Aratus of Soli in Cilicia is quite probably not the only heathen root that the inspired biblical writers tapped when they sought verbal vehicles in which to transport divine ideas. The book of Jashar finds an honored place on the pages of the Bible in at least two poetic passages. It is not certain who this Jashar was or if Jashar was a person. David, the "sweet singer of Israel" was obviously influenced by this book of Jashar. At the time of the tragic death of Saul and Jonathan the young David seized on the imaginative words and style of Jashar to sing his funeral elegy (II Sam. 1:17ff.). A statement from the book of Jashar appears in the song of Joshua when the men of Israel fought the Amorites pursuing them through the valley of Aijalon on that long day when the sun stood "still over Gibeon." At least we know that either Joshua influenced Jashar or Jashar furnished literary food for Joshua. It is one more instance that reveals that divine inspiration did not prohibit inspired writers from using human sources.

Under the influence of God's Spirit old material became new—new in adaptation to different problems for a later generation. Even more than direct quotations from earlier scribes are the innumerable borrowings of ideas, figures of speech, stylistic devices and vocabulary. No doubt most such use of material was not plagiarizing but an honest subconscious absorption. As a sponge soaks up the water in which it is submerged, so the sensitive spirits of prophetic souls engorged the words, ideas, style, figures, beliefs and notions of prophetic literature on which their minds fed from childhood. As it flowed through the streams of their own souls it became colored by their own personalities and the crises of their own times.

A masterful example of an impelling impact of one prophet's work on another's is that of Hosea on Jeremiah. When God first called Jeremiah to his service the prophet objected on grounds of his youthfulness. He protested, "Look, Lord, I don't know how to speak. I'm only a boy!" The late teens

(Jeremiah was probably 19 at the time) is hardly the age when sage wisdom is at its highest in a human being. Besides, the social, economic, political and moral conditions of the nation were like a threatening dark cloud before a violent storm. Even a mature man would shrink from single-handedly standing in the breach to stem the onrushing flood. God bolstered the young man's boyish insecurity by the promise, "I will be with you." Then from a memory indelibly carved the prophet recorded, "The Lord reached out his hand and touched my mouth and said to me, 'Now, I have put my words in your mouth . . .'" (1:8, 9). This is a clear-cut promise that, in spite of his inexperience, Jeremiah need not fear for a message pertinent to the crisis. God would surely supply the manifesto of judgment.

Without question God furnished much of his message by what may be termed direct insight. Perilous circumstances of a given moment demanding immediate word or decision often confronted the prophet. In Jeremiah 7:1, 4 we may read, "The word that came to Jeremiah from Yahweh: 'Stand in the gate of Yahweh's house and there proclaim this word . . . Do not put your trust in that lie: "This is Yahweh's temple, Yahweh's temple, Yahweh's temple!"'" But it was Jeremiah's sad task to point out that it was the low moral level of the people that occasioned the coming storm of judgment. Political events, natural calamities, tragedies of war, particular personalities — these and other factors shape the forms in which any given messenger delivers his word from God. But another factor involves the words, phrases, ideas of earlier men of God.

In Jeremiah 4:3 the prophet says, "Plow up your un-plowed ground! Do not sow among thorns. . . ." This is a vivid concrete image of land that has lain fallow so long that it is like solid rock. In order for such soil to produce a fruitful crop it must be broken up by the plow and harrowed down until the seed will take root. On this image the prophet was appealing to the people to break up their callous hearts, to prepare themselves inwardly for adjustment to a new more godly lifestyle. This was spoken to Judah, the southern kingdom, sometime after 627 B.C. when Jeremiah was called to his public ministry. But more than a century previous Hosea had said, "Sow for yourselves righteousness, reap the fruit of unfailing love, and plow up your unplowed ground; for it is time to seek the Lord." So we see appearing in Jeremiah the very same words expressing the same idea that Hosea had used. It is quite possible that Jeremiah was directly quoting Hosea. Certainly inspiration does not overrule quoting. In fact God's Spirit actually might even remind one where and what to quote. However, it is equally possible that such ideas and forms of expression became a part of the subconscious thought of the younger prophet. One becomes what he reads, what he memorizes, thinks on and meditates. Without question Jeremiah had been reared on the literature of Israel so far as reading habits were concerned. He was of a godly, priestly family. He had access to all the hallowed traditions of God's people. It goes without controversy that he absorbed all these traditions and literature which stretched far behind even to the pen of Moses.

One of the most lucid pictures of the utter corruption of Jeremiah's times is that of the wayward wife who has adulterated her marriage by going "whoring" with other men. This is the image painted by Jeremiah in scarlet colors aglow with coarse, repugnant details. In chapter three Jeremiah portrays Israel as an adulterous wife. "Yet you, who have whored with hosts of lovers—you would return to me? . . . You've polluted the land with your whorish depravity."

13

And a number of times he pursues this analogy. Yet it was the personal tragedy and consequent writings of Hosea that gave the earlier classic form to this image of Israel as a faithless wife. "Their mother has been unfaithful and has conceived them in disgrace. She said, 'I will go after my lovers, who give me my food and my water, my wool and my linen, my oil and my drink'" (Hosea 2:5). Hosea's graphic descriptions of wanton depravity which tarnished the affluent northern kingdom of Israel furnished Jeremiah his vocabulary and imagery for sketching dying Judah's death rattle. And what is to our point here is that this dependency of one biblical writer on another reveals much about the scriptures in the unfolding story of God's redemption for man.

In this brief chapter we have but glanced at the tip of the iceberg. God breathed on all the Bible scribes from Moses the lawgiver to John the revelator. Remove from John his quotes and allusions to previous books in the sacred volume and there would be no book of Revelation as we know it. Just to quote the quotes from scriptures, especially Old Testament prophets, would extend this chapter beyond the point of reason. But by way of example read Revelation 4:1-3. In that brief passage are at least six references drawn from Old Testament writings. They are Ezekiel 1:1, 26, 28; Daniel 7:9; Isaiah 6:1; and I Kings 22:19. And the remainder of the Revelation is sprinkled throughout with just such a deluge of Old Testament ideas and quotes.

The writers of the scriptures did at times use human sources as well as inspired writings in producing their books. Furthermore, it seems equally true that they were borne along by the Holy Spirit of God as they turned to these other writers as a fountainhead for ideas and vocabulary that could express what burned in their own hearts.

14

Chapter Three

HOW THE AUTHORS OF THE NEW VIEWED
THE SOURCES IN THE OLD

In childhood the Bible comes as a single volume with the aura of inspiration attached. That it represented two separate bodies of literature, Old and New Testaments, was part of early education about the book. Still later that God's book had a variety of human authors (about 40 in number), that it spanned fifteen centuries in the writing, and that the human writers were not only scattered over various geographical locations but were not conscious that others were writing— these facts became part of expanding consciousness. But ripe maturity arrived with the discovery that if one would read THE Bible he must become involved with three languages quite foreign to childhood lispings. And not only foreign tongues but the knotty problems attendant on translations from any language into another.

On first thought this enlarged body of information about the Bible looks forbidding, mountainous, even frightening. What can be done with limited capacity, restricted time, and a very circumscribed educational background? Has not God placed his inspired word beyond me? Even intuitive knowledge about God frames "No" for an answer. The very fact that forty writers, not one, were involved in writing suggests that God wants to use every possible kind of person to reach as many kinds of people. That its writing covered 1500 years intimates that He would not limit his revelation to one era of history. The writing of the literature of the Bible cropped up from Ninevah on the Tigris to Rome on the Tiber. This fact recommends the universality of the message from God. It never was intended to be confined to one nation, culture or people. The languages, Hebrew, Aramaic,

15

and Greek, were not foreign to the first hearers of the initial word spoken by prophet or apostle. The language in which God spoke at any point in history was the language of the common man, the everyday speech of the people in the market place. It was not the stilted parlance of scholar, schoolroom, temple or priest. It was the vernacular of field and farm, of trade and commerce. Whenever reduced to speech or writing it was the little man to whom God addressed his revelation.

And it is well to remember that God still wants his written word to be reproduced in the language and thought forms of common people. It does not lessen respect or reverence for the Bible to hear it read in the speech which one uses with a familiar friend. For God to communicate with us he must speak to us in the vocabulary of the kitchen, the barracks, the grocery store and the repair shop. God speaks from his heaven but he addresses people who live on this earth. For this reason it is good to bring the written word of God down from its starched thee's and thou's and its artificial -eth's to the warmhearted you and the perfectly human and modern verb endings for come and go rather than cometh and goeth. The multiplicity of modern translations may seem at times to be confusing. But the intent is constructive and good. If God wants to communicate to common people he must do it in common language. This is one of the meanings of the speaking in a variety of languages on the first Pentecost after the resurrection. God wanted the various peoples present to hear the message in the language of their nativity. Men always grasp ideas easier in the language of their childhood.

This places on the modern Bible reader a responsibility for honesty. Translation out of one culture into another has built-in problems. And we refer not only to language but the broader aspects of the culture. The climate and contour of a land in which a biblical author lived his life and gave his message leave their imprint on his written history, prophecy, epistle or gospel. Institutions and customs in family, government, religion affect the personal development of every Bible author as he grows up within their determining influences. If one really wants to hear what God says in his written word he must be willing to remove the differences between himself and the life-style and thought patterns of the ancient author. If one would be completely honest there is no escape from this responsibility.

One important factor of the biblical authors' background is their view and use of biblical writings other than their own. The passage in II Timothy 3:15, 16 uses two words that throw light on the author's view of the scriptures of the Old Testament, ". . . that from childhood you knew the *sacred* writings. . . ." The word translated "sacred" is *hieron* (ἱερόν). It may refer to places, things or people who because of their outward relationship to God are held in reverence. At the time of the penning of II Timothy the various pieces of literature comprising the New Testament were yet in the process of being circulated. There was not yet a single volume called "New Testament." It is possible that the Timothy passage is not limited to our Old Testament scriptures. But there is no doubt but that the apostle at least includes our Old Testament books. So these writings were looked on as "sacred" by the author of II Timothy. They were writings that had a special relationship to God. They were as sacred as the temple. As a matter of fact the same Greek term "sacred" is often translated "temple."

In what relationship these "sacred writings" were connected to God is spelled out in another word, this time in

17

verse 16. ". . . Every scripture [is] inspired of God and [is] profitable. . . ." The word translated "inspired" is more distinctively translated "God-breathed." The breath of God saturated these scriptures. The Spirit (breath) of God drenched the spirit of the Old Testament authors. Hence the Spirit of God sparked the writings of these ancient prophets.

That the Old Testament literature is "sacred" and that it is "inspired" is set forth with restrained dignity in II Timothy 3:15, 16. No anxiety of partisan dogma, no creedal coercion taints Paul's exhortation to Timothy to "abide in those things which you learned and in which you were established. . . ." The "sacred" writings are "God-breathed" and "profitable for teaching, for reproof, for correcting error, for discipline in righteousness, that the man of God may be complete, equipped for every good work." The scriptures are not an end in themselves. They are an equipping tool for the man of God. It is enough to know that the breath of God superintended them. To dogmatize and creedalize about them is divisive, sectarian, and contrary to the spirit (breath) of God. The Old Testament writings should be left right where the apostle set them, "God-breathed."

A variation from the apostle's "sacred writings" in II Timothy is his similar, though not identical, expression in Romans 1:2, ". . . which he promised beforehand through his prophets in the holy scriptures." Here the word "holy" is *hagia* (ἅγια) rather than *hieron*. The root idea of *hagia* is that of separation, dedication, consecration to a pure purpose associated with divine purity. It even came to apply to God himself as pure, majestic, glorious. So it came that things or people which were entitled to reverence as being sacred to God were termed "holy." If *hieron* was sacred

18

because of its external relationship to God, *hagia* was holy because it held an inward quality kin to divine sanctity. Thus in Romans 1:2 the Old Testament writings are appropriately designated "holy scriptures." In this Romans passage Paul is speaking of the gospel of God "which was announced beforehand through his prophets." Both gospel and prophets were separated to God and his calling for them. They were "set apart," "dedicated," "sanctified." It is fitting that their writings about God's purposes and plan are styled as "holy."

These two passages (II Timothy and Romans) set the tone and furnish a standard of measurement by which the books of the Old Testament may be gauged. One can sense the reverential awe in which the people who penned the New Testament literature held the Old. Usually the words "holy" or "sacred" are not specifically employed. In fact only these two times are these adjectives actually put into service in connection with the scriptures. But that God is the ultimate source and that the writings were held in exalted veneration is plain enough. For example in Romans 3:4 the apostle Paul, with deep feeling quotes from the 51st Psalm to sustain his statement that "God is to be true but every man a liar." He quotes, "That you may be justified in your words and that you might prevail when you judge." Paul was perfectly aware that the Psalm sprang from the penitent heart of David after Nathan, the prophet, had confronted the adulterous king with his sin. The words were David's; the idea is God's! But the manner in which Paul echoed David shows that the apostle looked upon God as the real source.

Or turn to Hebrews 9:7, 8 in which the author says, ". . . the Holy Spirit this signifying, that the way into the holy place has not yet been made manifest, while the first tent is yet standing. . . ." In the early portion of chapter 9 the author has depicted the furniture of the first room in the tabernacle as Moses arranged it in the wilderness. Then he described how the priests "go in continually into the first tabernacle [the Holy Place]." But that "into the second [the Holy of Holies] the high priest alone, once in the year, not without blood. . . ." The meaning of all this, the tabernacle, its furnishings, the serving priests and high priests, according to the author of Hebrews, is a message from God's Holy Spirit. He is signifying "that the way into the holy place has not yet been made manifest." In other words the pattern of the Old Testament tabernacle worship finds its source, meaning and divine authority from the Holy Spirit. The description in the Pentateuch of priestly worship has God for its wellspring and authority. This description is found in the "sacred" and "holy" scriptures, a word from the "Holy Spirit." At least so says the author of the Hebrew letter.

New Testament authors use various devices to introduce their supporting quotations from the Old. Often they refer explicitly by name to the Old Testament source. When Matthew saw in Herod's slaughter of the babes of Bethlehem a fulfillment of the sorrowful weeping of the mothers as they watched their sons being led off into Babylon he said, "Then was fulfilled that which was spoken through Jeremiah the prophet, saying, . . ." (2:17). Then there are those instances in which both the direct source of their message and indirect agent are identified with no name being specified. ". . . All this came to pass, that it might be fulfilled which was spoken by the Lord through the prophet, saying, 'Behold the virgin shall be with child . . .'" (Matt. 1:22f.). The Lord is the direct agent, the prophet the indirect through whom the word originally came. Besides this, one of the most frequent methods adopted for introducing a New Testament quote of an Old Testament passage is the bare, unadorned "it is written." This is a favorite among New Testament authors. Just to mention one example when Paul decries "the wisdom of this world" as being "foolishness with God" he sustains his point by proposing a passage from Job 5:13, "For it is written, 'He that takes the wise in their craftiness.'" The apostle fortifies his idea by adding from Psalm 94:11, ". . . And again, 'The Lord knows the reasonings of the wise, that they are vain'" (I Cor. 3:19, 20). There should be no doubt that Paul looked upon both these quotations as being God's words. In verse 19 the proposition he is advancing is that "the wisdom of this world is foolishness with God." His quotes from Job and the Psalm are no buttress to his point if they are not examples of God's revelation in Old Testament history.

The epistle to the Hebrews affords a distinctive touch in its method of ushering in Old Testament passages. In keeping with what we have already observed when the word, "he says," (l5egei) appears it is normally wedded to the prophet or to the "scripture." Paul uses "it stands written" or "just as it stands written" 16 times in the book of Romans alone. But when it comes to Hebrews the quotations are anonymous. No mention of the human author is made anywhere. God is registered as the real reporter. At the very outset in Hebrews 1:5-13 the author introduces his quote from Psalm 2:7 with the rhetorical question, "Unto which of the angels said he at any time . . .?" Who is the "he" to whom the Hebrew writer refers? That he alludes to God is made clear by the context. Indeed, a number of later English translations insert the word "God." However, it ought not be overlooked that neither the name of the Psalmist nor

21

"God" is specifically designated in the epistle. By ignoring the human instrument through whom God brought his message in the older covenant the author of the Hebrew letter would seem to be headlining the fact of the *divine* source.

This reverent regard for the celestial source of the Old Testament passages displays itself more emphatically when the words quoted are delivered by the prophet in his own person as his own words. In Genesis 2:2 the word reads, "God blessed the seventh day . . . because in it he rested from all his work. . . ." It seems quite clear that the author of the Genesis account is *himself* telling his readers what God did upon the completion of his creating work. "He rested from all his work." But when the author of the Hebrew letter quotes this Genesis narrative he ascribes the quote to God. "For he has said somewhere of the seventh on this wise, And God rested on the seventh day from all his works." Again, the context makes plain that the "he" of "For he has said . . ." refers in Hebrews to God although in Genesis it was the mortal man who actually authored the words.

An even more striking example is that of Isaiah 8:18. In this citation the prophet is quite conspicuously pointing to himself and his children as "signs" given of God. "Behold, I and the children whom the Lord has given me are for signs and for wonders in Israel from the Lord of hosts. . . ." In the midst of the threatening flood of Assyrian intrusion into the little land of God's people the princely prophet, Isaiah, was attempting to arouse both king and people to resist an ungodly compromise. Damascus of Syria and Samaria of Israel, the northern kingdom, had joined together against Judah to force her into their war against Assyria. King Ahaz of Judah was considering, as a means of resisting their menacing advances, inviting the massive armed forces of Assyria to be his ally. Isaiah saw such a move as fatal to the future of God's people not to mention a faithless fear on the part of the king. Should not trust in God's power offer more real strength than the marching might of mere man's sword? At least so thought the prophet and so advised he the king.

And thus it was that even within the framework of his family relationships Isaiah's message became prophetic. To enforce his views upon king Ahaz the prophet named his recently born son Mahershalalhashbaz meaning, "spoil speeds, prey hastens." The name of the son would be a daily reminder on the streets of Jerusalem that "the riches of Damascus and the spoil of Samaria shall be carried away" (Isa. 8:3, 4).

Furthermore, besides this second son an earlier had been labelled Shearjashub which means "a remnant shall return" (7:3). This, of course, indicated that the prophet saw beyond the present tragic times to the future when a righteous remnant would be set free from its bondage in Babylon not to say its release from the shackles of sin. So it would seem quite clear to any reader of the Bible that Isaiah 8:18 was the words of the man Isaiah as the instrument of God's revelation to Ahaz and that eighth century B.C. audience. Nevertheless, when the author of the Hebrew letter echoes Isaiah's words about his two sons he cites the prophetic passage as though they were Christ's word. And further- more Christ's words referring really to the brotherly sonship of Jesus and Christian believers. Hebrews 2:11-13 is show- ing that both Christ and Christian believers are "children" who share a common father. Having already quoted the 22nd Psalm to fortify his point the author advances to the Isaiah passage when he says "And again, Behold I and the children whom God has given me." How could anything be more pointedly insistent that the real source of Isaiah's words was divine?

Esteem, respect, reverence are mild terms when it comes to the New Testament authors' ideas about Old Testament scriptures. They saw in these writings not only that which was "sacred" and "holy" but the veritable words of God himself. In fact they were more than just the "words of God." They looked beyond the descriptive words of the Old Testament situations. There lay buried in these old circumstances a meaning and message that could only find genuine fulfillment in the ministry and message of the Christ himself. The significance of a foundation is seen only in the finished building. The root gets meaning from the fruit.

Thus far in this chapter we have observed how the New Testament authors viewed the literary sources of the Old. They cited the human penmen but reverenced them as channels for divine ideas. God was the ultimate source. But having found the voice of God in the Old they did not think of the Old merely as a message for the past. A necessary effect of God's having spoken in the Old is its aftereffect for present needs. The word of God *to* the old was living in the sense that it was the word of God *for* the present, that is, for the need of New Testament times.

God is spoken of in the Bible as "the living God." God is not stick or stone or house, temple or altar. He is Spirit; living Spirit! He cannot be imprisoned in a place, carved into marble, whittled out of wood, nor can he be limited to the confines of a written dogma. Though God created the world and the universe and is "in" it in that he energizes, empowers, directs and sustains it, he is never identified with it. He is transcendent! Above, outside, he asserts himself and his life in and on the world and its history, including

24

man. The Creator is not the prisoner of his creation. He is the "living God" who is involved in his creation. He gives moral guidance, directs to purposeful goals, exerts spiritual pressures, and by being personally present in the *events* in history reveals his moral and spiritual character. At no time nor in any event is he absent from a "living" engagement.

So God revealed his "livingness" in the *events* of the Old Testament times. These events stand recorded in the Old Testament literature. But nowhere do the scribes of the Old show any expectation that there would be a *written* New Testament. In fact, while all display a consciousness that God's Spirit impels their own message and a number of them refer to earlier authors as spokesmen for God, they themselves weren't even aware that their words were destined to be part of a single volume canonized Old Testament. Therefore it is no surprise that they don't anticipate, predict or think of a body of literature to be acclaimed as New Testament. God would always be the "living God" who would act in the critical events of the new era toward which their times, crises and messages pointed. So they, the Old Testament prophets, scribes of God's word, wrote in the indelible ink of events, whose paper was history and whose pen was the sharpened point of their own personal sufferings. Their message, spoken and written, was *to* their generation as well as *for* later times.

In these later times the living God spoke, as always, in the incidents of the later times and in the people of such times. In the lives of men God was acting out on the plane of their experiences certain objective truth that matched life experiences of Old Testament people. Event matched event like an engraving matches the die and foot mates with footprint.

Furthermore, it is worthy of note that it is not the New Testament *written* word that shadows forth the Old Testament *written* account. It is rather the event recorded by the New that achieves the sketched outline of the earlier person or incident. The writer of the New Testament in a brilliant flash of insight caught the inspired connection between the event before his eyes and the recorded affair of the Old. Thus it is that Matthew 11:10 registers the words of Jesus as he quotes from the Old Testament. Jesus saw in the ministry of John the Baptist and the events surrounding his message a bringing to fulfillment the Old Testament words of Malachi 3:1. Yet it was more than just matching the words of an old prophet. The words of the prophet reflected not only a custom current in Eastern diplomacy of sending a herald before a coming king but they also enunciated an even older fact of divine revelation. Exodus 23:20 testifies "I am sending an angel [messenger] ahead of you along the way and to bring you to the place I have prepared." The custom of announcing an approaching potentate was rooted in divine practice. The New Testament event of John the Baptist matched the *words* and *practice* of Old Testament experience, both secular and sacred. It was the genius of the New Testament author to see in his event the significance of the Old Testament event. God, who saw the end from the beginning and the meanings of both "breathed" into the writers of each event. Thus the breath of God safeguarded the divine message as reported by both human authors.

We have observed that the New Testament writers looked on the Old Testament writings as "sacred" and "holy." And they did so because the older chroniclers publicized and described events that were sacred and holy. For it was God himself in those events that made them sacred and holy.

Chapter Four

WHAT SCRIPTURES SAY *BECAUSE* OF WHAT SCRIPTURES SAY

What the scriptures say about the scriptures is one question. But what some scriptures say *because* of what other scriptures say is equally important. Such a subject can unlock somber secrets imprisoned from a casual observer. Such an investigation will disclose not only what God reveals but something of the method of his revelations to men. Ancient scriptures were inspired of God. When later scriptures become saturated with ideas, allusions and words from the earlier scriptures then the mind is arrested by the importance of what is said in both. That also underscores the fact that God spoke through some men because he had already spoken through others. Later servants were given maximum revelations because earlier prophets were given less complete visions of truth. A full painting fills out the pencilled sketch but a sketch furnishes the frame for the full portrait. A sponge dropped into water becomes soaked with the substance in which it is submerged. And what water is to the sponge so earlier Bible writers were to later. The writers of the new covenant soaked their minds, hearts and souls in the scriptures of the first. Ideas, vocabulary and even style of the old appear in the writings of the new. Besides, all the authors, old and new, were penetrated, permeated and pervaded by the Spirit of God. Thus it is quite true that what some scriptures say is significant *because* of what others said.

For a single chapter necessity demands that we limit ourselves to a select area of investigation. So we propose the first chapters of Genesis as they surface in some New Testament passages. At certain important places in New Testament literature we find data first published in the early chapters of Genesis.

27

The public ministry of Jesus had advanced far enough that opposition no longer sought in his words truth but a trap. At this juncture the Pharisees brought to him a troublesome question hoping "to ensnare him." "Is it lawful for a man to divorce his wife for any and every reason?" Jesus didn't allow their malicious motive to turn him away from an opportunity to teach the truth. In his answer the Lord referred to both Genesis 1:27 and 2:24. "You have read have you not that he who created from the beginning made them male and female?" Then he added, "On account of this a man shall leave his father and his mother and shall be joined to his wife and the two shall become as one flesh" (Matt. 19:3-5).

A number of details need to be noted in this use of Genesis by Jesus. First, he treats both passages as reporting realities. Moreover, the facts reported reveal God's original intent in the marriage relationship. Adam and Eve were partners as man and woman, husband and wife, different but equal. They were designed as two component parts of one whole. Each was individual but together both were "man" (mankind). As an individual, in point of time, the woman arrived after the male (2:21, 22) yet in the intent of God, she existed from before the beginning. Together "they" formed one humanity. So far as "man" was concerned each was fractional, partial. Together they were a sum, a whole, a man; they constituted humanity.

God created a social being with a difference in sex. It is worth more than passing note that this duality of sex is explicitly stated in the *first* chapter of Genesis. In it the "heavens and earth" are presented as the stage on which the human drama is to be enacted. And it is the first chapter that peoples the platform with all the principal characters. The reader does not have to wait even till chapter two to discover that "woman" is vital to the story, equally vital because an equal partner. God did not create "a" man. He created "man" and by that is meant "mankind." In the *first* chapter it is announced, "Male and female he created them . . ." Neither the female nor the male was an afterthought or a secondary sub-man. A single male or female member of the species did not constitute the original purpose of God. That purpose, eternal from before the beginning, included both female and male members. Paradoxically there was no "one" until he made them "two." And as two they were one man! This one in two is confirmed in Genesis 5:2 where it is reported, ". . . At the time they were created, he blessed them and called them, *man.*" God gave the generic name "Adam" to them, both the male and the female, for they both were "man." Different sexes but equally man (אדם 'ādām).

In chapter one the author of Genesis told of the creation on history's theater and with what a plentitude of life it was staged. Chapter two does not repeat chapter one. Here the dramatist rather tells the reader of the basic ingredients of man. He is both the "dust of the earth" combined with "the breath of life," divine life. Man was at once of the earth earthy and of the spirit spiritual. Heaven and earth produced a heavenly-earthly creature, in moral capacity "the image of God." In material frame and substance limited to "the clod of the ground."

Furthermore, chapter two specifies that God set man in a "garden in the east, in Eden," the garden of delight. It was man's opportunity and responsibility to work the garden, to dress, embellish and be creative in it. He was to cultivate its esthetic beauty. In it he was to reach his highest destiny. There he would become like his Creator, holy, good, with pride of performance and purity of character.

But on this earth, even in this garden, man discovered no one in whom he could recognize himself. He was neither fish, fowl, or mere mammal. He might have dominion over these but they were not like him. He saw no common bond on which to build fellowship. When God brought the animals before Adam for naming it was to stir in him the realization that he was "alone" and in dire need of one in whom he might see himself. Self-identification for a human comes through social relationship with another human. If this world were populated by only one person he or she could never know what it meant to be human. The plants and animals could give a sense of superiority but could never define the depth of human nature. That is the reason why it was "not good that man be alone." That is why the opposite sex (man or woman) was and is to be a helpmate. Each is to be a "mate" for the other and in so doing "helps" the other to realize his or her full potential as human. By being there and interacting each acts as a mirror to reflect the other. And without both neither one could see himself for what he really was. So, when the man finished naming the animals the need was plain and the way prepared for God to provide the needed helpmate.

God neither created (ברא bārā') the woman, nor did he form (יצר, yātsar) her from the dust of the earth. But he built (בנה, bānâh) her from the essence, the texture, the vital elements, both matter and spirit, of the Adam. He was already an organized being. The unity and superiority of the human society is guaranteed by her origin out of him. Adam observed the truth of this fact by saying, "This is bone of my bones and flesh of my flesh; she shall be called 'woman,' for she was taken out of man" (Gen. 2:23). In nature she was one with him.

30

It is on the basis of this vitally human union that the intimacy and permanency of the marriage bond rests. On this bedrock foundation marriage becomes a most, if not the most, intimate, personal, spiritual and bodily merger. "Bone of my bones and flesh of my flesh" implies without saying, "monogamy." It is a more binding bond than blood descent for because of it a "man shall leave his father and mother and be united to his wife, and they shall become one flesh."

If man created in the image of God is a social, creative being, then God Himself must be a social, creative being.

Furthermore, the unity of the marriage relationship reveals something of the nature of man, especially in his marriage relationship. Whether male or female, man finds the fulfillment of life, his or hers, in marriage. Whether that fulfillment be in his own personal identity or in the projection of the self in children, marriage offers the opportunity for that fulfillment.

But in keeping with the subject of our present consideration this Genesis revelation concerning man is the underlying foundation of Jesus' remarks to the Pharisees about marriage and divorce. Jesus' teaching about the perpetuity of marriage finds its roots in the nature of man as created by God. The New Testament scripture says what it says because of what the Old Testament said in Genesis.

In the title of this chapter the term *because* is made prominent. By use of this word it is not meant that New Testament authors, reading the Old Testament, simply began to write willy-nilly because they ran across a statement that appealed to them as fit subject on which to comment. Other reasons stimulated God's Spirit to guide them to take up the pen. An immediate need in some life, or some group's problem resulted in letter or prophecy. However, it was the fact that Genesis passages were at hand pertinent to the problem the authors faced that induced them to bring these scriptures into existence. The presence of the older passage and its relationship to the present point at issue was one reason why an allusion or quote was made. Listed below are a number of New Testament citations that refer to the early chapters of Genesis:

Colossians	1:16, 17
II Peter	3:5
Revelation	4:11
John	1:10
Hebrews	1:2, 10
Acts	7:50
Acts	14:15-17
Hebrews	11:3
Romans	1:20
Acts	17:24-29
Romans	4:12-17
Revelation	22:2, 3, 7, 14
Hebrews	2:6, 7
I Corinthians	15:38-45
Hebrews	11:4
I John	3:12
Hebrews	4:9, 10

This list is not exhaustive, particularly when the mere allusions are considered. However, it is representative and it is worth the effort at least to give thoughtful attention to these.

The first ten of the above references may be sheltered under the general umbrella of creation. In the Colossian passage the apostle asserts that it was God's Son who was the one "in whom all things were created." As a further indication of his meaning he added "all things have been created through him [as agent] and unto him [as the ultimate end in view]" (1:16). The basic problem faced in the Colossian letter was the person of Christ. Was He a subordinate intermediary aeon or was He the supreme embodiment of the Godhead here in flesh and blood? Did He stand here as a lower creator? Or was He himself the real direct agent and end of all creation?

The problem in II Peter was different. Paul was concerned about the theological implications of denial of the supremacy of Christ. Peter seems more disturbed about the insidious false teachers and their denials of the "last days." In answer he says, "They deliberately forget that long ago by God's word the heavens existed and the earth was formed out of water . . . " (3:5). The use of the "word [λόγος] of God" here reminds one of the opening verses of the Gospel of John, "In the beginning was the Word [λόγος] . . . all things were made through him; and without him nothing was made that has been made" (John 1:1, 3).

It is true that each of these New Testament writers, Paul, Peter and John, were dealing with different specific problems. Yet they all found ammunition suitable for their purpose from the early verses of Genesis. "In the beginning God created the heavens and the earth" (Gen. 1:1). Paul, Peter and John were weaned on the "sacred writings" of the Old Testament. The educated Paul was the man of letters and literature. Peter and John were unschooled, unlettered graduates of the wild waves of Galilee's stormy waters. Yet each had his mind and heart tempered by the knowledge of chapter one of Genesis. That "God created the heavens and the earth" flowed through each heart as readily as waters of the Nile flow to the sea. Be it the exalted person of Christ, traitorous teachers, or cosmic world view, each problem must face "In the beginning God created . . ." as that truth filtered through the lettered scholar or the unschooled fishermen. Moreover, each of these men latched on to the Genesis idea because it was there available.

The fact that this world and the universe of which it is a part finds its origin in the creative action of God furnishes the foundation for Isaiah's teaching and in turn for the faith of the first Christian martyr. Isaiah affirmed creation when he said, "Heaven is my throne, and the earth is my footstool: what manner of house will you make me? . . . For all these things has my hand made . . ." (Isa. 66:1, 2). Stephen, in the course of his startling vision of the unlimited universality of God's action throughout history, rebuked his blind generation for trying to box God into a certain land or imprison him in a Jewish temple. "The Most High does not dwell in handmade houses." Then he enforced the fact by quoting Isaiah, "What manner of house will you build me? . . . Did not my hand make all these things?" (Acts 7:48, 50).

As Isaiah was to Stephen so was the 102nd Psalm to the author of the Hebrew letter. The Psalmist, unknown by name, was languishing in sadness on the eve of return from the long years in Babylon. He remembered Zion as she was before the captivity and now he contemplated the city's present broken stones and rubbish-like heaps of dust. Yet his was a sadness broken by a shaft of hope for the "set time" to favor Zion "is come." And his hope enlarges when he considers the vast eternity of God in contrast to the brevity of his own years. And the created universe is but a blanket to be rolled up and put away when it has served its winter's use. "Thy years endure through all generations. Of old you founded the earth, and the heavens are the work of your hands" (Psalm 102:24, 25). As threads woven into a cloth form both the substance and design of the fabric so the idea of Genesis 1:1 that "God created the heavens and the earth" form the vocabulary and faith of the Psalmist.

And many centuries later the author of the epistle to the Hebrews in confirming the exalted position of the "Son" over angelic creatures tapped the 102nd Psalm. "Thou, Lord, in the beginning did lay the foundation of the earth. And the heavens are the works of thy hands . . ." (Heb. 1:10). Creation of the heavens and the earth at the hand of God serves biblical authors like a musical theme which constantly reappears in every movement of a symphony.

It helps us appreciate the Bible as a beautiful whole when we learn how the various portions of scripture view and use other parts of scripture.

The Pentateuch furnishes the setting in which the remainder of the Bible books are placed. A rough, uncut, unpolished diamond is a drab grey dull unattractive stone. But when cut, polished, honed to a brilliant luster it sparkles with dazzling splendor, especially when set in a ring of gold. It is Moses and his work that provides the setting for the cluster of books that follow him. Without the Pentateuch to give them meaning the historical, devotional and prophetic books are lacking in luster. But when set in the background of God's design as revealed in the Genesis through Deuteronomy accounts each succeeding work sparkles with divine light. And as surely as there would be no apple were there first no apple tree, so no New Testament could have been written without first an Old. Once produced the apple has some taste and nourishment apart from the tree. But all its present taste, pulp, and strength derive directly from root, trunk, branches, blossom and leaf.

The life-giving power in the New Testament has firm roots in the divine revelation of the Old Testament. Eliminate from Paul's thought the Genesis 1:1 idea. And how could he even approach idolatrous, gentile, heathen people by saying, "We also are men, of like nature with you, and bring you good news, that you should turn from these vain things to a living God who made the heaven and the earth and the sea and all that is in them" (Acts 14:15). Or to the intellectuals at Athens, though equally heathen, "The God who made the world and everything in it is the Lord of heaven and earth and does not live in temples made by men" (Acts 17:24). And to Christian readers he could appeal to the same creation idea announced in Genesis. "For what can be known about God is plain . . . ever since the creation of the world his invisible nature, namely, his eternal power and deity, has been clearly revealed in the things that have been made" (Rom. 1:20).

But there are other ideas, fundamental to the Old Testament revelation, other than creation which find a lodging in the New Testament scriptures. Genesis 2:2, 3 contributes the basis on which the author of Hebrews could say, "There remains, then, a Sabbath rest for the people of God; for anyone who enters God's rest also rests from his own work, just as God did from his" (4:9, 10). God certainly was not physically tired, nor emotionally drained, nor spiritually exhausted after his creative activity. There is something more involved in rest than ceasing from work. But the whole argument of Hebrews 4:1-11 rests on the historical reality written in Genesis 2:3, ". . . God rested from all his work." Man enters into God's rest, not by observing a day without work once a week, but by entering into the recreative experience of redemption in Christ. When God capped His creation by "making man in his own image" He fully expected man to enter into His, God's rest. But sin entered to thwart this design of the Creator. Though short-circuited God would not be defeated from obtaining His original purpose. So He began the work of redemption that eventually would lead man to "enter into the divine rest" which God himself enjoyed. Neither Joshua, nor David, nor any human historical experience could fulfill the meaning of God's entering into his rest. The weekly Sabbath itself was but a shadowy symbol of the real rest of God. Thus the entire thesis of Hebrews 4:1-11 stands on the profound concept of God's rest first voiced in Genesis 2:2, 3.

What is man? his nature? his destiny? These are acute questions with which men have wrestled from ancient times. In the 8th Psalm the poet, apparently David, raised the question, "What is man that you are mindful of him, or the son of man that you visit him?" (Psalm 8:4). Man seems so little, so insignificant when measured by the vastness of the universe. What is there about man that could possibly interest God in him? The Psalmist's answer to his own question reveals a thorough acquaintance with Genesis 1:26, 27. According to the Genesis account man was not only made in the "image and likeness" of God but as such was a creature shaped to rule. As the Creator is sovereign over his creation so he molded man capable of sovereignty over "the fish of the sea and the birds of the air, over every living thing that moves upon the earth." So we see that *in nature* he was to be the same as the deity himself. Man was not God but he was like God in the essence of his being. He was made in "the image of God." So when the Psalmist gave answer to his question, "What is man that thou art mindful of him?" his response sprang from the Genesis concept. "Thou hast made him little less than deity [some versions say "angels"] and crownest him with glory and honor. Thou hast given him dominion over the works of thy hands; . . .

37

all things . . . sheep and oxen . . . beasts . . . birds . . . fish
. . ." (Psalm 8:6-8). God's interest in man is that of a parent
who has a kinship with the son he has begotten.

Thus it is that when Hebrews 2:6, 7 sought to explain
why redemption interest lay in man, not angels, the author
quoted the 8th Psalm. Mankind's intended dominion had
been foiled by sin to the extent that "now we see not yet
all things subjected to him." But we do see Jesus who in
his person fulfilled the intention of God when he made man
a "little less than deity." And we see this Jesus, in nature a
divine-man, crowned with glory and honor because he
"tasted death for every man."

Once more we note that later scripture speaks with un-
hesitating insight into the nature of man and his divine destiny
because Genesis laid the foundation in its opening revelation, "Let us make man in our image, in our likeness . . ."
(Gen. 1:26).

One figure presented for the reader of the Bible is that of
the "tree of life." It is an idea that is fundamental to the whole
story of redemption. It is the reason why, the ultimate purpose for having any Bible at all. And yet the expression
itself, "tree of life," actually shows up in written form only
in the first and last books in the Bible. The author of Genesis
described how God "planted a garden in the east, in Eden"
and that he "made all kinds of trees grow out of the ground."
Then he specifies by name two of the trees. "In the middle
of the garden were the tree of life and the tree of the knowledge of good and evil" (Gen. 2:8, 9). After man fouled up
his prospects for the good life by rebellious sin he faced the
frightful prospect of going out into an unknown future. Because man had chosen death rather than life and had cut
himself off from the source of life God "drove man out"
and placed on the east side of the Garden of Eden cherubim

and a flaming sword flashing back and forth to guard the way to "the tree of life" (Gen. 3:24). Harsh sentence as it seems it was really a blessing in disguise under the realities of life as man was doomed to live it. God was gracious enough toward the rebel not to allow him access to life while living in a state of sin. Life in a sinful condition would be far worse than death. Hence, until sin could be eradicated, the flaming sword kept man back from the tree of life. But once redemption became possible, once history has run its course to its divine destiny, once sin becomes only a bad memory, a thing of the past, then the way to the tree of life opens up again. Thus it is possible for the author of Revelation to say in the final chapter, "The angel showed me the river of the water of life . . . flowing from the throne of God and of the Lamb. . . . On each side of the river stood the tree of life . . . yielding its fruit. . . . And the leaves of the tree are for the healing of the nations. No longer will there be any curse" (Rev. 22:1-3). And later in the same chapter the blessedness of the redeemed is set forth in glowing terms. "Blessed are those who wash their robes, that they may have the right to the tree of life . . ." (Rev. 22:14). When redemption has reached its climax and God has obtained his goal of creating man "in his own image," when death and sin have been vanquished, *then* all barriers to life are removed. Once again man may partake of the tree of life without hindrance.

Certainly these passages from the book of Revelation were penned by the apocalyptic author *because* the ancient Genesis author who wrote of the dawn of history introduced the idea of the "tree of life." Here was the underlying foundation upon which the whole Bible is built. The "tree of life" discloses itself in the beginning and again at the end of the Bible. Like an underground river it flows untrumpeted from

39

Genesis to Revelation. And its presence is unveiled at the end *because* it generated such promise at the beginning. God, who saw the end from the beginning, planted the "tree of life" at creation that its fruit might be gathered at the consummation. The writer of the Revelation wrote of the conclusion of human history because the writer of Genesis wrote of the capacity of the human heart at the beginning of history.

The early chapters of Genesis leaven so much of the teaching of the New Testament, and often in such subtle unheralded ways. I Corinthians 15:38-45 is a case in point. A thorough-going skepticism about the resurrection of our mortal bodies was one of the problems faced in this letter. "How say some among you that there is no resurrection of dead [bodies]?" Then the author refers more specifically to one of the incredulous negativisms raised by some of the Corinthians. "How are the dead raised? With what kind of body will they come?" Here, as so often, doubt springs from rational conclusions based only on the limited experiences to which mortal man is exposed. There may not be enough molecules of matter to furnish bodies for the un-numbered millions who have inhabited this globe! Or, a sailor lost at sea whose body has been devoured by a number of fish, how can this body ever be reassembled for a resurrection? Or yet again, a loved one is buried under the refreshing shade of a fruit tree. The roots stretch out to feed on the decaying body and transmit its plasma into the fruit. Someone happens along, plucks and eats the fruit. So the material of one human body becomes a part of a second human body. In the resurrection whose shall it be? After all, it was a part of both bodies — yea, over millenniums, innumerable bodies?

40

In meeting such foolish skepticisms the apostle uses from nature an analogy based on the creation account in Genesis. One expression in the first chapter appears almost as a refrain. Genesis 1:11 says, "Let the earth put forth grass, herbs yielding seed, fruit trees bearing fruit after their kind." And then verse twelve confirms God's ordinance, "And the earth brought forth grass, herbs yielding seed, fruit trees bearing fruit, wherein is the seed thereof, after their kind." As the creative process rises to other levels we read, ". . . the waters swarmed, after their kind. . . ." And the sky was inhabited with "every winged bird after its kind." Verse 25 repeats the phrase three times. "And God made the beasts of the earth after their kind, and the cattle after their kind, and everything that creeps upon the ground after its kind. . . ." So it is that each of the various gradations of the created order found an expression for its own particular kind of life in a body "after its kind." Since celestial life-style was different from terrestrial each was given a particular kind of body which could best demonstrate that kind of life. "All flesh is not the same . . . there is one of men, another of beasts . . . of birds . . . of fishes," hence there are a variety of kinds of bodies. In other words, when God created the world and all that in it is he designed a special kind of body to house and show forth each special kind of life. In the words of I Corinthians 15:38, "God gives it a body as he willed [determined at creation] and to each kind of seed he gives its own body." So, the "natural" life of a human being has a natural physical body to express life in a world of pain, poison and death. So too, the reborn spiritual life of the new creation in Christ must have its resurrection body in order to express best the life of the spirit. "If there is a natural body, there is also a spiritual. Also it is written, 'The first

41

man, Adam, became a living soul.' The last Adam, a life-giving spirit. . . . As is the earthy, so also are those who are earthy; and as the heavenly, so also are those who are heavenly. And just as we have borne the image of the earthy, we shall also bear the image of the heavenly" (I Cor. 15:44-49).

But the point of our contention here is not so much the resurrection body as it is the attitude and outlook which Paul as author of I Corinthians had toward the Genesis account of creation. He quite obviously believed that the Genesis record was an accurate account of God's creating for each kind of life a body "after its kind." He based his whole argument as to the Christian's resurrection body on that Genesis narrative. It was not Paul's purpose in this Corinthian context to elaborate a doctrine of inspiration. But it is quite clear that he respected and reverenced the Genesis account as God's truth. In other places where it was appropriate the apostle would speak of "the holy scrip-tures" (Rom. 1:2) or the "sacred writings" (II Tim. 3:15). But in Corinthians he used the Genesis passage as God's truth as a means of revealing another of God's truths, namely, that the Christian need not doubt the reality of a resur-rection body.

The thorough-going ugliness of sin is depicted in the insidious motive of the first murderer. The actual motive of Cain comes out clearly in I John 3:12. The author in this context is exhorting that "we love one another." And in order to show clearly just what love is he first reveals its opposite by showing the hate of Cain. Sometimes a positive truth can best be seen on the background of its negative. "We should love . . . not as Cain was of the evil one, and [violently] slew his brother. And why did he murder him? Because his [Cain's] works were evil, and his brother's

[Abel's] were righteous." For a person to hit back at someone who has done a wrong is understandable even if it isn't
exactly right. But when one hits back, not because of some
wrongdoing, but because a friend or brother has done *right*,
that is the lowest form of degraded perversion. Once again,
the force of this New Testament revelation of what it means
not to love finds its foundation in the facts of the first murder
as mirrored in Genesis 4:2-8.

The time came in the lives of the brothers, Cain and Abel,
when they felt impelled to offer sacrificial gifts in worship
to their God. Each brought the very best that he possessed.
Abel of his flocks; Cain of the fruit of his fields and orchards.
It is reported that "the Lord looked with favor on Abel and
his offering, but on Cain and his offering he did not look
with favor." It is important to observe that the acceptance or
rejection did not rest in the offerings. They were equal in
that they were the only thing either man had. Furthermore,
each gave the best of what he had. Thus, so far as the thing
offered was concerned there was no distinction. Since it was
not in the offering, then the acceptance or rejection rested
in the inward motive of the one who offered. Cain's angry
resentment and downcast face was rooted in the wrong condition of his inward heart. This is confirmed by Hebrews
11:4 in which the author says, "By faith Abel offered unto
God a more excellent sacrifice than Cain." According to
this Abel's was offered in faith; Cain's was not in faith but
in some self-assertive motive of self-sufficient pride.

Cain's failure to make his offering "in faith" is surely no
justification for his moral misbehavior in the murder of his
brother. But though it cannot be justified morally it can be
understood psychologically. Cain felt the full force of being
rejected. Ignoring his lack of faith, seeing himself as a rejected
person, while at the same time observing a brother basking

in the joy and approval of acceptance, jealousy rose as a consuming fire in his heart. He did not hate himself for his wrongdoing. Paradoxical as it seems, he hated Abel because Abel did what was *right*. It was a terrible inversion of moral values. It was God who had rejected him, not Abel. Yet his hatred was turned against his brother who was innocent of wrongdoing against either Cain or God. Cain sought to strike back against God by slaughtering his brother. Such is the psychology of sin and the confusion into which it leads.

Our basic concern is *What Does the Scripture Say about the Scripture?* In John's attempt in I John 3:11, 12 to make clear the meaning and obligation of love we do not see a direct teaching about inspiration. But John draws from the Genesis account of the first murder to give a prudent perception of human nature and its rejection of love. It stimulates him to a penetrating insight into the real meaning of love as its opposite rises to the surface in the hatred of Cain. God and God's methods of judgment and grace were present in the Genesis records. They were obviously "God-breathed."

Chapter Five

PETER ON THE PROPHETS

Though the New Testament authors do not refer to a single-volume book named "The Old Testament" yet all of them draw their message from the various literary writings of our present Old Testament. Like the roots of a fruit tree extract nutrients from the soil and channel the life sap into branches, foliage and full grown fruit so the New Testament writers use ideas, vocabulary, and style from the history, culture, geography and climate of Old Testament authors. The apostle Paul never looked upon his message as in any way contradictory to its Old Testament roots. Before King Agrippa he claimed, "I stand unto this day testifying both to small and great, saying nothing but what the prophets and Moses did say should come" (Acts 26:22). In his view Paul said "nothing" except what the "prophets and Moses" said.

Two passages from Peter offer valid statements about the view of Old Testament literature which New Testament authors held. One is I Peter 1:10-12, while a second is II Peter 1:20, 21. At least the ideas which the author of the Petrine letters had about "the prophets" of the Old Testament are clearly set forth in these two pronouncements.

The occasion that drew forth I Peter was the breaking out of fierce governmental persecution against the Christian movement. It was certainly unpopular if not illegal to be a Christian at the time of the writing of I Peter. Incentives to patient endurance of the harsh attacks by officials of Rome are being set forth before the readers. I Peter 1:3-12 is a paragraph in which the author presents God as one who in Jesus Christ, has begotten us to a "living hope through the resurrection." There is a divine purpose of good growing out of the severe persecutions which the believers were now

45

called on to endure. That is, ". . . that the proof of your faith . . . may be found unto praise and glory and honor at the revelation of Jesus Christ." Having thus presented God, the Father, and Christ, the Son, in verses 10-12 our author introduces the function of the Spirit in bringing the salvation "prepared to be revealed in the last time."

It is in these verses that Peter discloses some revealing ideas about his view of the Old Testament prophets.

> Concerning which salvation the prophets sought and searched diligently, those who prophesied the grace which was for you, searching what time or what manner of time the Spirit of Christ in them was repeatedly pointing to, when testifying beforehand the sufferings of Christ and the glories after. To whom it was revealed that not to themselves but to you they were ministering these things, which now have been declared to you . . ." (I Pet. 1:10-12).

A listing of Peter's ideas may be helpful before analyzing them in detail.

1. He identifies the prophets—"those who prophesied concerning the grace for you" vs. 10b.
2. These prophets "sought and searched . . ." vs. 10a.
3. That which the prophets "sought and searched" for was "what time and what kind of time . . ." vs. 11a.
4. These prophets had "the Spirit of Christ in them . . ." vs. 11b.
5. They "testified of the sufferings of Christ and the glories after these things [sufferings] . . ." vs. 11c.
6. The life ministry of the prophets was "not to themselves but to you" who now have heard the gospel which is the fulfillment of their prophet ministry.

Peter has a particular group of prophets in mind when he was writing this passage. He describes them as "the ones who prophesied concerning the grace for you. . . ." In a broad sense the entire literature of the Old Testament is prophetic. In fact history itself is prophetic. That is, it has a divine message for men whose minds and hearts are tuned to the divine wave length. The so-called historical books bear God's message as he "in divers portions and divers manners" unfolded his eternal purpose of redeeming love. And the Jewish law, the Torah, was prophetic in content and purpose. Moses, the great lawgiver, is called a prophet in biblical literature. The biblical historical books interpret the events which they record as prophetic messages from Yahweh, Lord of Israel and the God almighty. He, from their perspective, makes Himself known in history. The events of history are God's word for the ancient generation as for all future generations.

When God called Abraham out of Ur of the Chaldees and followed that call by insisting the patriarch follow through by getting out of Haran (Acts 7:2 and Gen. 12:1-4) it was more than just one man's personal word from God. It was for his family and generation. And for every succeeding generation of men. How many words from God Abraham's history reflects are on many of the New Testament pages, messages for the first century generation of the people of God. And he "being dead yet speaks" the revelation of God to us of this twentieth century. Abraham's life was a prophetic interpretation of his times as well as a prophetic forward looking to later times. Jesus understood Abraham's life as being of prophetic vision when he said to the Jews, "Your father Abraham rejoiced to see my day; and he saw it and was glad" (John 8:56).

As with Abraham so with all the law, prophets and Psalms ("the writings"). Prophecy is a great deal more than mere

47

prediction. It is that. Through prophetic revelation God gave His interpretation of the crisis of the time in which the prophetic voice was living. The law, the prophet or the Psalm first and foremost addressed itself to its own time, particularly whatever crisis drew forth the need for a word from God. But in addressing that immediate need the word of the prophet would of necessity reveal principles and definite ideas that could only be fulfilled in some future crisis beyond his own.

That the 22nd Psalm was written by David, a suffering servant in ancient Israel, is often overlooked. The first words of Jesus from the cross quote the first sentence of the Psalm, "My God, my God, why have you forsaken me?" Even details of the death experience are mirrored in the Psalm: ". . . they pierced my hands and my feet" and "upon my vesture do they cast lots." In Christian history and literature these words are so closely linked to the Christ on the cross that we almost lose sight of their origin in the Psalm.

Nevertheless, the Psalm springs from a very virile, earthy, human ordeal in the multicolored life of David. As a youthful shepherd guarding the flocks on the Bethlehem hills David had been anointed to be God's designated king over Israel. He was aware that he was "the Lord's anointed"! In the affair of Goliath he knew the thrill of victory as God's representative. And the accolades of a grateful people merely served as a foil to his present depression. Torn from his family and home, robbed of his "vesture," eating, as it were, hand to mouth, wondering if each meal would be his last, fleeing the murderous wrath of king Saul, a price on his head, his only companions, outlaws, betrayed by "friends," how could he be human but wonder whether God too had forgotten and forsaken him?

It is true, this Psalm is predictive. Jesus fulfills it. He gives meat and meaning to the Psalm as solid substance creates and makes a shadow have meaning. But the fact remains that it was in David that God initially spoke His word. And that in a very trying, personal privation. God spoke through David's life of trials and triumphs. Israel, its history, its kings, priests, institutions, law, wars and peace treaties — all were channels for God's prophetic word.

A footnote on the 22nd Psalm should include the fact that the Psalm is not one that reports just the dark valley through which David's trough of depression is detailed. As a means of revealing in verses 22-25 God's faithfulness to his servant the psalmist writes the first 21 verses. Verses 26-31 set forth the universal victory that comes to God's "anointed" because God has not forsaken him. "The kingdom is the Lord's and he is the ruler over the nations [gentiles]." Through the discipline of David's suffering the nations of the earth would come under the rule of God. And it is only through David's Son, Jesus the Christ, and through His valley of suffering that the "nations of the world" realize the promised reign of God. Only in Jesus is the Psalm truly "fulfilled." Was not Jesus thinking of this victory as he hung on that cross, that God indeed was with Him through it all; was He not "heard for his godly fear" (Heb. 5:7f.)? God forsook neither David or Jesus.

It seems certain that in all Israel's history God was revealing Himself, His nature, man's nature, and His methods of dealing with man. Yet in I Peter 1:10 the author gives hint that the prophets he has in mind are limited to a select group. He probably has in mind chiefly those whom we moderns designate as the major and minor prophets, the writing prophets. He very well might be including Moses, Samuel,

Elijah and others. But Peter's reference to the fact that they "sought and searched" and they prophesied of "the grace which was for you" would suggest those giants of prophecy who lived and spoke during the later crises of Israel's history. In the ever-developing and ongoing revelation of God the writing prophets represent the height and culmination of God's self-revealing activity. These are the prophets that give evidence of speaking most clearly of "the grace" and "glory" that followed and spring from the sufferings of the Christ.

Assuming that we have identified the particular group of prophets of which Peter speaks we affirm with confidence that Peter believed them to have "in them the Spirit of Christ." That is saying the same thing, though in a different context, what he says in II Peter 1:21, "No prophecy ever came by the will of man: but men spoke from God, being moved by the Holy Spirit."

But these prophets are not to be thought of as mere trumpets, flutes, lyres through which or on which the wind of God blows. They were more than megaphones, unfeeling funnels, unthinking robots, unwilling pawns. They were not mere machines to be started or stopped at the whim of the divine hand. They were men! Wholly and totally men made of the same dust, animated by the same breath of God that produced the "image of God" in every human "living soul." How human they were is nowhere more sharply revealed than in Jeremiah. Tortured and torn between the constraint of his calling to deliver God's word of doom to a reprobate people and his private longings and hopes for personal fulfillment, his inward tension grew unbearable. "Cursed be the day I was born. . . . wherefore came I out of the womb to see labor and sorrow, that my days should be consumed with shame" (Jer. 20:14, 18). And in words hardly short of blasphemy he accused God of deceit and strong-armed methods in calling him to the prophetic function. "You seduced me, Yahweh, and I let you; you seized and overcame me. I've become a daylong joke, They all make fun of me" (20:7). In his depths Jeremiah accused God of misleading him, "Why, O why, is my pain without end, My wound ever worse, defying all cure? Ah, truly you are a dry wadi to me, Whose waters have failed" (15:18).

No doubt attention must be given to the inspiration of these prophets. Peter plainly professes that the Spirit of Christ was *in them;* and that they were "borne along by the Holy Spirit." The hand of God pressed heavily upon the prophet even in the depths of his human despair. At one time Jeremiah resolved to abandon his prophet's task. He made up his mind to "speak no more in his name." Yet so saturated with the Spirit of God was he that he could not restrain himself from speaking. "Then it is in my heart like a fire that burns shut up in my bones. And I struggle to hold it in, But—I can't" (20:9).

But in the face of the fact of inspiration no prophet was called on to forfeit his personality. Neither in intelligence, feeling or will were they mere passive puppets jumping at the pull of heavenly strings. God always uses men but he never abuses any man's manhood. Not even his "servants, the prophets." Inspiration does not mean that faculties, capacities and powers of men are anesthetized or dulled in any way. In fact just the opposite. The mind is alerted, investigative powers are sharpened, feelings are heightened, all abilities and powers are stirred to uncommon energy. In the prophets this response is heightened to a peerless sensitivity. But even though God revealed divine truth

51

to the prophets He did not keep them from sin in their personal lives.

Some things the energizing Spirit of God left undone in the prophet. Hence he would have to "seek and search" if he would know certain things. So Peter declared that these Old Testament men of God in spite of divine help had to do research, consult others, investigate, weigh probabilities and arrive at conclusions. The prophets knew precisely what they prophesied. In the context of I Peter the subject of prophetic preaching was "the salvation of souls" in Jesus Christ. It was this salvation which the ancient prophets announced. But they were not able to learn all they wanted to about the very salvation which they themselves proclaimed. So they sought and searched but were never able quite to reach the high point of their desire for knowledge. Both inspiration and their human efforts left them short of unbounded knowledge. It was left to later apostles and prophets to fill out the sketches they drew of the salvation they saw "from afar." The grace, the time, the kind of times, and the sufferings of the Christ plus the glories which would follow —all these the prophets incorporated into the message they delivered to their own times. But the greatness of the grace, the point and nature of the times, and how the Christ's suffering could bring such salvation glory lay beyond their searchings. It left them wondering! The Spirit of Christ in them interpreted the revelatory events in which God was speaking in the prophet's time. He furnished too the form in which the revelation was to be passed on to coming generations. But to them the Holy Spirit left specifics of fulfillment as much in murky shadows as to any other men living.

These prophets, as men, had the normal curiosity of all men. And this curiosity thoroughly captivated them.

They wanted to find out "what and what kind of time" this salvation of grace would appear. As prophets they could announce God's salvation to come. But as men they were left in the dark as to when or what circumstances would surround the arrival of the salvation.

Men of every age seem to possess a consuming interest in details about the "last times." Whether this is an escape from present harsh realities or genuine faith in the future as a basis for present hope one cannot be sure. The fact is that the future consumes an extravagant amount of spiritual energy. After three years following Jesus his chosen twelve asked, ". . . When shall these things be? and what the sign . . . of the end of the world?" (Matt. 24:3). And on the day of ascension when they inquired of him, ". . . Do you at this time restore the kingdom . . .?" Jesus replied, "It is not for you to know times or seasons . . ." (Acts 1:7). Yet in spite of these pointed words men of the Christian age have yielded to the same temptation as those godly men of old. We have "sought and searched . . . what and what kind of times" surround the end of the ages.

The Old Testament prophets and authors were "moved by the Holy Spirit." The Spirit of God in them "moved" them to understand and to speak to their generation God's will in their special crisis. The Spirit in them also "moved" them to a clear perception that what God was saying through them belonged to some future critical people and time. But what epoch or period of human history that was, or what kind of physical, cultural, moral and spiritual conditions it would entail the Spirit in them did not reveal.

Abraham's "seed" was to "bless all the families" of the earth. It was to outnumber the stars of heaven and the sands of the seashore. But that his seed was not to be merely his physical descendants was not clear. That the patriarch's "seed" was to be those possessing the "faith" of Abraham became graphically lucid only when Messiah emerged. Even then it took the Spirit working in and through the apostles to make plain "if you are Christ's, then are you Abraham's seed, heirs according to promise" (Gal. 3:29). The fact was revealed to Abraham. But "what and what kind of time" was left to other generations to discover. Jesus could say, "Abraham rejoiced to see my day; and he saw it . . ." (John 8:56). Abraham saw as a traveller sees mountain peaks on the horizon across the broad valley. He knew the mountain of hope lay ahead and that it would be scaled. But the details could only be speculated about on the basis of his immediate environment. He could "see" that distant mountain peak in the light of the mountain on which he was now travelling.

When David was established as king over all Judah and Israel, Nathan the prophet announced, "Yahweh will make you a house . . . I will set up your seed after you . . . and I will establish his kingdom . . . I will establish the throne of his kingdom forever" (II Sam. 7:11-13). The fact that David was to inaugurate a dynasty that would last "forever" would naturally be understood to mean an enduring political dominion. David's "son" as perpetual ruler over the people of God became a fixed part of Old Testament Hebrew theology. In fact, that idea has influenced much thought that purports to be Christian. That Christ as David's son will yet rule with a "rod of iron" over a political kingdom with its capital at Jerusalem colors a generous amount of evangelical theology. It certainly affects modern Israeli political theory to this day.

To communicate to men whose minds are conditioned by life in a material world God must speak in material terms. In essence truth cannot be changed. But the forms in which

54

it blossoms must be adapted to the level of life in which the learner dwells. So God spoke to David. King David was one who hewed his kingdom out of the raw materials of warfare, marriages of expediency, and other forms of diplomatic maneuvers. God had other things in mind than just a powerful political empire ruled over by Jewish kings, even though they be sons of David. But God's kingdom was presented to David's generation and those immediately following as the kingdom of David. Belief in a kingdom of God did not rise in a vacuum. Prophetic pointing to the kingdom of God was painted on a canvas of historical fact. Before there could be an expectation for a son of David's line there must be a David. A kingdom of Israel must first rise on which might be patterned a kingdom of Messiah. For people on this earth a kingdom on this earth must be a reality before a kingdom of God could take meaningful shape.

God had in mind a different kind of kingdom than that envisioned by David and his immediate successors. It took several centuries and generations of prophets before it became clear that the political state of Israel was to be divorced from the idea of the kingdom of God. It was not until Jeremiah in the 6th century B.C. that this divorce was clearly disclosed by his revelation of a "new covenant." A covenant not written on tables of stone but as the prophet announced, "I will put my laws on their mind, and in their heart will I write it . . ." (Jer. 31:33). Then the day arrived when the angel spoke to Mary of the babe of her virgin's womb, "He shall be great, and shall be called the Son of the Most High: and the Lord God shall give unto him the throne of his father David: and he shall reign over the house of Jacob forever; and of his kingdom there shall be no end" (Luke 1:32, 33). It is in reality Jesus, the Christ who is David's son, the king over God's kingdom and whose reign shall last "forever."

Jesus acknowledged before Pilate, "My kingdom is not of this world" (John 19:36). But how could David "see" all this? How could David know "what or what manner of time" the Spirit of Christ "in" him spoke? The time, the nature of the kingdom, the course of events or predicaments of the first century he could hardly be expected to find out even if he "sought and searched." The Spirit inspired knowledge of the fact. But it did not divulge how it was to be fulfilled. Only time plus new prophetic vehicles would be able to do that.

The letter of I Peter, written in the second half of the first century at a time of persecution, spoke about the prophets of the Old Testament. One thing he said about them is that there were some things they did not know. They knew what God wanted their own generation to know about his will. They knew that later generations would be the beneficiaries of their messages. But they did not know "what [period of time] and what manner of time" to which the Spirit of Christ in them pointed.

Yet another allusion about these ancient prophets Peter makes. The prophets had "the Spirit of Christ in them." Our minds are so accustomed to the limitations of time and space, of dates for births and deaths, of up and down, forward and backward, of weights and measures in terms of pounds or grams. If we dare to talk about "spirit" or "spiritual world" it often degenerates into magic, ghosts, hob-goblins, and phantoms of the mystical mirages of hallucination. Spiritual things are shelved as being of the irrational, unreal. Yet Jesus indicated that "God is spirit." Those in the "image of God" would be constitutionally spirit also. And the things of the spirit cannot be judged by material methods of measurements.

When Peter refers to "the Spirit of Christ" as being "in them" he certainly is implying more than just an influence similar to that of Christ. It was more than like the "spirit of 76" lives in a 20th century patriot. The idea is kin to that of John when he says, "In the beginning was the Word, and the Word was with God, and the Word was God [deity]" (John 1:1). In other words the "Word" had being before his birth of the virgin; He existed in and from eternity. This idea is also similar to that voiced by Paul when he wrote of Israel passing through the sea under the leadership of Moses. They ". . . did all eat the same spiritual food; and did all drink the same spiritual drink: for they drank a spiritual rock that followed them: and the rock was Christ" (I Cor. 10:3, 4). There seems little doubt that these New Testament authors believed in the pre-existence of Christ. Even a passage such as II Corinthians 8:9 implies that Jesus Christ *was* something other than that which he *became*. "You know the grace of our Lord Jesus Christ, that, though he was rich, yet for your sakes he became poor. . . ." There is no calendar date that can mark any point when he "was rich" though men do attempt to date when he "became poor." He was rich in eternity; he became poor in time. And what I Peter 1:11 reveals is that this eternal Christ was actively present "in them," the prophets of old who spoke of the promised salvation. That which the prophets could not discover by "seeking and searching" the Christ "in them" surely saw and understood. The Christ saw the end from the beginning, the fulfillment from the form; He knew the substance which cast the shadow. This pre-existent Christ who was "in" the prophets stirred them to proclaim the shadowed form of the coming salvation. They spoke in terms of their times and understanding but in language easily transposed into terms of the age of fulfillment. This is what I Peter 1:11 says about the Old Testament prophets.

In addition Peter is quite explicit about the method which God ordained for the Christ to bring this announced "salvation." He says that these old prophets "testified of the sufferings of Christ and the glories after these [sufferings]" (I Pet. 1:11). From God's point of view suffering is a prerequisite to glory. As cause is to effect or planting to harvest so suffering is to glory. A law of God's grace, not to say a law of God's creation, is: no cross, no crown; no pain, no promise; no suffering, no glory. The Old Testament prophets were quite certain of what they announced. The eternal Christ in them testified that the Christ yet to emerge in history would abound in pain — excruciating, humiliating, shameful, shocking sufferings. Yet after these distresses, yea, as a result of such anguish this Christ would be crowned with a halo of glories. Jesus gently rebuked the two walking on the Emmaus road the day of his resurrection because of their failure to "believe upon all which the prophets spoke." Then he asked a question, so worded as to reveal he expected "Yes" for an answer. "It was a logical necessity wasn't it, that the Christ should suffer and enter into his glory?" Then it was that "having begun from Moses and from all the prophets he explained to them all the scriptures concerning himself" (Luke 24:13-27). This linking suffering with glory is in keeping with Peter's remark about the prophets who testified about "the sufferings of Christ and the glories following." God sees suffering as vitally bound to glory.

From Isaiah comes the most pointed of these prophecies of Messiah's sufferings. More than a third of the book of that prophet is dominated by the God, Lord of history, who is to bring Israel back from the tragedy of Babylonian captivity, back from the painful judgmental consequences of national sin, back to a new beginning, a new exodus, a new covenant, a new king and a reconstituted kingdom. The final twenty-seven chapters of Isaiah are saturated with joy, triumph and hope. The people of God, chastened, refreshed, rededicated were to be the "Servant of God." This Servant would carry light to the Gentiles, the isles of the seas and, of course, all the tribes of Israel.

This Servant appears in the prophet now as the nation of Israel, now as some towering individual leader; sometimes the picture becomes too large for nation or individual. He is an ideal person! But however portrayed, He is to bring God's redemption to God's people. And they are to come from the ends of the earth and together be God's people.

The strangest fact about the Servant is the method by which He gains success. In fact his victory startles us as being the exact reversal of what men call success. The way in which he gains his goal guarantees failure by man's methods. For God's Servant is a suffering Servant. And the victorious destiny He has for God's people is won by disgraceful, disreputable, contemptible suffering. The Servant is not to overcome by physical power or military might. Isaiah says, ". . . he will not cry, lift up his voice, nor cause it to be heard in the street. A bruised reed will he not break, and a dimly burning wick will he not quench: he will bring forth justice in truth" (42:2, 3). His progress will not be by means of picketing nor his reign by rabble-rousing.

This Servant in face and form was so "marred more than any man" and so startling was he that "kings shut their mouths at him" (52:14, 15). Rulers of the earth simply gulped in amazement. "He grew up like a root out of dry ground" (53:2ff.). Who would go to a drought-stricken dust bowl for a luscious life-giving crop? "He had no form nor comeliness; and when we see him there is no beauty that we should desire him . . . despised, rejected, a man of sorrows, acquainted with grief: as one from whom men turn their face he was despised. . . ." What union man could stomach that kind of a leader or expect from him any kind of victory? "He was oppressed, yet when he was afflicted he opened not his mouth; as a lamb that is led to the slaughter . . . is dumb," He didn't even bleat! He made no defense for himself. Can this prophet's picture possibly be that of a successful servant who is to attract, court, convert the captive tribes of Israel? Much less the power-hungry Gentiles in foreign lands and the isles of the sea? Yes! That is precisely what Peter says that Isaiah meant!

I Peter 1:10-12 plainly agrees with the Old Testament prophetic portrait of the suffering Servant. Furthermore, the suffering of the Isaianic Servant gives valuable insight into Divine use for suffering. In this world suffering is inevitable. But it comes from one of three different causes. First, as a consequence of sin. His disciples asked Jesus, "Rabbi, who sinned, this man or his parents, that he should be born blind?" (John 9:2). The question reflects basic Jewish theology: if anyone suffers, it is obvious someone sinned. Recall Job's extremes of affliction: loss of family, loss of wealth, loss of health. His friend came to comfort with this neatly-packaged theology, ". . . whoever perished, being innocent? Or where were the upright cut off? . . . they that plow iniquity . . . reap the same" (4:7, 8). In other words, "Job, you're hiding some secret sin; for none suffers like this except first he sinned." While such a viewpoint fails to cover all the sources for suffering there is some truth in this notion that sin breeds suffering which eventually issues in death. The New Testament affrims, "The wages of sin is death" (Rom. 6:23). And it speaks of many "hurtful lusts, such as drown men in destruction and perdition" (I Tim. 6:9).

On the other hand it is equally true that some suffering does not come from having sinned. Suffering often springs from having done what is right; from having carefully and fully done the will of God. The Old Testament heroes of faith are permanent examples that obeying the word of God exacts a costly price in pain. Stephen challenged, "Which of the prophets did not your fathers persecute?" (Acts 7:52). In this same letter Peter exhorts, "Let none suffer as a murderer, or a thief, or an evil-doer. . . ." In these suffering comes as a result of sinning. Avoid the sin and we avoid the fruit. But Peter adds, "If any man suffer as a Christian, let him not be ashamed; but let him glorify God in this name" (I Pet. 4:15, 16). So here we take note of a second reason why we suffer. We suffer because we do right. He who would live godly in Christ Jesus shall suffer persecution.

There is a third cause for pain. We suffer because suffering is God's vehicle of victory. The man of God *chooses* suffering because it is the handmaid of God's power, the redeemer of the lost, the servant for the sinful. If one goes swimming he chooses a swimming suit, not a tuxedo. If one goes to a formal party or wedding he chooses, not a swimming suit, but a tuxedo. Which is to say that we elect the kind of clothing that fits the occasion. That is why God's servant freely chooses humiliation in sacrificial suffering. The Servant of Isaiah's prophecy did not suffer *merely* as a result of doing God's will but as a means of succeeding in God's assigned task. The Old Testament Servant could not deliver Israel from captivity nor reach the world of Gentile corruption unless and until He embraced suffering as the tool of victory. Suffering is to God's servant as the sword is to the ancient soldier—the means of conquering. Without it he could not conquer for God. Such a prophetic view of suffering makes of it no longer an agony without meaning but rather God's charter of freedom, Christ's, ours, and others'! Peter says

61

the prophet "sought and searched" to see what kind of a time in this mundane order of things such a condition would obtain. Can there be a kind of time when to get up one must go down? to be victorious one must be defeated? that life must be shackled that death may be conquered?

A final thought Peter presents about these Old Testament prophets embraces the idea that the ministry of the prophets was "not to themselves but to you" (1:12). Without question the prophets addressed their immediate generation. The pressing realities of their own social failures demanded a threatening message of judgment. Sin in high and low places was eating as a cancer to destroy the people at every level of life. Hopes and dreams had to be recast in new forms. We cannot read the prophets and ignore these moral, social, political, economic and human factors that drew forth the word of God from these men of God. Amos addressed eighth-century Israel in the north in its prosperous days of affluence. Yet his keen prophetic eye saw the darkening moral cloud, "as small as a man's hand," on the horizon. The particular times in which he lived dictated the form in which Amos shaped his message. On the other hand the prophet Jeremiah in the 7th-6th century delivered his word from God when the enveloping cloud darkened the entire sky over the southern kingdom of Judah. It was no time of affluence. Sin was reaching its full fruitage. The nation was toppling on the brink of devastating destruction. The northern kingdom was only a memory, howbeit a vivid one. Jeremiah was living through the failure of reform, the world-shaking fall of Ninevah, the death of the promising young king, Josiah, repeated rebellions of his own people against the rising juggernaut of Babylon, the actual decimation of Judah and the final ultimate national calamity of Jerusalem's destruction. Even the aftermath of that debacle furnished fodder for his word of doom. The honest student of the scripture would be the last to question the fact that the particular times of each of the prophets cut the pattern for his own peculiar emphasis.

But having said all this it remains that the message and ministry of these prophets was designed to serve other generations than their own. This is what Peter explicitly affirms. It was these prophets "to whom it was revealed, that not unto themselves, but unto you, did they minister these things, which now have been announced unto you through them that preached the gospel unto you by the Holy Spirit sent forth from heaven . . ." (I Pet. 1:12). For the Old Testament prophets the figure of the future was woven into the fabric of their present. Hence they could not minister to their own generation and solve its problems without enfolding the future. Divine principles of judgment and salvation which would serve in the days of Israel's fall and restoration could only find their ultimate meaning and fulfillment in the days of Jesus, the Christ and "the glories that should follow" his sufferings. To the first readers of I Peter the message of the Old prophets was the shadow; the message of Christ and "them that preached the gospel unto you" was the substance that cast the shadow. The old was like the stars shining in the night; the new like the full-orbed sun that lights up the day. The old was the seed; the new the harvest. The old was the root; the new the fruit. The old was the reflection; the new the reality that is reflected. The old was the picture; the new the person whose picture was snapped.

In a day of personal doubt and political distress king Ahaz wavered between abandoned trust on Yahweh and practical trust on Assyria's sword. God, through the prophet Isaiah, offered to give Ahaz a sign that would shore up his fluctuating faith: "Behold, a virgin shall conceive, and bear a son, and shall call his name Immanuel" (Isa. 7:14). For a mind open to truth and a heart desirous of finding a basis for trust such a marvelous miracle would satisfy a vacillating king. But this message to the disturbed heart of Ahaz had a far richer significance than just that 8th century crisis. Isaiah not only ministered to Ahaz's need but by so doing he "ministered these things" unto us who have had the gospel preached unto us "upon whom the ends of the ages have come." Matthew confirms what the prophet said to Ahaz but expressly states that its definitive fulfillment comes in the birth of Jesus to the virgin Mary of Nazareth. God's highest meaning and ultimate intent as expressed in the incarnation lay buried in the personal travail of king Ahaz's doubting heart amid the political crisis of his times. Peter declares that Isaiah ministered to "us" as well as to Ahaz. As indeed do all the other of God's Old Testament servants.

In summation as to Peter and the prophets we may note that though the prophets of old were very human, limited in culture and encased in their own stirring times, yet because of the "Spirit of Christ in them" were enabled to rise above their human limitations and the confinements of their circumstances to see beyond their horizons. They were not able to understand even all of their own prophecies and their implications. But they were quite conscious that their lives and messages were meaningful to peoples yet unborn. The apostle Peter lived in the "latter" times of fulfillment. He looked back upon the times of prophetic preaching and could see that the literature of the older covenant was to be woven into the fabric of the new. And Peter was one of the craftsmen who helped do the weaving. So in the apostles and the prophets we have one whole cloth, one whole pattern, one beautiful divine design in God's tapestry.

Part II — What the New Testament Books Say About Themselves

Chapter Six

THE SYNOPTIC GOSPELS

The New Testament was authored by several different penmen writing in widely separated areas of the Graeco-Roman first century world. So one would hardly expect to find within the book any reference to itself as a single volume. However the separate writings do contain at least a minimal mention of themselves. Depending on the nature, author, content and purpose, any given book might embrace some allusion to itself. If the content failed to include some self-identifying statement, at least the title or salutation would offer an appropriate self-defining characteristic. Even closing remarks could give some penetrating insight to the book, its content, design, destination, origin or nature.

But there are other ways than direct statements in which a given piece of literature may reveal something about itself. What a person says about himself is one way to evaluate what he is. But it is not the only way. What a man is comes through by what he does as much as by what he says. This is particularly true if what he does springs spontaneously without premeditated plan. One may conform to an outward deed hypocritically. He conforms in order to deceive. But when one reacts without premeditated thought he acts in keeping with his essential self. When John and Peter raced to the empty tomb of the risen Christ John stopped at the open door. With growing wonder he reverently gazed into the void now destitute of a body. But when Peter came, he never hesitated for one moment. He rushed pell-mell into the gaping cavern. The outward act of each reflected the inner quality of spirit of each. Restrained, thoughtful,

65

gentle meditation was in keeping with the soul of the younger John. Rash, impulsive, impetuous, unbridled haste was equally reflective of the character of precipitous Peter. What one does unconsciously mirrors the unseen soul. So it is with the books of the New Testament. They seldom openly declare anything about themselves. But what they contain speaks eloquently what the authors think about their works.

What has been professed above is not meant to imply that New Testament authors did not give forethought to what they wrote. As a matter of fact they provide most excellent logic and for the most part structured design. It is the spontaneous outpouring of their feelings and thoughts as superintended by the Spirit. The content of what they write reflects the vital experience of their redemption in Christ. Some athletes are so insecure and so unsure of themselves that they feel constrained to announce to the world, "I'm the greatest!" Others are content to *be* great and demonstrate it on the field of play. So, the greatest literature, inspired or otherwise, declares its greatness by its message, the way it heralds it and the good it stimulates. As we turn through the New Testament pages we search for two particulars. First, direct statements, allusions or intimations which a book displays about itself. Second, any points that betray what the author thinks his book is disclosing to his readers. Such "points" might include outline, organization, selection of content, style, key words, sources and how the sources are used. From this point of view our topic, *What New Testament Books Say About Themselves,* could be better worded, *What New Testament Books Say!*

If one be only a casual reader with but a minimum acquaintance with the New Testament he is aware that the first four books are commonly known as Gospels. At first the term "gospel" referred to the good news from God revealed in the life, ministry, death, burial and resurrection of Jesus the Christ. But with the passing of time and the development of a growing literature the term shifted to include a type of writing in circulation throughout the Christian community. So we have The Gospel According to . . . Matthew . . . Mark . . . Luke . . . John. These books are not biographies of the life of Jesus. They are "Gospels." That is, they consist of selected material, weighed, sifted, evaluated as to what it would contribute toward a particular interpretation of the *meaning* of the life of Jesus. The word "gospel" literally means "good news." The *Gospel of Matthew* is the good news of redemption in Christ as the author of that book arranged and presented that good news. It is an interpretation of the life, death, and resurrection of Jesus. And thus it is with the other Gospels.

Among modern students of the Bible the first three Gospels have become known as the "Synoptic Gospels." Of these three, the third, the *Gospel of Luke,* is the only one that gives an extended direct statement about itself. The first two, Matthew and Mark, confine any such direct declaration to what may be termed the title.

Consider the book of Matthew. The opening words are: "The book of the genealogy of Jesus Christ, son of David, son of Abraham" (Matt. 1:1). This is the heading of the book as given by the author. It should be remembered that the title as it now appears, *The Gospel According to Matthew,* was placed by later editors and translators. The original author either had no title or verse one served as the title.

A question immediately arises. Does this heading of Matthew 1:1 refer only to 1:2-17? or to the entire first chapter? or to the first two chapters? or to the entire book of

Matthew? Reputable scholars advocate each of these views. So there is little unity among serious students as to which view one might appeal for an answer. For a solution we must turn to the purpose of the book, the precedent set in Jewish literature, and the text of 1:1 in its context.

Does this heading refer only to 1:2-17? One thing is unmistakably clear. Under any of the proposed answers 1:2-17 is included in the expression, "The book of the genealogy of Jesus Christ." The idea developed in verses 2-17 is a well-defined segment of thought. It is one buttress lending support to the basic teaching of the whole book. It is one of the underpinnings which holds up the author's outlook that the crucified Jesus really is "son of David, son of Abraham." thus it is a safe conclusion that whatever else Matthew 1:1 includes it does incorporate 1:2-17 within its scope. But is this geneological list the extent of the concern of verse one?

So far as the present author is concerned the notion that verse one refers to the first chapter, or embraces the first two chapters, may be dismissed as untenable. The whole of the first chapter is not a single, comprehensive unwrinkled unit of thought. There is a definite break in the unfolding theme beginning at verse 18. On the other hand at chapter two the issue at hand does not branch off into another channel as at 1:18. On the contrary, the story flows on unruffled by any turn of idea. If this be true then we are left with the remaining option, namely, Matthew 1:1 encompasses the entire book. Furthermore, if verse one does not serve as title to the whole of Matthew, then the book itself has no title, not even an opening salutation. At the beginning or end there is no statement of purpose.

Besides all this, there are examples of this expression in Hebrew literature. In those examples the "book of the

68

generation of _____" indicates more than just a genealogy. It embraces also "that which is generated by _____." The Septuagint, the Greek translation of the Old Testament, at Genesis 2:4 reads, "These are the generations of the heaven and the earth." And in Genesis 5:1, "This is the book of the generations of Adam." Ten times this expression enters the picture in Genesis, not to mention other times in the Old Testament. And it certainly means more than just a genealogical list. It includes a history of what the person or persons involved generated. It denotes the offspring of a progenitor; that which is generated, begotten, birthed by someone. Most likely this is included in the meaning of Matthew 1:1. Thus a more adequate translation would be, "The book of the generation of Jesus Christ, son of David, son of Abraham."

It is true that the book of Matthew presents Jesus as rooted in the past history and expectations of the Old Testament people of God. But it is equally true that the entire book of Matthew exhibits the past prophetic history as finding fulfillment in a Messiah-king who has come in the person of a rejected, crucified, God-man. This is what Jesus as "son of David, son of Abraham" has generated, has begotten, has brought to fulfillment. So says Matthew. Therefore, Matthew 1:1 means: a book on the meaning of the ministry, death, burial, resurrection of Jesus in view of his Old Testament heritage as "son of David, son of Abraham." Moreover, even if Matthew 1:1 refers to 1:2-17, it cannot be denied that it fits like hand in glove to the actual content of the whole book. This Gospel tells not only of the genealogical descent of Jesus but also that gospel which He himself generated.

So, what does the book of Matthew say about itself? It says that though Jesus has a pedigree from the past He is

69

the present and perpetual fulfillment of the foregleams of that past. That the power of His person as King-Messiah brings the only real redemption. That by His death and resurrection He fulfills man's longing and God's promise of a humanity in the "image and likeness" of God.

Turning from the only direct statement (1:1) to the all-inclusive message of Matthew, two texts stand out which embody what Jesus generated. They are 5:17 and 21:43. These give concentrated focus on the message of Matthew.

The Old Testament closes with the Jewish people looking for the coming of a promised King-Messiah who would reign in all the earth in righteousness. The prophets sang of this golden age; each generation longed for it. But in the third quarter of the first century after Christ no signs of the anticipated Messianic grandeur were visible. Jerusalem and the nation were being brought to ruin. Believers were fleeing the doomed city. The temple was about to be levelled. The people of God, to whom the national promises, privileges and responsibilities had passed, were now not a nation but a church. The membership largely Gentile; the Mosaic rites ignored. The fellowship entailed no national limitations since all varieties of race, culture, social level, sex and color shared equally. Can these facts match with God's promises? Is Jesus, rejected and crucified by the covenant people, the long awaited hope of Israel? How can the path Jesus walked be reconciled to the Old Testament? Can present conditions be harmonized with old expectations? These questions Matthew faced and answered.

"I came not to destroy but to fulfill" is a key idea that unlocks the meaning of Jewish history. The first of the Synoptics shows that the deeds, teaching, and church which Jesus assembled were the intended goal toward which every law, precept, priest, prophet, king or commoner pointed. Matthew is not a jumble of individual, isolated events of incomparable wonder. It is a well-designed, organized, coherent whole of carefully selected and logically arranged material. Chronology is ignored in the interest of logic. It creates its impression by topically arranged events and teachings. The book is characterized by unity, progress and symmetry. Its touchstone is *fulfillment*. Though rejected as Messiah, Jesus is set forth as the *real* fulfillment of prophecy, history, hope, and promise of the Old Testament. Even rejection is explained as a real fulfillment of Old Testament principles. In fact, rejection is another key idea in Matthew. But always, even in rejection, Christ fulfills the real content and meaning of God's purposes set forth in the Old Testament.

But it is also true that the "people of God" concept and the "kingdom of God" sovereignty are to be removed from the historic Hebrew to a new nation made up of "believers" whether Jew or Gentile. So Matthew reports Jesus' judgment on the Jewish people, "The kingdom of God shall be taken away from you, and shall be given to a nation bringing forth the fruits thereof." For certain there is a fulfillment of all the old prophetic dreams and hopes. But that fulfillment is not to be externalized in a cultural, national, political unit. Neither natural birth, economic philosophy, nor the power of the sword is to be the cohesive force of the new people of God. The new people are citizens in God's kingdom because of their personal faith, not by reason of their physical heritage. And the object of that faith is not an ideology but a person, the Person of the incarnate God, Jesus the Messiah. The center of unity is not a law but the Lord!

So! This is what the message of Matthew reveals about the book of Matthew. Christ really *is* all the fulfillment of of Old Testament expectations we need look for. God's people are no longer to be identified with a segregated race but rather are to be found in an assembly of believers. And the center of faith of the believers is God as seen in Jesus "the Son of the living God."

Consider now the book of Mark. The author's own title is established in verse one: "The Beginning of the gospel of Jesus Christ, Son of God." And this is the only direct statement which Mark contains about itself. But it says a lot for it is full and rich in suggestive ideas.

The first idea to take note of is the phrase "Son of God" with which the verse ends. In spite of the fact that most modern translators include this phrase some of the best of the underlying Greek manuscripts do not have it. Later copyists may have added it. Mark himself may have entitled his book simply, 'Beginning of the Gospel of Jesus Christ!" And so we would inquire, What is gained or lost by including or omitting the words "Son of God" to Mark's title? If it is an addition by the very addition, the scribe who added "Son of God" would testify that the first author of the whole book did a first-class job. When a reader picks up Mark and leaves the channels of his thought unencumbered he gains one overpowering impression—that the gospel of Jesus Christ consists of this: *HE* is "Son of God." In other words, when the author set about to write the essentials of the gospel, the ABC's, without which no gospel could exist, they were summed up in the Person of Jesus Christ, "Son of God." If Mark did not originally state "Son of God" as part of his title, he wrote with such clarity and force that any reader would himself consciously or unconsciously add "Son of God." So, the fact that the expression "Son of God" was added by some unnamed scribe is a significant witness to the power of the book of Mark to convey its intended message. And that message is: This is the elemental substance of the gospel of Jesus Christ; he is God's Son.

Mark's use of the word "beginning" in his title is enlightening. He does not mean "beginning" in the sense of a chronological beginning. As a matter of fact, from the viewpoint of chronology Mark does not begin at the beginning. No genealogy, no birth story, no antecedents of any kind delay an immediate confrontation with the hero of the account. Verses 2-8 serve as a brief vestibule that opens into the main narrative. Even the quotation in verses 2b, 3 is the briefest of hinges on which hangs the forerunner, John the Baptist, as the one who brings to public notice the chief character. It is neither the past nor the future with which Mark is primarily concerned. It is the present power of the Person of Christ, the "Son of God" that occupies his entire vision. Hence, the word "beginning" refers to what Mark considers the elemental, fundamental, ABC's, footing and foundation of the gospel as he conceives the gospel The word "gospel" may and does contain other elements but the one basic element which Mark presents is Jesus Christ. Furthermore, Jesus Christ is presented in such proportions as men will be impressed with him as "Son of God."

Another fact to be noted in Mark's title is the construction "gospel of Jesus Christ." The term "Jesus Christ" is in the genitive case, that is, the case which describes or characterizes the noun with which it is used. It is the gospel characterized by Jesus Christ. Furthermore, it is an objective genitive. That is, Jesus Christ is the object of the gospel; he is the content of what is to be believed as good news; he is the object of faith, the sum and substance of Christian belief! Without Jesus Christ as the all-inclusive point and power in life there is no good news, no gospel! Thus we see that the title speaks quite distinctly as to what the book of Mark says.

When we turn to the message of the book itself apart from the title it becomes a vividly dramatic extension of the title. The outline is simple. The Son's ministry in Galilee with an emphasis on discipleship stretches from 1:9 through 10:52. The second part of the book dramatizes the Son's ministry and conflict in Judea. The cross and the resurrection become its most prominent feature. No lengthy sermons, a limited amount of teachings, are found in Mark. Deeds, miracles, movement, action, power leave an unmistakable sign of energy and force on the book. The author of Mark introduces Jesus full-grown who starts his ministry in high gear at full speed. There is not the slightest intimation of Jesus' personal past. He just begins his task of redemption like the full-orbed sun at noon. It is as though he had no beginning; he just appeared! He strides through his brief years like a colossus, preaching, winning disciples, arousing opposition. He selects, teaches and trains a designated twelve and amid conflict and controversy is crucified. But this is not the end. Compatible with such a person and program he rises bodily from the grave. As a final touch consistent with such a character he commissions his faithful to herald the good news world-wide. There the story ends.

Such a story, such a Person is the "beginning," the essence, the elemental ingredient of the gospel of which Jesus Christ is the object. From Mark's standpoint if God would come into this world for saving purposes, this is the way he would come; this is how he would introduce his good news for man. In fact, according to Mark, that's the way he did come.

We turn to the last of the Synoptics, the *Gospel According the Luke*. The first four verses form one beautifully

74

balanced sentence. It is classic in style. It is the one direct statement in which Luke evaluates his own treatise and sets forth what he is trying to achieve in it. We hesitate to call it a title yet it performs that function and more. Without it no formal title is present. It is worthy of careful examination. Here is one translation:

> Inasmuch as many have taken in hand to arrange a narrative of the things which have been accomplished among us, just as those who from the beginning were eyewitnesses and ministers of the word delivered to us, it seemed good to me also, having followed all things carefully back up (to their origins), to write to you an orderly sequence, most excellent Theophilus, that you may know the certainty concerning the things of which you have been instructed.

Nine particulars may be listed as deserving some detailed comment. They are:

1. Many others preceded him in the task of writing.
2. These others left much that needed yet to be said.
3. His sources were "eyewitnesses."
4. The narratives of these earlier ones reported "things that have been *accomplished* among us."
5. They "passed them on to us."
6. He was writing in a "vital sequence," an orderly arrangement.
7. His purpose was "that you may know fully with certainty."
8. ". . . most excellent Theophilus . . ."
9. The first reader was a catechumen, who already had some knowledge of Christianity but needed more. He needed a fuller insight, a less fragmentary knowledge.

Luke was not the first to document the facts about the Christian faith. In truth, it was the fact that "many" had already drawn up narratives that stimulated him to write,

especially when he saw the incomplete, if not sketchy, fragmentary stories being circulated. Who these earlier writers
were Luke does not specify. A generation later John would
make an observation that "the world itself could not contain the books" about Jesus if "all" the marvels he did or
said were written (John 21:25). So, before Luke took up
his pen "many" unnamed scribes told a variety of incidents
about the life, miracles, message and meaning of Jesus.
Who could witness the feeding of the five thousand, the
raising of Lazarus, or hear the penetrating parables and
not tell relatives, friends and acquaintances about what they
saw and heard? And many of them put their experiences in
writing to send to more distant contemporaries. Those fragmentary stories were circulated through many hundreds of
hands until they were dog-eared. They were reproduced,
tacked onto other episodes, eventually grew into longer
connected narratives. It is quite reasonable to think of many
thousands of remnants, both oral and written, being circulated before the more structured, well-designed Gospels
took shape.

In view of Luke's positive declaration that he was aware
of and investigated earlier narratives what should we think
about his examining Matthew and Mark? We may assume
that the first two Synoptics were written earlier. Matthew
and Mark are parts of the inspired New Testament. If Luke
would count it worthwhile to examine non-inspired writings
would it seem likely that he would deliberately ignore the
inspired ones? It is a matter of common sense researching
and investigation of all sources. So it is safe to say that some
sources of Luke included these earlier canonical Gospels.

Thus these others left something important that demanded
yet to be told. As a Greek writing to a Greek the "good

physician" saw a side to the tale that had not been adequately chronicled. Without question Jesus was deity, the "Son of the living God." But He was equally the son of man, that is, quite truly human. As deity, God begot Him; but as a human, Mary conceived Him. Both the unborn Jesus and the mother endured all the human dangers, pains, and human uncertainties of a nine-month pregnancy. So the birth stories of Luke are those that reflect a woman's particular concerns. At the manner of begetting the baby she was humble before God yet humiliated before man. Her cousin Elizabeth, the prophetess, Anna, and prophet, Simeon, lent support in all her ordeal. Angels' songs and shepherds' witness increased her amazement and sustained her soul. These are distinctive *human* touches that would appeal to the sense of universal humanity that Greeks would especially appreciate. For God to be so human would charm and impress a sensitive, noble-hearted Greek like Theophilus. These and other such things alongside what had already been written would complete the picture of who Christ was—and what God did in Him.

Luke relates that he sought out "eyewitnesses and ministers of the word" for his sources. Luke was a professional man quite used to thorough-going investigations. Before he drew conclusions upon which human life depended he must have a complete diagnosis. The available literature about Christ not only left some gaps in knowledge, it needed to be thoroughly examined, evaluated and verified. For example, Luke felt the need of the mother's side of the birth story. From which eyewitnesses could he get that except from the virgin herself, either directly or from a close companion? Because of Luke's assertion about "eyewitnesses and ministers of the word" it would suggest a personal approach to Mary. Quite possibly he enlisted the apostle John to whom Jesus committed his mother at the crucifixion (John 19:26, 27). He would be the one who could introduce Luke to Mary. Or he himself could repeat Mary's first hand description of Gabriel's announcement of her virgin pregnancy. Not only the facts but Mary's delicate feelings about her experience would color and temper Luke's telling of the story. Mary could give insight into her sense of wonder, amazement, awe and submission at the angel's tidings. And she could recount the supportive strength of Zachariah and Elizabeth's marvel at the birth of their own baby in their old age. And the many thoughts she kept "pondering in her heart" — angels' songs and shepherds' praise — Luke learned from the lips of the virgin or some close sensitive companion of the virgin.

That which earlier authors had arranged were budding narratives of "the things which have been accomplished among us." The word translated "accomplished" marks an unusual, seldom used term. Outside the Septuagint and the New Testament it is rare in Greek literature. Examples appear in the papyri and inscriptions of the first century era in which the meaning is to "bring to a full finish." When used of things, as indeed it is here, it contains the notion of attaining completion or an arrival at the finish. Luke apparently deliberately chose this term for it reveals his philosophy of history. The "matters which have been accomplished" were not those that naturally in the surge of the flow of history would by hook or crook accomplish themselves. On the contrary, Luke, who also authored Acts, says about his Gospel that it deals with what "Jesus began both to do and teach . . ." (Acts 1:1). The divine-human Jesus "began" something and *He* brought it to its "full finish." As a builder brings to its symmetrical completion the architect's design so Jesus brought to accomplishment God's plan in history.

78

What does the third synoptist say about his book? When we consider that Acts is a second part of a two-part narrative (a second volume of a two-volume set) then Luke's choice of "have been accomplished" (πεπληροφορημένων) is doubly significant. In his Gospel Luke portrays the good news of redemption as it was wrought in the person of Jesus of Nazareth, the incarnate God, as He tabernacled in human nature in the land of Palestine. The facts of the gospel were accomplished in His flesh and blood person. Judged by its contents the book of Acts unveils how Jesus (in the Spirit) expanded the work He "began." Acts continues the story of how, now ascended and exalted, Christ gets the good news of human salvation to all the world. Acts traces the course of the gospel from the small fountainhead of apostles on Pentecost until it reaches Rome. When it reaches Rome the divine plan "has been accomplished" in and by Jesus, the Christ. So this is what the third synoptist declares about his own two-volume work. Furthermore, he indicates that his work is more complete, not fragmented; the full story, not abridged.

But he says more about his book in 1:1-4. Luke vouches that his eyewitness sources "delivered to us" those "matters which have been accomplished." That is, "they passed them down to us" from person to person, witness to witness, generation to generation as any people deal with tradition worthy of preserving. In the ancient Orient, not to mention modern remote tribes, "tradition" is not a bad word. It does not suggest carelessly repeated personal opinions, or imaginative myths colored by deep-seated feelings, desires or prejudices. It rather refers to a well-established method of conserving cultural and national history, institutions, records, customs and memories. Keeping oral traditions became a profession that gave a permanence as reliable as parchment or as fixed as carved stone. In some cultures to alter the tradition was punishable by death. It was an acceptable, dependable process by which venerable beliefs, practices and conventions were passed on. A responsible reverence hovered over the heart of those who passed on the hallowed traditions. It was in that spirit that the apostle Paul wrote, "I commend you because you remember me in all things and hold fast the traditions even as I delivered them to you (I Cor. 11:2). To pass on faithfully the traditions was an honorable, commendable act worthy of community recognition and praise.

So it was that Luke looked on what was "passed on to us" as reliable tradition. Such a view accords with Paul's view of Christian teaching. "So then, brethren, stand! and hold fast the traditions which you were taught whether through our word or letter" (II Thess 2:15). And when dealing with the very heart of the gospel, the death, burial and resurrection, the apostle used the same verb used by Luke. "For I delivered to you . . . that which I also received" (I Cor. 15:3). Luke says that the eyewitnesses faithfully delivered the traditions "to us." Luke's facts, interpretations and meaning were well founded.

We next consider in Luke's titular prologue his proposal that he write "an orderly account." The word translated "orderly account" suggests the idea of "successive" events. It represents ideas or acts which follow in consecutive order. The word does not necessarily imply a chronological sequence as much as a vital sequence. In fact "vital sequence" would seem to be an excellent translation. Luke sifted through his accumulated material. As his over-all goal determined his specific selection he proceeded to choose marrow for his narrative. An outline shaped in his mind as a building forms on a blueprint from the architect's imagination. First the footing for the foundation; then appear the studs of the frame to which is attached laths, siding and wall board. Paints brightens the outside. Windows, doors, wiring and baseboards impart a sense of finish to the inside. But through the entire process each single task has prepared for that which follows. And every fresh job rises on what preceded. Such is the concept of a "vital sequence." In the writing of the Gospel of Luke the chain of recorded events is logical and psychological more than chronological. First the sprout, then the blade, the stalk, the ear and finally the corn in the ear. So Luke has submitted a story of exquisite symmetrical beauty. By its balance and well-groomed arrangement it generates conviction, an inescapable impression. Some have felt Luke to be "the most beautiful book in the world." Certainly its orderliness would favorably impress the Greek sensitivity to beauty and balance. Theophilus was a "most noble" Greek trained to appreciate ordered beauty. And Luke provided exactly that.

This leads to the purpose of Luke's writing. He clearly states his design to be "that you may know fully with certainty . . ." (Luke 1:4). Full accurate knowledge on which a solid, sound certainty could grow is the end in view.

Sound knowledge rests on experience. If Luke's highly educated, broadly cultured, sophisticated friend is to be fully persuaded of the truth, then faith must not stand on hearsay. The fuzzy uncertainties of vagrant rumors are not enough on which accurate knowledge is to be built. Hypothesis, conjecture, speculation, surmise are not sufficient to weather the cold winds of doubt. Knowledge must not be suppositional; it must be experiential. Knowledge does not arrive just from reading directions but from experience in practice. If I'm drowning I prefer a life guard who has actually rescued some drowing people over one who has only visited a life-saving class. So Luke proposes to give his reader that kind of knowledge which comes from experience. It is the experience of those who not only listened *to* what Jesus taught but who *did* what he said. It is the knowledge that comes from the testings of life in the market place; not the sheltered, sequestered isolation of academic postulate. Such knowledge leads to the assurance of faith.

Concrete footings hold up buildings. Bona-fide ideas hold up faith. Structures rest on block foundations; faith stands on well-evidenced fact. And underlying such facts is good communication. Faith, order and peace is fathered by good communication. Doubt, confusion and turmoil are generated by poor communication. Because of this Luke labored long in order to communicate clearly, fully and accurately. After all, it was not a material, physical brick building he was erecting but a human soul whose faith he was fashioning and whose ideas he was grounding. If doubt is fear; trust is surety. So the author must develop his book to reach both intellect and feelings of his reader. The mind must see clearly; the feelings must respond positively. Then certainty would pervade the soul of Theophilus. This was the aim of the Gospel of Luke: to remove doubt; to establish faith by a full report, by a faithful report, by a well-researched report, by an eyewitness-based report, by a traditions-oriented report and by a vitally arranged report. Such a report appeals to the mind and heart and so brings conviction.

The first reader of Luke's Gospel is designated as "most excellent Theophilus." The name means "lover of God." The epithet "most excellent" would seem to lift him out of a plebeian class to that of the more highly cultured if not a noble breed. The vocabulary and style of the writing bears this out. Luke, the author, was obviously a man of letters and targeted his treatise to a man of cultured taste. For an educated, trained man it is just as easy to write well as to write poorly. And for a reader of the same quality it is easier, more winsome, more convincing to read a book of energetic style.

It is not meant to imply that the Gospel of Luke is bookish or pedantic or stilted. Quite the contrary. We have already pointed out that this is the most down-to-earth, human, of all the Synoptics. But it is the work of a consummate artist who knows how to submerge both art and artist to the practical end in view. The techniques of clear writing, including arrangement, vocabulary and style, are brought under the artist's control that a noble disciplined mind may be convinced of the author's thesis. The eminence and social distinction of Theophilus helped determine the plan and style of Luke in writing his beautiful witness to the person of Jesus.

Through the centuries some students have asserted that the name "Theophilus" was intended to symbolize a class of people rather than an individual man. But under careful consideration this is unlikely. Any book whose content is aimed at a specific individual will have some themes of general interest. Any person has certain factors common to all humanity. And this is true in the Luke-Acts work. And it is because of this that Luke (and Acts) is best described as written to an individual. In Theophilus, the man, was embodied certain attributes belonging to the Greek people, in fact, to the whole human race.

It is easier to grasp abstract universal traits when seen in specific, normal, typical human beings. "Fruit" is best appreciated when I have an apple in my hand or a banana in my mouth. The particular gives concrete meaning to the universal. The same is true in literature. To address one man and his mind, emotions and will, inevitably touches

83

on what affects mankind in general. When an author writes to convict one human being he is quite likely to convert a whole herd of human beings. So it is more sensible to think of Luke as addressing a particular Theophilus than a general class of unnamed people. Without question Theophilus was indeed a "lover of God." As such, any "lover of God" would find in the book a convincing message. But the book itself was written to one individual person.

To this conclusion a bit of supporting evidence comes from the opening verses of both Gospel and Acts. A variation in the way the author addresses his reader appears in the two volumes. In the Gospel it is "most excellent Theophilus." In Acts the salutation is the unadorned "Theophilus." As indicated above the "most excellent" probably refers to the lofty culture or blue-blood nobility of the recipient. Some kind of change is implied in dropping of "most excellent." If Luke-Acts were addressed to a class it is difficult to explain the change. But if to an individual then there is more than one reason for such an alteration. Some have suggested that after Luke but before Acts was written Theophilus had changed from being studiously interested to a convert to Christ. That is a possibility. Another is that Theophilus was one with whom Luke had, as a physician, formed a professional acquaintance. But by the time he wrote Acts the relationship had grown into a warm personal friendship. By then Luke felt free to drop the more formal title. This too is a possibility. But for whatever reason we conjure up the indisputable fact is that there is a change. And whatever the reason, it suggests a person, not a class, as the initial reader.

The ninth and last of the particular points gleaned from Luke 1:1-4 is that the first reader was a catechumen who had some knowledge of Christianity but needed more.

By the term "catechumen" no thought of a regularly organized class of novices is entertained. At this stage in the development of Christianity it is uncertain that such catechetical groups existed. But people everywhere were "inquiring" about Christ and his meaning for life. They were asking questions, seeking answers, sifting evidences and accepting or rejecting the Christ of the gospel. It is just this kind of inquirer that Theophilus was. He was a serious student of Christ and the Christian movement.

How and where Theophilus first learned of Christ is not known. The safest conjecture is that he heard the gospel story from Luke the "good physician." It could have been because of an already existing friendship between the two men. Or it might have come by means of some ailment for which Theophilus sought the services of Luke's medical skill. At any rate this distinguished Greek was more than just a passing acquaintance of Luke's. And for sure Theophilus had already made progress in his knowledge of Christ. This is clear from Luke 1:4: ". . . that you may know the certainty concerning the things of which you have been instructed." Theophilus had already received some "instruction." And apparently he had enough sympathetic response to what he had learned that Luke felt that it was critical that he have more. The result of that feeling produced the *Gospel According to Luke.*

The fullness of this Gospel sets it apart. In this third Synoptic more actual content material is given than in the other two. They all present Jesus as the Christ of prophetic expectation, the deity of Christ's nature, his supernatural power, his more-than-human insight into God, man, sin, redemption. They all appeal to his genuine humanity, that which is universal in him. But the broad human touch, the sensitivity to suffering humanity, the perception of *human* need marks Luke's Gospel as distinctive. So we note its fullness not only in material but in its broad appeal to all strains of humanity. All three have a universality. But Matthew gives a special nod to Hebrew history and its promise of a Messiah. Mark picks up on the overwhelming power of the Son that appeals to the power of Roman might. Luke is delicately human in a way that attracts the heart of *man* be he Jew, Roman, Greek or barbarian.

What Luke says about Luke comes alive in a few clever strokes of his pen. He alone tells what place women held in the evangelistic campaigns of Jesus with his twelve (8:2, 3). It is Luke who paints the memorable picture of God as a *feeling* father watching and waiting for a prodigal's return. And Luke alone paints word pictures of a "good Samaritan," of a woman who is a "sinner," of an importunate widow before an unfeeling judge, of ten lepers healed only one of whom returned to give thanks and he was a Samaritan. And Luke's collection of masterpiece portraits includes one of Zacchaeus the scorned tax-collector, of a beggar comforted in Abraham's bosom, of a banquet in which "the poor, the crippled, the blind and the lame" became guests of honor. These and many others reveal the burden on Luke's heart with which he appeals to the inquiring soul of Theophilus. To write that God can be so human as to *feel* with the most miserable of humans is a stroke of genius. Of God in his painless isolation of heaven men may be affrighted. But a God on this earth enduring suffering with all kinds of humans is something else! God as a Creator! That's to be expected. But God among the sawdust and shavings of a carpenter's shop or handling the odorous filth of a leper's flesh is a revolutionary thought. At every turn of the road Luke reveals God in Christ as a sensitive, feeling human being. This is that which Luke declares in his book. And in that sense this is what the book says about itself.

The Synoptics!

We have taken a glance at all three of the Synoptic Gospels. A brief look at the Synoptics as a whole is in order. Three individuals make anything the same dissimilar. Can three women possessing dresses with the same print, color and style stroll on the same street and long remain the same? Three Volkswagens purchased by three people, even though the bug is the same model, will not have the same lines for long. Oversize tires soften the ride of one; a souped-up motor speeds up another; psychedelic paint reflects the taste of a third owner. Human experience establishes that three people shift three identicals to three distinctives.

Matthew, Mark and Luke hardly see together the person of Jesus. They embrace portraits painted by three artists using much the same colors, having the same model, yet they display three different masterpieces. Attempting to force the three into one, blurs the sharpness of each picture as much as a triple exposure produces a blurred image on a film.

The term synoptic as referring to the first three books of the New Testament is well fixed in biblical studies. Although not rigidly so, the books of Matthew, Mark and Luke exhibit similarities in structure, material and locale. Take locale. After an opening flash in which John baptizes Jesus in Judea's wilderness, Mark hastens the action to the Sea of Galilee. The cities bordering this depression and the high-lands overlooking Galilee's blue waters furnish the platform on which Jesus teaches friends and combats enemies. Beginning at 10:1 Mark propels Jesus toward Jerusalem, there to work out the tragedy of his death and the announcement of his resurrection. These two areas of Palestine frame the stage settings for all that Mark has to say.

As far as the scene of activity is concerned Matthew is no different than Mark. Matthew is not chronological; he is topical. Still, the Great Galilean Ministry, followed by the Jerusalem conflict remain the geographical theaters of the story of Jesus.

Luke enriches his narrative with an extra section of totally fresh material. He shuttles Jesus along the "borders of Samaria" and beyond Jordan. Yet in spite of this added terrain, Luke does not forsake the familiar Mark-Matthew environment of Galilee and Jerusalem. Thus, so far as locality is concerned all three "see together" the ministry of Jesus. They are synoptical.

The Synoptics use much material in common. More than three-fourths of Matthew (816 verses of 1068) show up in Mark's Gospel. Above two-thirds of Luke (798 of 1149 total verses) enliven our second Gospel. If the final twelve verses of Mark are not part of the original book (omitted by some mss.) then only twenty-three verses of Mark belong to him alone. Out of a total of 88 separate incidents heralded in the Synoptic Gospels, 71 of them adorn all three. Of the 661 verses in Mark's Gospel all but 23 form the fabric of the other two. If this be true, the word "synoptic" fittingly designates these three gospels. They are synoptical.

Also consider that in many sections which occur in all the Synoptics identical words appear in their descriptions. This fact clinches synoptic as quite suitable as a label for our first three gospels. Such verbal identity in over 50% of the material firmly verifies synoptic as an apt epithet.

But in spite of all similarities many differences force the question "Are the Synoptics synoptical?" In fact, the differences have created the synoptic problem of modern scholarship. How may we account for so much identity and yet so much divergence? But for the past two centuries scholarly attention has been fastened on the problem of literary origins and inner relationships. The peculiar messages of the Synoptics have been shunted to the side. Since they represent a Word from God, the main interest ought to be the messages more than origins. A starving man is less interested in the processes of the baker than in the bread he bakes. Famished humanity needs to hear *what* God says more than to settle questions as to God's method of speaking.

The fact that there are *any* differences between the Synoptics immediately sets each apart from the other. While the general structure is similar in all three, the specific use of the material separates them in their roles. Each adds *something* which the others don't have. That something lifts each account into a slightly different category. The annexing of a different incident to the Galilean ministry is like hanging a new picture in a gallery already filled. It supplies additional color and instills new character to the room. When Matthew alone relates how Jesus paid the temple-tax, he is touching up the color on his portrait of Jesus. He is clarifying his personal version of Messiah.

Even the differences of the three are different. Luke's differences from Mark are different than Matthew's differences from Mark. All three include Jesus' call of the four fishermen. But Luke characteristically surrounds the call with details which sharply enhance his sketch of Jesus as understandingly human. And consider how each opens his book. Mark knew more of the origins of Jesus than he reports.

89

But what he does *not* say is his literary device by which he stresses what is to be his principal point. "The beginning [elemental] of the gospel of Jesus Christ." Matthew provides the birth of Jesus but more than just the fact. He connects all to the shadows cast in the Old Testament. Jesus is "son of David, son of Abraham" as indeed Messiah must be. Luke too tells of the birth but with an entirely different approach. The thrill and grandeur of motherhood, the excited exchanges of joy between relatives, the ominous threat of overpowering, bureaucratic government, crowded highways, overflowing inns, humble shepherds, parental longings, and growing virgin — these accumulated snapshots fill the memory book of the story of Jesus, Son of man.

To reduce the three messages to one word each is an aid to memory. It also answers the mind's desire to package ideas in short, clear propositions. Even though this can be unfair to what each and all have said it is worth the effort. They all have presented Jesus as God's son, history's Messiah, and man's Saviour. Yet each has his own paramount idea. It is Matthew who says, "Behold, Messiah!" It is Mark who proclaims, "Behold, God!" And it is Luke who urges us to "See, the Saviour!" None denies what the others disclose. In fact, they supplement each other so the complete picture may include Deity, Messiah, human — all in One! Mankind needs a sense of history, a feeling of roots bearing fruits, of fulfillment. Man needs to know that God *is* and that he is powerfully present to help. Man needs as well a God who feels with us and suffers with us because he is one with us. To these needs the Synoptists write their books. Are the Synoptics really synoptical? They see the same thing differently!

Chapter Seven

THE JOHANNINE WRITINGS

The expression *Johannine Writings* here includes only the Gospel of John and the three epistles. But because of the uncommon content and the singular situation of the book of Revelation it is not included in this chapter.

The Gospel and epistles of John admit to a number of statements within them which refer directly to themselves. This is noticeably true of the epistles. Both the Gospel and I John provide clear, unclouded statements of purpose. While the two shorter letters, II and III John, are less clear they do say enough about the situation that brought them forth that we may determine something they say about themselves.

A tabulation of references to themselves in the Johannine writings impresses both the eye and the mind. This list may also serve a framework for our present inquiry. Such a cataloging includes the following:

1. John 20:30, 31

   Jesus did many other signs in the presence of the disciples, which are not written in this book, but these are written that you may go on believing that Jesus is the Christ, the Son of God, and that believing you may have life in his name.

2. John 21:24

   This is the disciple who is bearing witness to these things, and who has written these things; and we know that his testimony is true.

3. I John 1:1, 3

   . . . That which we have heard . . . seen . . . looked on . . . touched . . . concerning the word of life . . . we proclaim to you . . . that you also may have fellowship. . . .

4. I John 1:2

   And the life was manifested, and we have seen and are testifying and announcing to you the life, the eternal life, which was with the father and was manifested. . . .

5. I John 1:4

   And these things we are writing that our joy may be made full.

6. I John 1:5

   This is the message which we have heard from him and are declaring to you. . . .

7. I John 2:1

   My children, these things I write to you that you may not sin.

8. I John 2:7, 8

   Beloved I am not writing a new commandment to you, but an old commandment which you were having from the beginning. . . .

9. I John 2:12-14

   I write . . . I write . . . I write . . . I wrote . . . I wrote . . . I wrote. . . .

10. I John 2:21

    I am not writing to you because you do not know the truth but because you know it. . . .

11. I John 2:26

    I am writing these things to you about those who are leading you astray. . . .

12. I John 5:13

    These things I wrote to you that you may know that you are having eternal life, (that is), the ones believing in the name of the son of God.

13. II John vs. 5, 6

And now I beg you, Lady, not as though writing a new commandment to you, but one which you were having from the beginning; that we love one another.

14. II John vs. 12

Having many things to write to you, I was not wishing (to write) by paper and ink. . . .

15. III John vs. 1

The elder to Gaius, the beloved, whom I love in truth.

16. III John vs. 9

I wrote something to the church but the one loving pre-eminence over them, Diotrephes, does not receive us.

17. III John vs. 13

Many things I was having to write to you, but I do not wish by ink and pen to write, but I hope shortly to see you. . . .

When we consider the paucity of direct allusions of scriptures to themselves this is quite an extensive list. This is eminently impressive when we regard the brevity of the letters and that the Gospel has only two of the seventeen listed.

That these four pieces of literature arose out of the same millieu should not be overlooked. To read aright any New Testament book one must discover the problem that first prompted it. No book in the Bible, Old or New, would ever have been written had there been no need. And that is surely true of this body of Johannine literature. Furthermore, in a general sense they are all waves stirred up by the same storm, written by the same man, reflecting the same vexing question.

The scene of the aging apostle John's ministry in the late first century was in the churches of the Roman province of Asia. Reliable tradition reports this. The battles Paul fought with a Judaistic-legalistic Christianity were a matter of the past. A new threat was now disturbing the faith and ideals of the Christian community in western Asia Minor. It is known to us as Gnosticism. Teachers with Gnostic beliefs were infiltrating the churches disrupting the faith, peace and moral power of the Christians. Gnosticism incorporated in its presuppositions a strange mixture of Greek philosophy and Oriental mysticism. According to the Gnostics matter was in essence evil and Spirit in essence good. And the two were incompatible with each other. Hence this world of physical matter was inherently base, vile, foul, evil. Essentially it was and is evil and can contain no good. On the other hand God is good, righteous, chaste and virginal nor could he touch, admit or accommodate evil of any kind. If we grant their assumptions it is obvious that Christian faith as taught by Jesus and voiced in apostolic preaching could not be valid. Since Spirit is absolutely good and cannot share in evil an incarnation of God in which he became human was unthinkable. It destroys the deity of Christ. Furthermore, since matter is evil and spirit alone is good a basis for a moral ethic is also impossible. What Christianity pronounces sin is an inherent necessity of the flesh. Lying, stealing, adultery, murder are not sins. As certainly as gravity is ingrained in nature so these sins are the necessary outpourings of the physical nature of a man's physical body.

From this brief glance at the underlying tenents of Gnosticism one can see its negative, destructive nature. It negates basic Christian faith. Jesus could not possibly be the "Son of the living God." Besides, it discouraged any moral discipline in personal living. At the same time it encouraged selfish, sensual abandonment to lower animal tendencies.

94

Unethical behavior was not based in human choices but in the inevitable outcroppings of physical necessity. One could not have freedom of choice. Everything was predetermined by the involuntary hungers of flesh. In accord with this lecherous sensualism Gnosticism was loveless in practice. To feel responsible toward the hunger, poverty, nakedness, or feelings of other human beings was beyond the pale of Gnostic obligation. The words oblige or ought were not a part of Gnostic vocabulary. In Gnosticism there could be no genuine love, no duty, no sin. Life's goal was merely to get rid of the flesh in the handiest way possible in order that the spirit might be reabsorbed into the great World-Spirit.

Such was the problem that prompted the penning of the group of writings we term *Johannine*. And even this cursory overview of the problem illuminates many passages. For to hear what a New Testament book says about itself we have to listen against the background in which it was born. Gnosticism stimulated John's writings like disease incites a doctor's practice. If nobody gets sick, there's no need for any doctor. If Gnosticism had not invaded the churches of Asia, John would never have written. So his works must be read as a response to the Gnostic enigma.

The Gospel of John and the first epistle hold in common the same author, a similar vocabulary and style, an identical problem and the selfsame destination. They have also a doctrinal relationship. The Gospel of John frames the fact of history on which Christian faith rests. The first epistle formulates the experience in the believer of this fact of faith, the Christ. The Gospel presents Christ in history; the letter, Christ as experienced in the believer. The Gospel says, "Jesus is the Christ." The epistle says, "The Christ is Jesus" (in the believer). The Gospel roots God as a real man in real history. I John roots God in Christ as real in me. They say the same thing in the same words but from two decidedly different points of view.

The shorter epistles are two snapshots which picture one local congregation in its actual struggle to experience the historic Christ. II John was written to one of the local churches of the group to which the Gospel and first letter were sent. II John spotlights a particular congregation as it grappled with the Gnostic issue disturbing the churches in that whole province. It is an exhortation not to let the Christ of faith slip from them through neglecting to love. III John was directed to the same Christian community but to a particular man, Gaius, within the church. Gaius was a prominent member, healthy in soul, an excellent leader. But in addition to the unsettling influence of Gnostics the situation was aggravated by a certain Diotrephes. He loved to have the "preeminence." He was the kind of leader who must rule or ruin a church. He even did not "receive us." That is, he would not listen to John or his letter "to the church." So this private letter to Gaius was to encourage Gaius to persist with patience until he, John, could come and deal personally with Diotrephes. The two little letters give a vivid insight into the life of a first-century local congregation. How similar their problems to the 20th century!

No New Testament book has a more explicitly direct statement of purpose than the Gospel of John. And it reveals much more than purpose about itself.

> Jesus did many other signs in the presence of the disciples, which are not written in this book, but these are written that you may go on believing that Jesus is the Christ, the Son of God, and that believing you may have life in his name (John 20:30, 31).

The Gospel of John is a calculated, premeditated selection of signs. And the fact some were singled out implies that others were rejected. Not that they were any less real but they were less suitable for the author's purpose. And John does not leave this acceptance or rejection to the astute discernment of his reader. He plainly says that Jesus did "many" other signs. If his selected signs be limited to what is often labelled miraculous we note a total of seven, not including the resurrection.

But we need not limit John's signs to the seven selected miracles. John's recording of the miracles reveal his typical pattern of thinking. He viewed outward events as revealing inward realities whether those events were miraculous or the more normal expressions of the hidden energies of creation. Whether it was the cleansing of the temple, the betrayal of Judas, the washing of the disciples' feet, or the pouring of expensive perfume on the feet of Jesus, these all signified something beyond the outward act itself. In other words, they were signs.

Nevertheless, when the author in 20:30, 31 speaks of "many other signs" not written, and in saying "these are written" he has in mind the seven chosen miracles plus the resurrection. Like signboards along a highway, they direct the reader-traveler to something down the road that should be of concern to him. A sign is not an end in itself for it points to something other than itself.

Sometimes a commercial company advertises its product by a number of signs along a highway. Each separate sign contains a particular point of value about the product. When the passing traveler has read all the signs, has become impressed with each separate merit, he catches a total idea. He gets an overpowering sense of value. By the time he reaches the next town he is convinced, convicted, "sold." So he stops and buys the product. This is similar to what John has devised to convict his readers. He has a specific purpose in mind. In his experience with Jesus he saw many signs. Yet there were some that stood taller than others in the effect they had in nurturing his own faith about Jesus. So these he selected as being focal points around which he would tell the story of the Christ. Each sign has its own distinctive message. But each also is connected in meaning to the other six. Furthermore, the overall effect, the total message of the whole seven viewed as one, is vitally related to Jesus' greatest sign, his resurrection. The seven were classified ads; the resurrection was a full page display. It said it all! The seven gave the message piece-meal. But together they prepared the mind to comprehend the full message of the death, burial and resurrection of Jesus, the Christ.

We are not left to wonder about what John's purpose was. ". . . These are written that you may believe that Jesus is the Christ, the Son of God, and that believing you may have life in his name" (John 20:31). The expression "that you may believe" is about as explicit as one may get in stating purpose. But a word of caution is in order here. John was not written to initiate faith in unbelievers. It was written to Christians of longstanding faith, some of whom were second or third generation Christians. The Gospel of John was not written that men might get faith as though they had never had it. It was written that the readers "might go on having faith." That is, that they would not lose or let slip what they already had.

A deadly poison was eating at the flesh and morals of the church-body in Asia. Its cancerous growth was placing in jeopardy the health and stamina of the souls of those under John's pastoring care. The human, Jesus, was being denied by the subtle Gnostic infiltration as being the divine Christ. The pure God could never have a "Son" who dwelt in flesh — so taught these Gnostic teachers. They hung like leeches sucking the lifeblood of these Asian churches. So John says about his own Gospel that he proposes to describe seven signs from the many Jesus wrought. Moreover, his plan involves discussions, debates, clashes, teachings, tidings, confessions and claims of Jesus with various representative Jews both hostile and friendly. Each of these clashes or claims is related to the seven signs as meaning relates to fact. It takes only a few well chosen words to state the fact that Napoleon was defeated by Wellington at Waterloo. But it would take pages if not volumes to explain the significance to human history of that event. So John says about his own book that it consists of signs rehearsed in such a way as to embrace their meaning. Along with each miracle is narrative material. The sign throws light on the narrative and the narrative reflects light on the miracle. The fact is explained by thought and the thought explains the fact. John says, ". . . These are written that you may believe. . . ." Believe what? Believe something about Jesus, the man, that would lead to trusting Him as divine, "Son of God."

A listing of the seven signs with the briefest of statements of meaning or application will help the mind grasp what John says his Gospel is all about.

1. Water transposed into wine, 2:1-11. The *joy of life* restored, not by rituals of religion, but by the person of Jesus as the Christ.
2. Healing of an official's son, 4:46-54. Not time, race, sex, or social level but trust in Christ's word brings healing.

Not place but *faith* triggers the flow of the power of the person of Christ.

3. Healing a cripple at Bethesda, 5:1-15. The Sabbath was made for *re*-creation of man who has been ravaged by sin. Life is an unending Sabbath in which God in Christ seeks to repair man.

4. Feeding 5000, 6:1-15.
   Man has needs as well as stains, craving as well as cracks. Beyond healing he requires *support*. So, "I am the bread of life. . . ."

5. Walking on the water, 6:16-21.
   Man needs *guidance* amid forces over which he has no control. When they were willing to take him into the boat, "immediately the boat was at the land where they were going."

6. Sight given to a man born blind, 9:1-12. Besides support and guidance man needs sight since by birth he has been born into blindness. *Obedience* to Christ brings light to darkened eyes, truth to darkened hearts and minds.

7. The raising of Lazarus, 11:17-44.
   The Life in Christ is sovereign over life and *victor* over death.

When these seven signs of John's selection are stitched together as a single fabric they form one grand design. However much the faith of the first readers was sagging this portrait of the person of Jesus as the Christ would lift it, restore it, and sustain it. The glory of Christ shone through seven shafts of sunlight breaking through the gloomy clouds which hung heavily over faith.

But the seven were crowned by the resurrection of Jesus. As the beams of sunlight gain their brightness from the central sun so the resurrection holds within itself the pith and soul of each and all the seven signs. The resurrection reaffirms and confirms all that the seven say. Clear and loud it shouts that Jesus is the joy, the recreation, the support and guidance of life. And that His sovereignty over life and victory over death is open to all who trust and obey his person.

Furthermore, *every episode, every event, every discussion* from John 13:1 through 20:29 helps unravel the baffling mystery of the cross. The washing of the disciples' feet by Jesus was more than a lesson in humility. It was an objective demonstration of what the cross means in personal relationships between human beings. And this theme of the cross stretches through the betrayal, the trial, the tree itself, and the triumph of faith when Thomas exclaimed, "My Lord and my God."

And when we sum up what the sign of the resurrection says plus the seven it all adds up to *Jesus was a real man who lived a real life and died a real death.* Yet He was more! *He was the real God, living His divine life in human nature, in human limitations to the extent that He really dies a death!* "The Word became flesh . . . full of grace and truth" (John 1:14).

There is a yet deeper purpose underlying John's Gospel than to demonstrate that the man, Jesus, is the divine Christ. John has more in mind than merely to declare a doctrine. For doctrine is of little value until translated into redeemed life. So John says that the signs presented in his book have for their ultimate goal, ". . . that believing you may have life in his name" (John 20:31). Faith in the Christ of the past translates itself into present moral power. If I believe that the pure waters of a mountain spring will bring health to my fevered, parched body, then I will pipe it to my kitchen, store it in reservoirs, and drink it to cool my body and restore my health. Trust in the man Jesus as the divine Christ means

101

that the water of life is piped into the fevered soul and parched spirit of the sinning saint. Faith not only relieves the conscience bent low under the load of past guilt but it also releases moral power to resist the pressure of present temptation. This is what the apostle John says about the book of John.

To undergird his witness about his book the author adds what amounts to his signature in 21:24. "This is the disciple who bears witness to these things, and who has written these things; and we know that his testimony is true." Through the centuries many had denied to the apostle John his authorship of this Gospel. Yet the meandering speculations of critics, both destructive and constructive, have not been able to shake the solid internal and external evidence supporting the tradition of John's authorship. The major claim of verse 24 is, "and we know that his testimony is true." This is a very important allegation of John about his own book. It's not just a claim that the facts are straight, that the signs are accurately reported. Much more than that! It asserts that the true, genuine, real meaning of the facts is incorporated in this Gospel. John affirms that his facts are accurately reported. But he also affirms that his explanation of the significance of those facts is their real meaning.

The first fourteen verses of chapter six relate the fact of the feeding of 5000 from a little lad's fish and barley loaves. And the people who witnessed the sign, with excitement concluded, "This is . . . the prophet that comes into the world" (John 6:15). But Jesus perceiving that they would force him into their mold of king-prophet rejected their offer of the kingly crown. Then in that same sixth chapter verses 22-59 John interpreted for his readers the *kind* of king Jesus came to be. He would not support life by the power of the sword; not even with bread for the belly. But he was the "bread which comes down out of heaven, that a man may eat thereof and not die" (John 6:50). And, "I am the living bread . . . if any man eat of this bread, he shall live forever . . ." (John 6:51). Jesus came to enlighten the mind with truth, to purify the emotions with an unstained object of feeling, and to galvanize the will with an inward motive for obedience. In other words, He would be king of the spirits of men. His was a sovereignty over heads and hearts, not over real estate or governments. He would rule by love, not force, by persuasion rather than coercion. He would generate moral power, not military glory. He would feed the soul, not the stomach. He would feed the fountainhead of faith and blast open the log-jam of cynical doubt that was destroying humanity. He came to be king but it was a kingdom that conquered sin and its consequence, death.

So, when John wrote in 21:24, "We know that his testimony is true" he claims more than a faultless report of the fact that Jesus miraculously fed 5000. He is maintaining that his explanation of that report is the true one. And thus with all the signs.

I John

Two times in his first letter John makes a clear statement of purpose, once in 1:3 and a second time in 5:13. The passage in 5:13 leaves no doubt that his immediate point in writing *this* letter is that his readers may "know" with the certainty of absolute knowledge that they even now are in possession of life eternal. Tests of the presence of eternal life are as readily available as are the tests by which physical life is measured. That his readers may know these tests and how to recognize and use them is the stated intent of the apostle when he set about writing I John.

But John's pronouncement of purpose in 1:3 brings out a somewhat different idea. It also seems to include more than *this* immediate letter. He affirms, ". . . that which we have seen and heard, we declare also to you, in order that you may go on having fellowship with us." In 5:13 the author used the verb "I wrote" indicating his current letter that he was then in the process of writing. But in 1:3 he chooses the verb "we declare" or "announce." So far as the content of the epistle is concerned it does embrace three specific tests by which fellowship in divine life may be checked out. But it does *not* embody "that which we have seen and heard," that is, the apostolic witness to their experiences with Jesus. The logical explanation of this difference in purpose would seem to be that in 1:3 he refers to the proclamation of the historical facts of the Gospel. In I John 5:13 he refers to the present Christian experience of the Christ in the heart and life of the readers.

What does John say about his own works? He says that he is writing his letter to provide tests by which the reality of eternal life in their experience may be measured. Moreover, he wants their unbroken fellowship in the faith as proclaimed in the Gospel of John. The apostle seems to claim for his books a firm basis on which fellowship with God can be built, and on which a community of fellowship of believers can be reared. And the actual reading of John and I John will induce precisely that kind of faith and fellowship.

There is yet a third statement of design included in I John. It has a more intimately personal ring; less formal, less

104

theologic; quite warmly human. It unveils the concern of writer for readers in his anxiety for their spiritual health. In 1:4 he says, "These things we are writing that our joy may be made full." Now, that's the earthy, down-to-earth reason why he wrote. Even a textual variation in the Greek manuscripts cannot remove this verse as a revelation of the feelings of the author. Some manuscripts have "your joy" instead of "our joy." But in either case it was his feelings of concern about their welfare that prompted his literary effort.

Whenever we consider that the books of the Bible are inspired of God such earthy human motivations ought always be noted. Inspiration, among other things, denotes the activity of God working in and with weak, limited human beings to get His message across. He breathes on them in order to speak His truth through them. So, when John felt a deep, personal anxiety about the spiritual health of the readers under his pastoral care God took hold of that anxiety as a point in which he could speak his word to their need. John was motivated to find joy for himself and his readers; God used such human feelings to give certain assurance to believers of their redemption. Inspiration does not set aside the human personalities of the writers; it uses them.

From the list of 17 quotes from Johannine writings recorded above, ten of them (3 through 12) are from I John. And each of the ten represents a thought of the author about his writing. But they do not so much refer to the entire letter as they do to the limits of the context in which each appears. For example 2:1 reads, "My children, these things I write to you that you may not sin." While in principle the "these things" might pertain to the whole letter, its immediate reference is to what he has written beginning at 1:5. There is a unity of thought in I John from 1:5 through 2:6. The idea developed has to do with a test by which the reader may measure whether he is "walking in the light." This test is "righteousness." First, negatively (1:6—2:2) and then positively (2:3-6). We "walk in the light" when we "confess our guilt" and when we "keep his commandments. . . ." So, the "these things" of 2:1 refer primarily to the positive and negative ways of evaluating one's "walking in the light" of God's truth about oneself.

A similar reference to the immediate context holds true in 2:7-8 when he speaks of ". . . not writing a new commandment to you, but an old. . . ." He is alluding to the commandment of love under discussion from 2:7 through 2:17. And thus also in 2:21 and 2:26 in which the context indicates that it is the test of belief under consideration from 2:18 through 2:27.

If one is to take the Bible seriously and wants to read it with understanding he must be willing to make the effort to listen to what each author has to say about his own work. Sometimes it is clearly stated. Other times one must look beneath the surface and read between the lines. But every author betrays his own feelings about his own book some way or other. Simple honesty demands that we let an author say what he has to say. The reader has no moral right to impose his own opinions or force an author to say or mean what the reader may wish. One must look and listen while he reads.

And there are places in which we cannot be sure precisely what an author means by what he writes. This is true even when he makes a direct statement about his passage. A prime example in I John is 2:12-14. These verses involve a number of puzzling problems. First, how many classes of readers does he address? two or three? He uses three terms: "little children," "fathers," "young men." And were there no females in the churches to which he was writing? A second problem is: why repeat an almost identical threefold apology for writing—addressed to the same classes of people? Yet a third perplexity is the author's change of verb forms between the first set of three and the second set of reasons for writing. He says, "I write . . . I write . . . I write." Then he changes from present to what may be termed "narrative past tense" by saying, "I wrote . . . I wrote . . . I wrote." And still a fourth question is: why include this section at all? It is a parenthetical interruption in the flow of the author's thought. It intrudes with a seemingly illogical break in the author's argument. If inspired (and we are not questioning that) what contribution to God's word does such an apparent suspension of an author's logic make? Very honestly, these questions are difficult to answer *with certainty.* To seek answers we must rely on context, common sense, and a double sense of dependency on God's help.

The first problem we have indicated in 2:12-14 is that of the classes of people addressed. It is impossible to accept the idea that no girls or women shared membership in these congregations. After all these churches had been founded by Paul a generation or two earlier. And he had written about being "no male or female" in Christ. We know by name of one woman from one of these churches who lived in Paul's day, Lydia. Though Thessalonica was not of this province it furnishes a pattern for women in church membership; Acts 17:4 reports members there "of the chief women not a few." We are safe in assuming women as members, probably in equal if not greater numbers than men, in the churches of Asia. So we conclude that in a man's world such as first century after Christ was, the classes addressed as "father" and "young men" include within their scope the females of the churches.

But what does our author mean by "little children" coupled with "fathers" and "young men?" The content of I John is hardly the kind of thought-provoking material that would be written to kindergarteners! Nor to children of elementary grade level. Besides, the reason for writing to "fathers" is given as "because you have known the one from the beginning," that is, their long years of experience in Christ. And the reason appended to "young men" is "because you have conquered the evil one." In other words, the reason he wrote to each class was due to the stage of Christian struggle normal for that particular class. For "fathers" it was long experience. For "young men" it was their present battle with Satan. But the reason attached to "little children" is "because the sins have been forgiven to you." This is not very appropriate address for small children who are scarcely removed from childhood innocency. But it does fit *any* Christian of *any* level of Christian experience. Moreover, John uses the same term, "little children," when he is undeniably addressing the whole of the congregation(s) (2:1, 18, 28; 5:21, etc.). Thus, we conclude that John addresses the entire church by "little children." Then he breaks them down into two general classes, older and younger, including both men and women. Are not all churches, then and now, made up of older experienced and younger struggling people?

A second problem of our passage is "Why repeat a three-fold apology? Especially since it is addressed to the same two classes? And linked to this is the third question, "Why the change of tense from present to past—from 'I write' to 'I wrote'?"

Repetition is a teacher's best means of arresting, fixing, and impressing the mind. Whether that was John's reason for repeating or not his repetition here surely has the effect of emphasis. Clarity of thought is another reason for repeating. The threefold apology for writing is not an *exact* reproduction. There are slight, yet significant, variations in the repeated statements, especially for "young men." He reasons, "because you are strong and the word of God abides in you and you have conquered the evil one." By thus expanding the reason the author not only gains emphasis but lucidity.

In connection with the problem of repetition is that of the change from present to past tense. No problem exists with "I write." He obviously was referring to the letter he was in the process of writing. But, having decided to repeat himself for emphasis and clarity, why alter the verb form to "I wrote"? No answer to this enigma will satisfy everyone. But the most satisfying seems to be that as he concluded the writing of verse 13a he was interrupted. It was some hours, maybe days, before he returned to take up again his line of thought. As he retraced what he had written and was determining how to proceed with his ideas he was thinking in "past time."

The question as to why include this parenthetical interruption at all still remains. Why did John break his line of argument? The answer to this problem does not lie in the logic of the thought but in the psychology of human feelings. John is considerate of the feelings of his readers. He does not use apostolic authority or the power of his official position to force home truth. He wants to gain the willing cooperation of his people, not their abject capitulation to superior force. Nor would he have their resentful compliance even to truth.

The New Testament epistles sent to churches were designed to be read aloud in the public assemblies. As the congregation sat in assembly and listened to the reading of I John the topic of love and hate was unfolding. Suppose 2:12-14 had not been included. The reading of verse 11 followed without interruption by verse 15 could be easily misunderstood. It might conceivably build resentment and rejection upon the part of over-sensitive souls present in the audience.

> But he that hates his brother is in the darkness, and walks in the darkness, and knows not where he goes, because the darkness has blinded his eyes. . . . Don't be loving the world, neither the things in the world. If any man love the world, the love of the father is not in him.

In the social and theological disturbances bothering these Asian churches such severe words could sound harsh—even offensive. They could stir resentment. So, in order to guard against misunderstanding and in order to encourage his readers to greater efforts he inserted this complimentary interruption. In effect he was saying, "I don't mean to imply that you are walking in darkness . . . because you *are* experienced . . . strong . . . forgiven . . . etc. . . ." The tools of John's trade as an apostle included psychology as well as logic. And in I John 2:12-14 he was at his psychological best.

It may seem that an undue amount of space and energy has been taken with this passage of 2:12-14, particularly since it does not contribute any logical development to the theme of the epistle. But the space and energy is justified for two reasons. First, the psychology that initially produced these verses is still useful to modern readers as well as the ancient. And for the same reason. It encourages the modern reader to self-examination. Have my years of experience in Christ brought me to the knowledge of "the one from the beginning"? And as a younger one in Christ I am privileged to examine whether "I have overcome the evil one." And we all, younger and older, ancient or modern, need to realize that our "sins have been forgiven for his name's sake."

Even more important is the contribution this passage makes to a healthy view of how God inspires the men whom he used as penmen in producing the sacred scriptures. One should not forget that inspiration not only has to do with *what* is revealed from God to man but *how* it is said as well. God is not interested in smashing to smithereens the reluctant will of a potential prophet or apostle. Those who were to be literary channels of his spoken or written word must work with the utmost freedom of will. To be effective they must be willing. To be convincing they have to know the skills of persuasion. They do not need to be bookish but they do need to write books. They do not need to be grammarians but they do need to know how to articulate ideas, how to communicate clearly in words. They do not need to be professional psychoanalysts but they do need to know how to fire the emotions of men that will stir them to strong actions.

In other words, inspiration is neither wooden, mechanical or magical. God does not breathe into (inspire) heartless statues, or motorized machines, or witch's potions arbitrarily injected into an unconscious mind. The man through whom God breathes is alert to every talent, skill, literary device or psychological bit of information he can command. Medical skills (Luke), academic proficiency (Paul), the accountant's trade (Matthew), the fisherman's expertise (Peter and John) — these all felt the breath of God pulsating through their souls. God blew on their crafts and turned man and craft into one welded instrument of inspiration. This is the reason lying back of John's use of the passage at I John 2:12-14. The aged apostle had learned much

111

about human nature over his many years. He had an inspired message. But he must also be inspired to deliver it effectively in keeping with how he knows human nature will react emotionally.

There are two sides to inspiration; man who is inspired and God who inspires. Under God's inspiration a man is not wholly passive. He thinks, feels and wills in a specific cultural environment. This furnishes the alphabet and vocabulary of his works. So the Spirit of God which inspires him limits Himself to the man's cultural vocabulary. It is the man who does the thinking, the feeling, the acting. It is God's Spirit who does the breathing into the man's thinking, feeling and willing.

On the basis of these two principles John was inspired to include 2:12-14 in his first epistle. John recognized the practical wisdom of softening his harsh words of 2:11 and 15 without changing a single word of warning. John chose to write the interruption of verses 12-14. On the other hand the Spirit of God breathed (inspired) on John's effort to refine and purify that which needed to be said and how it should be said. So we see that what John says about why he wrote "children," "fathers," and "young men" opens up a whole vista of truth about inspiration. And that not just for his little letter but for all the other books of the Bible.

II and III John

The salutations in the two short letters, II and III John, open a window looking on life in a local church of the first century. Both letters ascribe themselves as drafted by "the elder." Some scholars have suggested that this "elder" was a John other than the apostle. But there is no valid evidence to lead to that conclusion. These two letters are more intimately personal and confidential than either Gospel or I John. That close, special warmth finds reflection in the author's use of "elder." And it is good tradition that identifies "the elder" with the apostle.

No doubt prevails as to whom the third letter was addressed. It was a respected individual leader in a local church. His name was Gaius. But a decided difference of opinion persists among students as to whom the second letter is directed. The salutation reads, "The elder unto the elect lady and her children, whom I love in truth . . ." (II John 1). Is this "elect lady" an individual or a local congregation addressed under the name *Kyria*? Without question that was a common name at that time. But it appears more rational to view this letter as sent to a congregation. Women occupied a more prominent role in the early churches than moderns are willing to concede. However, for the apostle to address a particular woman under such terms of universal affection is not likely. If this letter is not to a church then we have here only an intimate view into the life of one family. And a family with no husband or father, either through death, desertion, divorce or other such calamity. Why one such family would be singled out as deserving special description is harder to figure than that one local church would be depicted. Besides, when the author writes, ". . . whom I love in truth" he adds "and not only I, but also all they that know the truth." It is understandable and acceptable that an apostle should speak of his love for a particular woman. That's quite normal. But to assert that "all they that know the truth" also loved this particular individual woman is asking too much. Such a woman must indeed be universally prominent for "all" truth-lovers to love her as John did.

It seems much more natural to view this "Lady" to be a particular local congregation of believers.

In addition, verse 13 lends support to the idea of a church: "The children of your elect sister salute you." Was John writing a letter to act as a mediator between two sisters? hardly! That he referred to two congregations is much more plausible. So we conclude that John's allusions in his salutations are his way of calling attention to the fact that he writes in these two letters about one particular congregation of Christians. II John is to the church; III John is to Gaius, a leader in that church.

The basic problem as echoed in the letters was the need for reminding the readers "to love one another" (II John 5, 6). Such a need was made more visible by the agitation of Diotrephes in his effort to corner all the praise and power that comes from being Mr. Number One. He "loved the preeminence!" (III John 9). This lack of love and grasping after prominence grew out of Gnostic deceivers, "the ones not confessing Jesus as Christ as coming in flesh . . ." (II John 7). Doctrinal dangers were bearing fruit in a loveless ethic and a greedy grasping for power.

In evaluating what John says about his two brief letters we note that both declare his unwillingness to write everything that is on his mind about their current situation. A full unloading must await his personal presence when he could speak "face to face." Writing is better than ignoring the problem but there can be no substitute for face to face coping with the issue. So! What does John say about these two little letters of his? He indicates that writing, while a helpful device, is not adequate for resolving the congregation's present problems. He obviously felt the wind of God blowing through his soul, wafting through his heart. He must speak!

114

But he could not wait until he confronted them face to face, so he wrote. First, a letter to the church (III John 9). But in order to make the letter more effective he wrote a private letter to Gaius. By these letters the Spirit of God operating in the human qualities of the aged apostle could shore up the flagging love, rekindle the doctrinal perceptions about Jesus as the Christ, and dam up somewhat the flood waters which the disturbance of Diotrephes had released. These inspired words would have to do until he could come and deal with things "face to face." Then he would say many things which he was not inclined to say with paper and ink.

Without attempting to develop an answer we are led to raise the question, If this apostle's written words are inspired of God, would the words he spoke when he finally faced them face to face be any less so?

Chapter Eight

THE PAULINE EPISTLES

Epistles of Paul addressed to individuals and churches total thirteen. Hebrews is not included here because too much uncertainty exists as to its authorship on the part of too many scholars of every conceivable theological stance. Some of the thirteen have been questioned as to Paul's authorship, but we accept the traditional view. We do know that Paul dictated some of his letters, then signed them "with my own hand."

In this investigation into what Paul's letters say about Paul's letters we will first glance at the salutations. They say or imply something about authorship and destination. Then we'll cast a brief look at those letters in which he states that he signed with "his own hand." Following that, a glimpse at those passages in which he claims or implies God's guidance will be in order. A pause to examine Paul's adeptness in using without abusing his apostolic position will throw light on both inspiration and authority. Finally, a brief sampling of Paul's use of the Old Testament will add knowledge and insight on our theme of *What The Scriptures Say About the Scriptures.*

Considering that the first century was an age without printing presses, typewriters, teletypes, radios and televisions for rapid exchanges it was a time of extensive communication. Epistolary activity distinguished the first century. Letter writing was an art. But more than that, it was a means of linking society together. Had it not been for letter writing, government, commerce, and social stability could not have been strongly tied together. Provincialism rather than universalism would have marked the times. Roman highways facilitated rapid transport of mail, public and private.

116

Like other enterprises, the church of the first Christian century had its emissaries traveling the highways with mail from pastors to people. To be getting letters from apostle to people and from church to church nurtured a sense of brotherhood. Such interchange formed a vital cog in the wheel of Christian fellowship. Without it there scarcely could have been any unity. For a sample read Colossians 4:16. "When this epistle has been read among you, cause that it be read also in the church of the Laodiceans; and that you also read the epistle from Laodicea." Letter writing was a major factor in giving the early church a sense of fellowship on a world-wide basis.

In the light of this widespread use of epistolary communication the letters of the New Testament must be viewed. These sacred missives are not isolated cases of literary interchange. On the contrary, they are as domesticated to that early culture as an apple tree fits into a fruit orchard. In the driving speed with which modern life is dispatched a salutation gets no more than a "Dear Sir" or a "Dear Jim." But salutations in the ancient society were leisurely enough to reveal more about both writer and reader. It included who wrote and to whom. And it did so with an embroidered flourish. Enough so that the reader could get the impression that he was worth writing to. At any rate the salutations of New Testament letters follow the pattern of first century letters as revealed by thousands of samples found in papyri remains of the Graeco-Roman civilization.

All thirteen of Paul's letters enclose two basic elements. First, his name, Paul! In the different letters various identifying epithets are added. It may be, "apostle of Jesus Christ . . ." or "a slave of . . ." or "a called apostle. . . ." On occasion some of his companions in labor join him in his opening salute. When they do, they are included as responsible authors of the epistle's contents.

Another part of the salutation is the greeting, "Grace to you and peace from God our father" (Col. 1:2). Or in a more expanded form, ". . . grace, mercy, and peace from God our father and Christ Jesus our Lord" (I Tim. 1:2). The ideas of "grace" and "peace" are not exclusively Pauline, not even restricted to Christian circles. "Peace" (*Shalom*) was typically Hebrew as a word of address. The Greek χάρις (grace) in the Graeco-Roman world became the Gentile word of salutation. As in so many other areas of human life Christianity picked up a common cultural usage, poured new and richer meaning into the receptacle, and turned it into something quite distinctively Christian. The writings of Paul, Peter, and John lay hold of this duet of ideas, "grace and peace." The Christian gospel discovers the origin of grace in the very nature of God. As it pours unceasingly into man it brings peace, calm, tranquility to the heart and soul of man. None of Paul's letters could open without a recognition of such grace and peace which saturates both center and circumference of the man "in Christ." "Grace and peace" is at once the wish of Paul to his readers and the right of the readers to claim for themselves. As a salutation it invited writer and reader into a more intimate bond than the detached "Dear Sir" could suggest. So, the first fact we note about Paul's letters is their embodiment of the essence of the gospel in his salutation. They identify the author and suggest an overview of the entire Christian message.

Paul is the *author* of his letters. That might seem to be a wasted statement! Whom should one expect to be the author of Paul's letters other than Paul? Well, the answer to that depends on what the word "author" means. His letter to the

Galatians was apparently dictated to one of his assistants. In 6:11 he says, "See with how large letters I write unto you with my own hand." To pen other of his letters we know he depended upon secretarial service. Romans 16:22 provides us with the name of one such helper. "I, Tertius, who write the epistle, salute you in the Lord." And in three other of his epistles Paul indicates that he personally finished a letter the rest of which he had dictated. See II Thessalonians 3:17: "The salutation of me Paul with my own hand, which is the token in every epistle: so I write." To guard against forgeries apparently Paul had the habit of finishing each of his communications with his personal signature accompanied by an added gracious touch. (Cf. I Cor. 16:21; Col. 4:18.) So if we mean by author the one who actually penned the letters the apostle was not the author of most of them. But if we mean by the term author the one who was the source of the ideas then Paul was the author of all thirteen. And even should we concede to the judgment of some scholars that a few of his loyal helpers wrote in specific situations in the name of Paul that still leaves Paul as the basic source of the ideas. For example, a school of thought projects the idea that the apostle did not write Ephesians. Their views are based largely on vocabulary, style and the mature fullness of the ideas developed. But the chief point with which we are concerned here is that even if Ephesians (or other books) were in fact written down by students of Paul, the apostle still remains the author of the ideas. And in that sense he is the responsible author of all thirteen epistles which bear his name. And in point of fact there is *no* external evidence to contradict the tradition that Paul was the actual original author. The evidence to the opposite view is entirely subjective based on internal evidence within the books themselves.

119

One New Testament letter in which Paul states, "I Paul write it with my own hand" is Philemon. That the apostle personally penned this entire letter seems quite logical. It is intensely personal, written to one individual with whom Paul had enjoyed warm and congenial relationships. In fact Philemon "owed" to Paul his "own self," that is, his salvation in Christ. Because of the delicate problem with which this brief letter deals it seems best to think of Paul as having actually inscribed the whole letter. The verse (19) in which "with my own hand" appears has the value of a legal promissory note. Philemon's legal slave, Onesimus, had *robbed* his master of his services by escaping to Rome. It is quite probable that Onesimus also literally robbed Philemon of money and property. In the capital city the slave of Philemon came under the influence of the slave of Christ. He was converted to Christ and became one of Paul's trusted friends and workers. But rather than keep Onesimus at his side as a helper without the free consent of Philemon Paul felt it honorable to send the slave back to the master. Judging by the content of the letter Paul fully expected Philemon to set Onesimus free from his legal slavery. Furthermore, also to send him back to Paul as a worker in the gospel. To enlist Philemon's will, freely and unforced, was the design of the apostle when he determined to dispatch such a letter. He could not afford to entrust the penning of this letter to even his most trusted amanuensis. To confirm this we may note that Paul's expression of writing with his "own hand" comes in the midst of the letter. It is not in the salutation either at the beginning or end. It is at a point in which Paul raises the possibility, actually a probability, that Onesimus had stolen money and/or property. He wishes to guarantee to Philemon that his material losses will be made good. So he writes, "If he wronged you in anything or owes you any-thing, put this down to my account. I Paul write it with my own hand, I will repay it" (Philemon 18, 19). Since this is not a part of the salutation, it must be taken seriously as a promise to pay. And for such a matter it was imperative that Paul write his own signature. And as we have noted above, the circumstances of this letter make it probable that the entire letter was in his own hand.

What does Paul say about his own letters? Judging from his salutations alone, he claims authorship, he sets forth the essence of the gospel message, he enlists compatriots as co-authors, and he signs his letters himself even though he dictates the rest. And in at least one instance he penned the whole of it.

In a number of places Paul clearly claims God's guidance in what he is writing. In Galatians 1:20 the apostle dis-claims lying in what he is writing: "Now as to which things I am writing to you, behold, before God, I am not lying." That can hardly be classed as a claim for God's guidance. Most anyone would make such an assertion about his own writing, especially if he had been challenged as Paul had been. But the circumstances that prompted Paul to insert such a statement of "not lying" make it more than just a disclaimer of being a liar.

That which stimulated the writing of Galatians struck at the authorship of Paul as well as the gospel message as he viewed and preached it. Judaizing Christians had visited the churches of Paul's planting in the Roman province of Asia. Though believers in Jesus as the promised Christ they insisted, "Except you be circumcised after the custom of Moses, you cannot be saved." It was not only Christ who saves but Christ *plus* the moral code of Moses and religious taboos sanctioned by human traditions. These intruders attacked the validity of Paul as an apostle. They said that he was not one of the twelve; had never learned the gospel from Jesus in the flesh; was really a renegade from Moses and the law preaching a message at variance with that of Peter and the twelve. They believed his message of justification by grace undermined the restrictions, ethics and moral values of their historic traditions. They held that he had no authority as an apostle, his message was a liberalizing corruption of the true gospel. To them his gospel was of human invention, not of divine revelation. The Galatian brethren were rapidly "removing themselves . . . unto a different gospel" (Gal. 1:6).

To combat this personal and vicious attack Paul sent this letter. After his first missionary journey, *after* the council meeting at Jerusalem as reported in Acts 15, *after* the "apostles, . . . elders, with the whole church" at Jerusalem expressed their unity in support of the gospel as Paul preached it, but *before* he launched his second journey Paul posted Galatians. Paul believed he was a genuine apostle, called personally by Christ. He also believed his message was revealed by God to him, not given by men, not even from the twelve who were apostles before him. Consequently these are the two basic issues with which he deals in the epistle. In 1:20 where he repudiates the accusation of lying he is developing the factual history of when, where and how he got his gospel message. He did not get it "from men." He never visited the apostles to learn from them, he did not "confer with flesh and blood." On the contrary, "God . . . called me through his grace, to reveal his son in me . . ." (Gal. 1:11-17). After these things he spent three years in Arabia, alone. At least he was not conferring with "flesh and blood." It is in the midst of this line of argument that he makes his statement about "behold, before God, I am not lying" (Gal. 1:20). This may not be a positive claim of God's inbreathing. But it certainly appears in the midst of a context in which the apostle is ardently pressing the point that he got both his message and apostleship, not from men, but from God.

The whole of Galatians is saturated with this idea that God, not men, made him what he was and gave him what he had. The opening verse headlines both ideas. "Paul, an apostle (not from men, neither through men, but through Jesus Christ, and God the father . . ." (Gal. 1:1). In other words, he was an apostle by divine sanction, not human. Then in verse four Paul describes Jesus Christ as the "one who gave himself for our sins, that he might rescue us out of this present evil world. . . ." In these words his message of grace comes through clearly. As drowning swimmers are dependent on a lifeguard to rescue them from their own self-defeating struggles to be saved, so Jesus as the Christ rescues us. He did for us what we could not do for ourselves. Our efforts to save ourselves is like one sinking in quicksand. The more we struggle to be free the deeper we sink into the mire. Our rescue is of His grace, not our efforts. If God, not men, made him an apostle and if God, not men, gave him his message would not God, not human initiative, guide Paul in the deliverance of that word? Such an idea colors the context in which the apostle wrote, ". . . before God, I lie not."

Paul was not reluctant to hang out a sign openly declaring that he got his revelation from God. Galatians 1:1 claims he was made an apostle by God. Verses 11, 12 of the same chapter maintain that he got his message by revelation from

God. "For I make known to you, brethren, as touching the gospel which was preached by me, that it is not after man. For neither did I receive it from man, nor was I taught it, but through revelation of Jesus Christ." While such a statement does not allege that God directly prompted, guided, or helped him in writing this Galatian epistle it does say that God gave him his gospel message by revelation. And that message Paul sets forth in vigorous terms with deep feelings in this letter. It is difficult to conceive that God gave the message but withdrew from helping when the apostle set the message down in writing. Particularly when writing to believers under threat of denying and abandoning the very message revelation had given in the first place. If God guided Paul in such decisions as whether to go "again to Jerusalem" and under such guidance he went "by revelation" (2:1, 2), he would give the same guidance when writing about the same problem. Paul claims revelation, the twin brother of inspiration.

As in Galatians so in other of Paul's passages his words refer to the context at hand, not the entire body of New Testament literature. But his sense of God's guiding presence is everywhere to be noted. Pauls says, "We also thank God without ceasing, that when you received from us the word of the message, even the word of God, you accepted it not as the word of men, but, as it is in truth, the word of God" (I Thess. 2:13). I Thessalonians 4:1-7 mentions some "instructions" which "we gave to you through the Lord Jesus Christ." These instructions deal with sexual purity in married as well as other personal relationships. And the apostle declares "this is the will of God" (I Thess. 4:3a). To underscore the divine source of these "instructions" in verse eight the apostle attaches his allegation,

124

"Therefore the one rejecting [these instructions] is not rejecting man but God, the one who gives his Holy Spirit to you." The context would limit this claim to the teaching in verses 1-7 about sexual cleanness. Paul's teaching was God's teaching. If that be true, it would seem reasonable that Paul enjoyed God's guidance when he wrote the Thessalonians as much as when he originally spoke to them. This is what Paul thought about his teaching and by implication what he felt about his writing.

Beginning at verse nine in that same fourth chapter the apostle turns from sexual behavior to brotherly love as a Christian obligation. "Now about brotherly love we are not having need to be writing to you, for you yourselves are taught of God to be loving one another . . . but we are urging you, brethren, to abound more. . . ." Where or when had these Thessalonian brethren been "taught of God"? Paul was the one who founded the church and nurtured its faith. So we conclude that it was God using the apostle Paul who first taught the Christian virtue of "loving one another." If Paul's oral teaching was to be identified with being "taught of God" why then should his writing be any less a "taught of God" experience? Furthermore, Paul's disclaimer here that "we are not having need to be writing" was really a literary apparatus by which he could point up that his word, whether in person or in writing, was "of God." It was one way he could assert that God breathed on him in his apostolic activity. Remember, it is persons, not paper or pen, that God inspires to write His truth. God's teaching was in Paul's writing. And as an added confirmation of the seriousness with which he viewed his own letter Paul included an urgent oath "By the Lord, I put you on oath that this letter be read by all the brethren" (I Thess. 5:27). He wanted other believers besides the Thessalonians to have this "teaching of God." Because it was "of God" his written word must be channelled to other churches.

In his second letter to these Thessalonians Paul refers to the traditions "which you were taught, whether by our word or letter" (II Thess. 2:15). In Paul's vocabulary "traditions" were not just folklore picked up at random. They were teachings handed along from one to another as an accredited and accurate means of preserving God's truth. Paul's exhortation is that his readers "stand firm" and "hold fast" the traditions which he himself taught "whether through our word or epistle." The traditions he passed along Paul viewed as God's truth. His method of delivery embraced two methods: oral speech and written epistle. And one was as much of God as the other.

Paul refers to some of the Thessalonians who "walk disorderly" in that they "work not at all, but are busybodies." To such he writes, ". . . We command and exhort in the Lord Jesus Christ, that with quietness they work, and eat their own bread." And as to what attitude other brethren should hold toward such idle meddlers the apostle urged "if any man obeys not our word by this epistle, note that man, that you have no company with him, to the end that he be ashamed" (II Thess. 3:11-15). From the point of view of the apostle he did not "command and exhort" on his own authority. He did so only "in the Lord Jesus Christ." Whatsoever right of command Paul possessed it was because God was speaking in him. And that by means of the spoken word or written epistle. If this were not true then we would have to conclude that Paul was either sick in mind or was an overgrown, self-inflated egotist. But the better conclusion is that he spoke and wrote by the "inbreathing of God."

126

It is true that Paul was either deceived by Satan or saturated by the Spirit of God. Everywhere and in so many ways, by incidental casual allusion or by bold affirmation he insists that God works and speaks in him. Though eye, ear and heart of sage and prophet had never seen, heard or entertained "whatsoever things God prepared for the ones loving him" yet Paul avowed, ". . . unto us God revealed [them] through the Spirit . . ." (I Cor. 2:9, 10). Certainly he includes his readers as sharing in the indwelling of the Spirit of God. But his basic reference is to himself and other apostles as ones who were instruments of God's revelations. He goes on to say, ". . . We received . . . the Spirit which is from God, that we might know the things that were freely given to us of God. Which things also we speak, not in words which man's wisdom teaches, but which the Spirit teaches; combining spiritual things with spiritual [words]" (I Cor. 2:12, 13). And in the concluding sentence of this penetrating paragraph the apostle boldly claims, "we have the mind of Christ" (I Cor. 2:16). As a sponge soaks up water so Paul was absorbed with the idea of God's presence in his speech and writing. Even when he would offer some hard-nosed practical advice on the married or single state he would append with caution, "after my judgment." It was his opinion but he could not refuse to add, "and I think that I have also the Spirit of God" (I Cor. 7:40). He felt that even his personal convictions were affected and dominated by the Spirit of God.

In chapters 12 through 14 of I Corinthians Paul works his way through the knotty problem of the abuse of charismatic gifts. After writing his thoughts and making his appraisal on the matter he concludes with a piercing statement relative to his own place as a channel of God's "commandment."

"If any man thinks himself to be a prophet, or [to be] spiritual, he is to take knowledge of these things which I am writing to you that they are the Lord's commandment" (I Cor. 14:37). No question should arise here but that the apostle is positively affirming that *his* word is that of the Lord. In the original text the word "Lord" is very emphatic by position, ". . . they are the *Lord's* commandment." It was the apostle's opinion that what he wrote about the charismatic gifts, their use and abuse, was God's authoritative commandment.

But even more important, he is more than just the mouthpiece of the Lord, he is also the standard by which anyone claiming to be a prophet might measure his prophetic gift, not to mention his "spiritual" quality. "If any one thinks himself to be a prophet, or [to be] spiritual. . . ." Obviously in the eager jealousy and disruptive ambition of the contending members at Corinth many were trying to outreach others in their spirituality. Many were climbing the ladder of spiritual preeminence by trying to gain a higher gift than another. They were not as much interested in *using* their gift as they were in having a *better* gift than another. Nor were they as ambitious to reach their own personal spiritual potential as they were to be more spiritual than their Christian neighbor. To grow to one's highest capacity is true spirituality. But merely to outreach someone else is the very opposite of genuine spiritual character. Charismatic gifts are for service to others, not for self-exaltation. What Paul is saying in I Cor. 14:37 is that what he wrote in chapters 12-14 represent the Lord's command and that his teaching is the yardstick by which a prophet can determine whether he is a genuine prophet or not, and whether one's claim to being "spiritual" is real or phony.

Nor should verse 38 be ignored in evaluating what Paul thought about his own views as expressed in his own writing

—in this context, his writing about charismatic gifts. He says, "If anyone is ignorant, he is to be ignorant." In other words, "If anyone insists on his own opinion about his being a prophet, or about his own level of spirituality; if anyone refuses to recognize me and my teaching as being from "the Lord" and as being a rule of measurement, then I throw up my hands in amazement at his insistence on remaining in his ignorant state." In other words, the one who aspires to be great in the Lord but refuses to use the divine yard-stick of greatness just has to remain self-deceived. He who is little but thinks he is big will just have to stay little — even while he thinks otherwise. Spiritual pride is the worst kind of self-deception.

One might raise the question, Is not Paul himself an example of presumptuous, overweening pride? Is not his assertion mere self-assertion? Does he not demonstrate gargantuan egotism to claim for himself to be the absolute standard by which divine truth and growth is measured? This truly poses a real problem. It might seem to be a probable evaluation of Paul if he in fact were not God's mouthpiece. God, through centuries, has spoken to men in men. And if God is going to speak to men in men he must call men and designate them as his spokesmen. So the question reduces itself not to Paul's egotism but to God's choice. Did God in fact call and reveal "his Son" in Paul? If we look on the history of Paul as recorded in the New Testament as being true, then God did touch the persecutor's life and turn it around to his own divine purposes. Ananias of Damascus said to Paul, "The God of our fathers appointed you to know his will . . . you shall be a witness for him unto all men . . ." (Acts 22:14, 15). This sums up the source of

129

Paul's call and the object of his ministry. God "appointed" him; "all men" were the goal of his service. As far as the historical fact is concerned Paul was in fact the channel of God's message to "all men."

But when we turn from the fact of the divine call to the method God used in calling his servant then we open up the human side of the matter. When men set themselves to study God's creation, in the written reports of their studies creation disappears in favor of the word nature. By use of the term nature with everything evolving naturally from forces inherent within nature man has successfully eliminated God as creator. There is no supernatural. They say everything is natural and has a natural explanation. But the difference between man's observations of orderly uniformity and progress in the universe and the biblical view is not in the order or progress. The difference lies in the recognition of God as being involved in the orderly progress. Order and progress are pictured quite clearly in the first chapter of Genesis. Men who have expelled God from their thinking refer to that orderly progress as evolution. That is, the world of nature (creation) has evolved from forces inherent within itself. The basic difference lies in the Bible's including God as the person who acts in creation. The Bible says God created. Naturalists say it evolved. At the birth of Cain Eve said, "I have gotten a man with the help of the Lord" (Gen. 4:1). Eve was perfectly aware of how a baby comes into this world. So is the modern scientist. To Eve God was involved in the natural process; to modern man only natural procedures are entailed.

The same principle is present in the biblical view of God's calling men versus human explanations of any radical change from secular to sacred service. Conversion has been occurring universally throughout history. Every climate, country, culture, ideology, philosophy or religion knows what it is to have a convert. And within each system of thought men have felt called to dedicate themselves completely to the goal or god around which the system is geared. From a psychological view the change that takes place in one's call would be the same in any system of thought, religious or otherwise. The natural human factors would be unvaried. But, to the Christian, since God is personal, living and active in human affairs *He* must himself be a partner in the process. In fact, He is so intimately associated in the transaction the biblical writer often does not describe the human element. Paul could honestly say, "God separated me . . . and called me. . . ." Or a Jeremiah might claim, "Before I formed you . . . I knew you . . . I sanctified you . . . I appointed you. . . ." These men of God recognized and experienced the natural normal human elements in their divine call. But they also perceived that God was personally and actively a part of the psychology of change. HE, as creator of the psychological principles gave direction to their developing in actual living people.

If we describe the call of Saul of Tarsus we may paint it in divine colors as the Bible does. On the Damascus road God arrested, appeared to, called, appointed Paul to the apostleship. These are facts. We heartily agree with Paul's evaluation of himself that God "separated me from my mother's womb and called me through his grace to reveal his son in me" (Gal. 1:15, 16). But these facts in no way disturb the companion fact that God did His calling and appointing in harmony with universal psychological principles by which men are changed from one way of life to another. In fact God is the author of these human psychological

131

factors. So when He calls a man He is merely using his own creative devices by which to bring the man to a radical change in the way He uses his life.

Sufficient biblical evidence is available for us to recognize God's psychology at work in Saul of Tarsus. "It is hard for you to kick against the goad" reveals the intense deadly struggle that unquestionably went on in the life of the persecutor over many months, if not years. When Stephen, the first Christian martyr was stoned, "the witnesses laid down their garments at the feet of a young man named Saul." And thereby "Saul was consenting unto his death" (Acts 7:58; 8:1). To think that Paul persecuted Christians "even unto foreign cities" without any pressure on his conscience is unreal. When Paul later would say before the council "I have lived . . . in all good conscience" (Acts 23:1) he was affirming that he followed truth wherever it led. He certainly was not claiming that he never felt ashamed, embarrassed, or guilty. As a matter of fact he vividly describes how deeply guilty he often felt, ". . . not what I would, that do I practice; but what I hate, that I do . . . wretched man that I am! who shall deliver me . . ." (Romans 7:15, 24). No! When Paul said that he "lived in all good conscience" he was affirming that he was a man who followed his convictions consistently. Not that he never struggled with his conscience, but once the issues were clearly drawn and he had fought it out with his conscience he resolutely moved to do what was right.

But so far as God's call is concerned the Damascus road episode was a catastrophic consummation of many months, possibly years, of struggle with a conscience that refused to be quieted. At least from the day of Stephen's stoning Paul was "kicking against the goad." The fact of a crucified

Christ could not be reconciled to his education as a Pharisee. So he "consented" to Stephen's execution. By accepting the clothes of the executioners Paul publicly approved of that judicial killing. But it kept pricking his conscience from that day forward. Years later it burst forth from the hidden deeps of his soul. Before Agrippa the searing memory came out again, "And when the blood of Stephen . . . was shed, I also was standing by, and consenting, and keeping the garments of them that slew him" (Acts 26:20). Time heals! But time leaves scars. Grace forgives but even grace doesn't change scars from being scars. In fact, grace covers over cuts by making and leaving scars. Grace uses scars. Paul not only did not forget but like a splinter under the thumbnail it kept on hurting and irritating him until he turned his life without reservation to God's grace.

The message which Stephen advanced and for which he was killed was the germinal idea which later became Paul's obsession throughout his life. Stephen had debated in all the synagogues in Jerusalem. Are we to suppose that the best educated, most sophisticated, most knowledgeable and skillful of all the Pharisees would not eagerly seek debate with Stephen? Without doubt Paul debated the issues which Stephen summarized in the speech which triggered his death. The arguments which Stephen proposed in his debates lodged in Paul's mind and germinated in his heart more than the future apostle was willing to concede. Besides, the spirit in which Stephen died, added to the dying words of the martyr, left its stabbing barb in his soul (Acts 7:59, 60). The angry, frustrating fury with which he persecuted Christians was itself one method Paul adopted to stifle the truth of the gospel as Stephen preached it. The constantly pricking goad was like a knife in his soul with its unrelenting pain.

133

Even a strong-minded soul like Saul of Tarsus must yield sometime. So, when the risen Jesus appeared in person that was the final feather that made the weight on conscience too heavy to bear.

The call and appointment of Saul by God was abrupt if viewed only from the Damascus road event. But that is really the climactic crest of the wave. God was tugging at the inward monitor of Paul's heart from the death of Stephen onward. And possibly even from before that! What we are saying in all this is that God called Paul along the lines of human psychology, along those lines that make for radical change in any man's life from one loyalty to another.

Was Paul a monstrous egotist? Was he merely feeding his ego when he told the Corinthians that his teaching was the rod by which they could measure their spirituality? Even if he were then that was just one of the very human psychological ingredients which God exploited when he called the persecutor. No doubt Paul was a strong-willed person. He could and did assert his views against all who were "reputed to be pillars" both before and after he became a Christian. He refused to submit to any man if he felt the man held to false principles. Yet he was strong enough to be meek when it was right to be meek. He referred to himself as "slave" of Jesus Christ. Thus he knew how to be humble and submissive. He could fight furiously against circumcising Titus when others insisted that salvation depended on circumcision (Gal. 2:3-5). Yet a few weeks later he voluntarily circumcised Timothy that he might be a better servant of the Christ (Acts 16:3). So, rather than view Paul as titanic in his ego we would prefer to see him as being confident without overloading. As an apostle he was firm but did not exercise authority like a tyrant over vassals. Egotism reflects self-inflation; confidence comes from trust—trust in God's gifts to oneself! Paul was sufficiently confident of that which God was doing in him that he could rebuke Peter "before them all" (Gal. 2:14) and yet without overbearing arrogance. With certain self-assurance he would say, "I labored more abundantly than they all." But it was not bloated ambition overreaching itself, for with the same stroke of his pen he could write "yet not I, but the grace of God which was with me." And also he called himself "the least of all the apostles" (I Cor. 15:10, 9).

In this excursion about Paul, his conversion to Christ, his call and appointment to apostleship, we discover the rational explanation about Paul's confidence that his words are God's word. His assertion that what he writes is the plumb line by which prophetic or spirituality is measured is not egotism but faith—faith that God made him what he was and gave him what he had. In this confidence Paul's epistles claim and imply revelation and inspiration.

In his letter to the Ephesians the apostle voices his farewell summation of the Christian philosophy of history. The New Testament contains some of his later letters to certain individuals. The Titus and the Timothy letters were written later than Ephesians. But so far as correspondence to churches is concerned Ephesians concludes Paul's literary labors, at least as far as what remains to us. And when we consider the content of the epistle it has the sound of a swan song. After years of missionary church planting, after much nurturing of faith and growth, the apostle began looking toward the end of his career. He felt the need for a concise, pointed digest and encompassing the whole sweep of God's purpose and plan. The churches needed a clear statement of God's plan from the point of its inception in eternity past to its successful termination at the finale of history. God in human history progressively revealing himself in the Christ reconciling the world to himself — such is the theme of Ephesians.

Of six chapters the first three present the eternal purpose and plan of God, particularly as they are unveiled through the church. The final three chapters hold forth the challenge to the church as the fulfilling body, an instrument in God's hand by which he brings to perfection his goal for man. God is the architect, Christ the executor, the Holy Spirit the one who makes effective the work of God in each segment of the church, whether an individual or a group. The church is the community in which all fragments of humanity find faith and unity in a living, growing, redeeming temple of God. Having said this (chps. 1-2) Paul adds a clarifying word to expand the idea.

> . . . If indeed you heard [with understanding] this management of God's grace, that which was given to me for you, that by revelation his secret was made known to me, just as I wrote briefly [in chapters 1-2], to which as you read you are able to perceive my understanding in the secret of the Christ, which in other generations was not made known to the sons of men as now it is revealed to his holy apostles and prophets in the Spirit — that the gentiles are fellow-heirs and of the same body and partners of the promise in Christ Jesus through the gospel, of which I became a servant . . ." (Eph. 3:2-7a).

No statement in any of Paul's epistles in the New Testament surpasses this in content or clarity as to what the apostle felt about his own literary efforts. His reference to "this management of God's grace" alludes to the fact that God has not dispensed his saving action in a disjointed, helter-skelter method. God's grace has been directed and controlled

136

by selected managers called seers, or prophets, or apostles and such like. And Paul recognized himself as one of God's selected servants when he affirmed that "this management" "has been given to me for you." And then he underscored his confidence by appending, "his secret was made known to me." Paul believed that God had made him a trustee of the "secret" of redemption, that is, the gospel. But the secret had been given that he might make it known, in the present instance, to his readers — the same readers who had heard it orally from him when he first preached to them but to whom now he was summarizing it in writing.

This revelation which had been made known to him and destined for them, his readers, about which Paul says, "I wrote briefly." This "brief" writing to which he points is his exposition in chapters one and two of his present letter. The apostle thought that he had written plainly enough that they could see that he was a depository of God's gospel. Furthermore, that though this gospel had been sketched in a shadowed outline in "other generations" it had not been revealed unrestrictedly as the manner in which it has "now" been revealed. And that God's "holy apostles and prophets" were the ones through whom the unobstructed revelation has come.

But the most dazzling revelation which electrified even the "apostles and prophets" who transmitted the light is enfolded in verse six. The content of God's eternal secret is embodied in a three-pronged idea: gentiles are "fellow-heirs," are of "the same body," and are "partners of the promise in Christ Jesus." It definitely took an unblurred revelation for any Jew, especially a Pharisee, to arrive at the point at which he could write that "gentiles are fellow-heirs" with Jews. And we ought never forget that Paul was

"Hebrew of Hebrews" and a Pharisee. God lifted him above such narrow limitations so that in him as an apostle God's secret that gentiles were equal objects of his grace, equal servants of his plan, could be clearly known. Besides, though the gentile might not be an eye that sees, or lungs that breathe, he could be a leg that moves or an arm that reaches out. That is to say, the gentiles were "of the same body" as the Jews. Without the gentile the "body" of God was incomplete, less able to function in society. Nor should the readers ever forget that when God called Abraham and showered on him the promise to service and salvation for "all families of the earth" the gentiles were equally in God's promised goal. They were "partners of the promise in Christ Jesus through the gospel."

The brilliance of the contents of this revelation has become so commonplace in Paul's version of the gospel that we moderns may take it for granted. But it's the *statement*, not the practice, that is taken for granted. Our churches are as segregated in membership, narrowly limited as to outreach, restricted as to vision and program as were the churches with which Paul struggled. That someone other than my race is "fellow-heir" is as difficult for me to adjust to as any Jewish Pharisee. That someone in a different level of culture or economics is part of the same body in which I worship may be all right in theory but it isn't practical. And that they share in the same promise is true but let them share it in some other congregation than mine. So the secret of God has to be learned and relearned in every generation of human beings from the first century to this very hour.

But the chief point with which we are concerned is what the scriptures say about themselves. Paul's view of himself and his place and his writing is that "I became a servant" of this gospel. Paul was quite conscious that what he spoke and wrote was God's message for men. He wrote to meet particular problems in local situations. He wrote to answer universal questions that arose in men's hearts in every country, climate, and culture. And because he resolved the problems and answered the questions, that which he wrote has found a universal appeal throughout the centuries since. If the breathing of God was at work in the Old Testament prophets (I Peter 1:10-12 & II Peter 1:21) it is an instinct, commonly and widely held, that the same Spirit was breathing on the apostle to the gentiles. It should excite little wonder, therefore, that the Christian world has looked on Paul's writings as inspired of God. Or that Paul could write with the feeling that he wrote "in words . . . taught by the Spirit," and "we have the mind of Christ," or "if anyone thinks he is . . . spiritual, he is to acknowledge that what I am writing is a command of the Lord" (I Cor. 2:13, 16; 14:37). Nor should it create any wonder that he would urge that his letters be "read to all the brethren" in other churches. In his first letter to Timothy he could say, "I charge you in the sight of God and Christ Jesus and the elect angels, to keep these instructions without partiality . . ." (5:21). And in the same letter (2:14, 15), "Although I hope to come soon, I am writing you these instructions so that, if I am delayed, you will know how people ought to conduct themselves in God's household, which is the church of the living God. . . ." Whence came the apostle's soaring confidence that he could "charge" others to "keep instructions" of his? Or that his writing was an adequate measuring stick on how people should "conduct themselves . . . in the church of the living God"? It was because he labored under an awareness of the Spirit of God breathing through his soul. At least this is what Paul's writings certify about Paul's writings.

The way in which Paul used the power of his apostleship casts some light on what his writing says about his
writing. It was not by arbitrary power that he was made an
apostle. Nor was he expected to exercise authority as an
apostle arbitrarily. The power of moral persuasion is the
method God used and uses with men. And it is that same
method he expects his servants to use when dealing with
other men. The world's rulers "exercise authority *over*"
men. But in God's church using God's method the "leader
among you" is to "become as one who serves" (Luke 22:25-
27). Authority is real but it is exercised by moral persuasion,
not physical force.

Some of Paul's heaviest heartaches came from tension
that arose between him and his own converts. This was
especially true of the Corinthian brethren. Some ugly and
sharp criticisms were lodged against Paul. One was that
he was bold in his letters but weak in his personal presence,
that he was vacillating in keeping his word and could not be
counted on in his promises. In his answer (II Cor. 1:23ff.)
Paul explained, "It was to spare you that I refrained from
coming to Corinth. Not that we lord it over your faith; we
work with you. . . ." And, "I wrote as I did . . . that I might
not be pained by those who should have made me rejoice. . . .
I wrote out of much . . . anguish of heart . . . not to cause
you pain but to let you know the abundant love that I have
for you" (II Cor. 2:3, 4). We have already noted that when
occasion demanded he could rebuke a man to his face, and
that publicly (Gal. 2:14). Even such public rebuke to Peter
was an effort at arousing the conscience of Peter to obey
what he already knew to be right. In the case of the Corinthians Paul is obviously plucking on the strings of their
heart to arouse an emotional response. To get obedience

he must touch their feelings. "This is why I wrote, that I might test you and know whether you are obedient in everything." Surely, not "obedient" to him as one who "lords it over them" but as God's chosen vessel in whom the water of life was coming to them. He did not exercise authority with the whimsical will of a tyrant. On the contrary, he wrote "as one who serves." In the same letter he avows, "we persuade men" for "the love of Christ constrains us." God "gave us the ministry of reconciliation . . ." and "We beg you . . . be reconciled to God" (II Cor. 5:11-20).

As he dealt with congregations so the apostle appealed to individual believers when the situation demanded. We have already remarked about the personal differences that damaged the relations between slave and slave-owner in the case of Onesimus and Philemon. Before they were Christian, social and economic inequalities furnished the fabric of their personal relationship. When Onesimus fled from his slave obligations he robbed Philemon at least of his services, if not other property. Then when Paul in Rome introduced the runaway slave to Christ a radically new foundation for personal relations became an obligation on both the slave and the master. They were no longer just bondman and free; they were both slaves of Christ and both free in Christ. Their new relationship "in Christ" placed moral demands on them to recognize new personal duties toward each other. Paul was the God-appointed catalyst through whom the two men could be established in their new relationship. And Philemon was not even yet aware that he must exercise such a new rapport! How was Paul to wield his authority as an apostle to bring these men together in *brotherly*, not just social, relationship?

The letter to Philemon not only answers the question but also furnishes an example how the *written* word of God accomplishes its task. Paul must deal with two elements in resolving the problem. One, he must inform both men of the fact that they are now *"brothers."* Christ had changed their fundamental connection to one another whether they were yet aware of it or not. The apostle must enlighten their mind of the change of state; a family tie, not economic. And second, he must get them both to accept *voluntarily* this change to kinship in Christ. The gospel must not only be accepted as salvation but it must be applied in brotherly bonds. Faith in Christ must forge faith in each other.

No organist ever played with all stops out with more skill than did Paul play on all the emotions of Philemon. We have the written melody in the book of Philemon. We may assume he played with equal skill on the heart of the slave face to face. As we read the letter we hear these notes in perfect harmony. First, Paul sounds the note of his prayer for Philemon's faith, love and effectual works toward "all the saints." Because Philemon had "refreshed the hearts of the saints" Paul's own joy in his present discomfort in prison was lifted and sustained. As Philemon was reading, not yet realizing his missing slave was the occasion for the letter, his emotions were being prepared for a friendly response. To compliment a man's faith is not flattery unless insincere. So, Paul was rightfully recognizing Philemon's leadership among the brethren at Colossae.

In a flurry of notes in verses 8-14 the apostle constructs a harmony designed to move Philemon to bring into play his leadership in the case of his runaway slave. Paul indicates, "I could command" as an apostle but I prefer "to exhort on account of love." Paul appeals to his age and his imprisoned condition to help swing open the door of Philemon's heart. "I Paul, the elder [some mss. have "ambassador"] and now a prisoner for Christ. . . ." When the name of the missing slave is first introduced into the letter it follows "I appeal to you for my son. . . ." The word "son" was calculated to be more moving than "acquaintance." Besides, Philemon no doubt reacted with surprise to discover the slave who betrayed his trust was a "son" of the beloved apostle. There follows the note "he was useless but now useful to you"—a very practical note suggesting a more harmonious melody than physical punishment. The announcement by Paul that "I am sending him back" is accompanied by the strongest of chords, "sending my own heart." The apostle let Philemon know that he "would have been glad to keep him" as a working helper. A helper who really, since he was the legal property of the reader, would have been serving "on your behalf." But, says Paul, it must be by free "goodness" and not "by compulsion." What an accumulation of motivations! What melodious harmony designed to make Philemon's heart break out in a song of freedom and brotherhood for his erstwhile slave.

Another stanza is added in verses 15-20. Mysterious ways God has in working his will. In the providence of God Onesimus ran away a slave; he runs back a brother, "both in the flesh and in the Lord." Then Paul presses home three strong personal notes. Receive him, "if you consider me your partner." Whatever he robbed you of, "I will repay" so you won't suffer financial loss. And finally Paul's final appeal when he reminds Philemon of "your owing me even your own self." With all these accumulated emotional strings tightly drawn around Philemon's heart how could he refuse when he was reminded of how his own salvation had come from Paul's ministry? The same Paul and the same gospel had reached into the dregs of Rome and rescued Onesimus for Christ. The gospel makes brothers out of opposites whether they be racial, social or sexual. "In Christ there is neither slave nor free!" (Gal. 3:28).

The letter to Philemon says volumes between the lines about how God's word comes to man. Even as the man, Paul, exercised his apostolic authority toward the man, Philemon, so God expresses his divine authority toward the world of men. God does not force his will on the reluctant will of a man. But like Paul with Philemon, God appeals to the moral promptings of a heart created to be in God's "image and after God's likeness." The written word of God does not give vent to its authority by imperious, high-handed, haughty, irrational force. God appeals to the reason, the logic of the situation. He engages man's emotions, cultivating the deepest and noblest of human feelings. He solicits man to make right choices on moral grounds rather than racial, social or sexual bigotry. In other words God asserts his power and authority, not by outward force, but by his divine immanence within the moral quality of the act itself. "Thou shalt not murder" expresses a moral truism but not because it is written in the Bible. On the contrary, it is written in the Bible because it springs from the moral quality of God and consequently the nature of the thing itself. "You shall be holy for I am holy!" There is no way to rationalize, bend, break, or wiggle out of the built-in authority of divine command, "You shall not murder." But in spite of that fact God's all-powerful, universal, eternal authority is not exercised by means of coersion. It comes by moral inducement. God charms and invites people to do right. God could have commanded with overwhelming, arbitrary force but he did not and does not. God through Paul did not command Philemon but He did exert His divine authority by drawing on the moral sensitivity of the slave-owner. Furthermore, in inspiring Paul God did not crush the normal attributes of the apostle. No! He breathed into them His own divine qualities. Paul as one in the "image of God" was in tune with God and so was the instrument on which God could play his song of salvation. God is the living God. Inspired people wrote books hence the books are bathed in the breath of God. And His dominion is administered through the moral power of love not the external power of the sword. The iron rod of which God's sceptre is forged is *love* appearing in a sinful order as *righteousness*.

A few samples of Paul's use of the Old Testament scriptures will enlarge our understanding of how the scriptures employ other scriptures. Hence what some scriptures say, at least by implication, about scriptures.

Paul's handling of Old Testament texts may be separated into two groups. First, those in which the apostle places on the texts the same meaning as the Old Testament authors did. Second, those passages in which he utilizes the ideas, vocabulary, and expressions of the Old Testament and makes additional application.

As an example illustrative of the first group Romans 9:19 is sufficient. The apostle's imagined critic raises objection to God's sovereignty and justice as voiced by Paul in 9:14-18. "Why does he [God] still find fault? For who can resist his will?" The apostle answers his caviler by quoting Isaiah 45:9. "Who are you, a man, to answer back to God? Will what is molded say to its molder, 'Why have you made me thus?'" Paul's addition of the word "thus" does not alter the spirit or meaning of Isaiah's, "Does the clay say to him who fashions it, 'What are you making?'" Wonder fills the prophet's voice, "What are you making?" He is not asking for information. He is rather suggesting that the potter is botching up the vessel as he is making it. Much as one might say, "Beware, what are you doing? You're making a vessel with a flaw in it!" At any rate, Paul's use of Isaiah 45:9 is in harmony with Isaiah's original context. Most of Paul's quotes from the Old Testament would follow this pattern. He respects the content, context, spirit and meaning of the original author.

As an example of the second bracket of Old Testament scriptures we cite Romans 10:18. The first half of Psalm 19 describes the glory; of God in his created universe. It especially sets forth the universality of creation's witness. "The heavens declare the glory of God . . . their voice goes out through all the earth, and their words to the end of the earth." But Paul's point in Romans 10:18 champions something other than God's universal glory in his creation. He is declaring the universal character of the gospel and its unbounded proclamation. Paul used this passage to make an additional application. He used the beauty of style, the familiar rhythm, and vocabulary of the Old Testament psalm in which to convey his idea. He obviously employed these for two reasons. The authority of the Old Testament carried weight with both writer and reader. Furthermore, both style and words, being familiar to the readers, would tend to make the heart more receptive to the truth Paul was teaching.

Paul's view toward the Old Testament scriptures is that they reveal God's will, but not by mechanical means or in rigid, stiff form. Paul said, "God has done what the law, weakened by the flesh, could not do: sending his own son in the likeness of sinful flesh and for sin . . ." (Rom. 8:3). It gives absolutes on which to build life. It does not force righteousness. But it does invest a man with righteousness by forgiveness, acceptance, love and the inward working of the Spirit of God. So Paul accepted the spirit, meaning

146

and goal of Moses' law because he found in the New Testament gospel the means of fulfilling the aims of law.

> Is the law then against the promises of God? Certainly not; for if a law had been given which could make alive, then righteousness would indeed be by the law. But the [Old Testament] scripture consigned all things to sin, that what was promised to faith in Jesus Christ might be given to those who believe" (Galatians 3:21, 22).

The gospel Paul preached fulfilled the prophetic meaning of the Old Testament. This is what the Bible says about the Bible because it is what Paul said in his use of the older scriptures.

Part III — What the Old Testament Books Say About Themselves

Chapter Nine

THE LAW

The Old Testament is prophetic in tone, spirit and message. This prophetic feature coloring the Old Testament is not limited to the writing or preaching prophets. It pervades all the books. The records of Israel's history are as prophetic in meaning as are the books formally designated prophets. And Job and Psalms, classified as poetical, are no less prophetical than any book or class of books that make up our Old Testament.

If it be true that all Old Testament books are prophetical by nature, then that broadens the view which frequently attaches itself to the idea of prophecy. The term *prophet* or *prophecy* must not be confined to *predictor* or *prediction*. A biblical prophet is certainly more than one who predicts the future. While the prophet's understanding of the future was real, the predictive element was inseparably connected with the prophet's contemporary crisis. Whenever the prophet projects the future it is always in terms of the present or past. His message must have some kind of meaning to his own generation in order to form a basis for an intelligent understanding for any future generation. Most of the material of the prophets actually deals with the emergencies of the moment, their moment, not the distant nonexistent future.

For one concise sample the book of Joel will be adequate. The generation in which Joel lived faced a farmers' disaster of national proportions. It was a year in which Israel had endured "the swarming locust" that had "laid waste my vines and splintered my trees." The catastrophe was total.

No household, whether rural or urban, escaped the devastation of swarming locusts that darkened the land more than massed storm clouds. Both prophet and people were obsessed with fruitless fields, bare tables, unfed stomachs, and empty pockets. Despair was etched on every face. The future was only filled with fear! The future about which they were concerned was the next hour or day, not a century or a millennium hence. What is the meaning of a tragedy of such staggering scope? How can God look on such suffering? Has he no message for such an hour? Does God's man have any word of explanation?

The entire three chapters gives God's message to the people in that crisis. Joel found an explanation for their reverses from the locusts in the need to repent. "Return to me with all your heart . . . rend your hearts and not your garments" (2:12-13). But in interpreting those events, so real to the suffering people, the prophet held out hope of better days. God's Spirit, withdrawn in judgment, would not forever leave his people facing perpetual poverty and meaningless death. In fact God had a time in the future in which he would shower his Spirit on "all" flesh rather than on just a selected group of "prophets."

> And it shall come to pass afterward, that I will pour out my spirit on all flesh, your sons and your daughters shall prophesy, your old men shall dream dreams, and your young men shall see visions. Even upon the menservants and maidservants in those days, I will pour out my spirit (Joel 2:28, 29).

What could these words possibly mean to those whose ears first heard them? Their crops had failed, their children were hungry, their tomorrow was bleak! Even when Jesus the Christ came it took three years of daily teaching plus the fact of his death and resurrection to open his disciples' hearts to the meaning of the Old Testament scriptures (Luke 24:45-48). The fulfillment was so unexpectedly diverse from the mold in which the prophet cast it. When the pains of hunger fill the horizon of one's attention, spiritual values of sin and salvation lie too far beyond to grab the mind. Joel's people could comprehend when they heard, "The threshing floors shall be full of grain. . . . You shall eat in plenty . . . and praise the name of the Lord your God . . ." (2:24, 26). When they ate "in plenty" it would be easier to praise the Lord. In fact, such restoration of good crops could make even young "sons and daughters" to prophesy and old men to "dream dreams!" In the famine circumstances in which Joel preached his prophecy about pouring out my spirit even upon "menservants and maidservants" its most obvious meaning was that a return of material prosperity would buoy up morale to such an extent that even the most menial domestic would be a dwelling place for God's Spirit. But according to Peter on the day of Pentecost the Spirit of God in Joel had in mind the preaching of the gospel of salvation by, to and for "all flesh" (Acts 2:17-21, 36). Joel preached a practical hope for his own generation. The eventual fulfillment of his preaching involved a prediction that the Spirit had embedded in his message. The fulfillment was real but decidedly different than the form in which it was packaged by Joel. The form was temporal; the fulfillment spiritual!

What is true of the prophet Joel is equally true of the entire Old Testament. The Hebrew people divided their sacred canon into the Law (Torah), the Prophets, and the Writings (Hagiagrapha). The word Torah literally meant instruction or law. In the course of time it not only referred to the legal enactments designed as governing principles for the people but also the historical narratives in which the laws were given. In fact much of their law was what we might term history. It included the books of Moses from Genesis through Deuteronomy. And as a fixed body of literature it should be noted that it is not a code of laws. It does not come before the reader as the code of Hammurabi or the Justinian legislation. It actually reports the laws of the nation as they were given in the gradual, unfolding life of Israel. It is more a history which relates mostly the occasions in which the laws came to precise expression. As such it teaches (prophesies) that which did and will happen (predicts) if the laws are ignored in life. So the Hebrew Torah is prophetic in substance, intent and results. Every bit as much so as are the prophets!

As a body of laws, including the historical cloth into which they are woven, they were given by Moses. His successors were duly charged with the responsibility of heeding the commandments. The lessons of history amply illustrated the blessing of obedience and the curse of disobedience. As the time of his death approached the great lawgiver wrote "in a book" his commandments and prophesied reasons for so doing. "When Moses finished writing the words of this law in a book, to the very end, Moses commanded the Levites who carried the ark of the covenant of the Lord, 'Take this book of the law, and put it by the side of the ark of the covenant of the Lord your God, that it may be there for a witness against you. For I know how rebellious and stubborn you are . . .'" (Deut. 31:24-27).

The laws were conspicuously prophetic. Moses plainly pointed out that they were "for a witness against you." That is, they would act the part of a mirror reflecting "how rebellious and stubborn you are." That is the work of a prophet.

151

The laws had the sanction of God himself for the book of laws was entrusted to the sacred priests who were to place it by the most hallowed religious vessel in the holiest part of the sacrosanct temple. Hence from the earliest days of the nation these laws embodied the will of God in a sinful society. That's the task of prophecy, to reveal the will of God! So they were respected from the outset as the authoritative, divine word of God.

Furthermore, these laws were to continue exerting their prophetic power throughout succeeding generations. Moses enjoined that each seven years at national festivals "when all Israel comes to appear before the Lord your God . . . you shall read this law before all Israel . . . that they may learn to fear the Lord your God, and be careful to do all the words of this law . . ." (Deut. 31:11, 12). So far as what the scripture says about itself we are left in no doubt that it was thought to be the very word of God. "As the Lord commanded Moses his servant, so Moses commanded Joshua, and so Joshua did; he left nothing undone of all that the Lord commanded Moses" (Joshua 11:15). That Moses knew his laws to be God's word is clear; that Joshua believed those laws to be God's word is equally evident. During the depressive years of the judges the biblical writer explains the leaving of some Canaanites in the land as being God's way of testing Israel. As he declared, ". . . to know whether Israel would obey the commandments of the Lord which he commanded their fathers by Moses" (Judges 3:4). Thus it was through all Israel's history, the law of Moses held the value of God's word for man. And for that matter, even to this twentieth century after Christ a large segment of humanity looks to that body of law as the prophetic word of the Lord.

152

The word of God was not only externalized in the legal statutes of law but it was also ingrafted into the historical events which generated the need for the laws. Israel's rescue from Egypt under Moses is an objective event in history. That deliverance itself revealed something of the nature of God. At the same time it necessitated a written statement about God's nature thus revealed. "I am the Lord your God, who brought you out of the land of Egypt, . . . You shall have no other gods before me. You shall not make yourself a graven image, or any likeness of anything that is in heaven above . . . or earth beneath . . ." (Ex. 20:2-4). So we see that this epochal event signified for all time that the living God is exclusively God, that He alone is God, that He acts in happenings of history, that He cannot be boxed up in any image, created, painted, or sculptured by men. Whether one classifies Exodus 20 as history or law it performs the function of prophecy. It reveals, interprets, explains, exhorts and appeals to the conscience. All these things belong to the work of prophets. Both law and history teach, instruct, exhort so they are prophetic in meaning. At any rate the scriptures treat themselves, both historical narrative and legal statutes, as having prophetic significance.

The concept of history as being prophetic is most clearly revealed by the book of Genesis. At least this literature that reports historical events is of the nature of prophecy. Here is a book describing incidents which happened long before Moses. Indeed, long before Israel was conscious of itself as a nation. It reaches back to creation and extends its story to the threshold of the birth of the nation. Yet it was considered by the Hebrew people as among their books of the law. Though it contains few legal enactments it does tell the story of God's ways with men. After setting the stage for human history it follows God's eternal design as it unfolds in the lives of Abraham, Isaac, Jacob and Joseph.

The book of Genesis does not say anything about itself as a piece of literature. But there is no biblical book that surpasses it when we consider the content declaring itself. It's like a housewife who elects not to put a marker on the outside of the preserves she's prepared. She prefers that the taste itself shall reveal the quality and nature of the food. The author of Genesis relies on what he has written and how he has put it together to reveal the divine quality of the book.

He who reads through Genesis from first to last without interruption will become aware of a recurring turn of speech. It is: "These are the generations of _____." This expression, or a slight variation of it, occurs ten times in the book. It quite plainly furnishes the theme of the book while at the same time the ten statements form the scaffolding for the whole volume. If the present chapter divisions of Genesis could be eliminated this tenfold partitioning would be much clearer. What in fact we have is ten sections of unequal length each of which has at its head "These are the generations of _____." Each time it appears it serves as a title of the subject matter that follows in that section of the book.

For a proper understanding of what the book is saying this reiterated title needs to be defined. In Genesis 5:1 the title reads, "This is the book of the generations of Adam." Genesis 5:2 through 6:8 presents a listing of ten names from Adam through Noah. With each person named is included his age when an offspring was born, the name of the offspring, how long he, the parent, lived after the birth of his son and finally the total length of his life concluding with the fact that "he died." One exception to "he

154

died" is observed in the case of Enoch of whom it is said, "he was not; for God took him." Judging by this single section the inevitable conclusion would be that "the generations of Adam" intimates that which Adam generated, the line of descendants which sprang of his begetting.

As we move through Genesis to 6:9 we encounter again the title in a slightly variant form. "These are the generations of Noah." From 6:9 through 9:29 the author narrates the history of Noah's family until his death. In other words, the keynote of this section is that which Noah generated. What Noah generated patterns itself after the section on what Adam generated in that both give a genealogical descent. But the account about Noah offers a lengthy expansion about the flood. This cataclysmic event was vitally involved in that which Noah generated. It affected his family, his generation, his whole civilization. It revealed much about the nature of God, his moral quality and how he responds to righteousness and/or unrighteousness in men. It spoke of his universal judgment as well as the depth of his mercy. And it spoke (prophesied) of the future, both man's and God's. The section closes by resuming the genealogical feature of giving his length of life plus the refrain "and he died."

Besides these two, Adam and Noah, the remaining eight sections fully sustain the meaning of the title to be that which _____ generated! It does not refer to the origins of the progenitor but rather the offspring of a progenitor. The nature and amount of material in each genealogical link is determined by the contribution that section makes to the unfolding purpose of God. So Genesis is a book of genealogies; in fact, ten of them. Nine out of the ten include in its title the name of the person who generated the genealogy that follows in the narrative. Arranged with the genealogies are stories of a historical nature, shorter or longer as the need demands, that promote a better knowledge of God. These historical narratives deal particularly with the redemptive promise of God as he is handing it down from person to person. When it reaches Jacob's twelve sons God is ready to embody his prophetic promise in a nation. That's where Genesis stops and Exodus picks up the thread of the story.

If it is true that nine out of ten titles enclose the name of the progenitor, what of the other one? And why the difference? The tenth (really the first of the ten) appears immediately after the general introduction to Genesis. "These are the generations of the heavens and the earth . . ." (Gen. 2:4). Attempts have been made to attach this statement to Genesis 1:1 — 2:3. The arguments advanced to sustain that are quite unconvincing and unduly subjective in nature. A good deal of modern criticism smacks of speculation supportive of wishful thinking too often based on personal bias. If we allow this title to speak as the other nine without question speak it means that everything described from 2:4 through 3:24 was "generated" by "the heavens and the earth." God used matter to produce a human kind "after God's image" as well as of "the dust of the earth." Furthermore, being "like God" the human could evaluate right from wrong and feel the pull and tug of conscience. Mankind could choose; he was not mechanically predetermined. At the same time his senses responded to beauty, taste and wisdom. He was capable of being tempted to the point of yielding and choosing the wrong. And in point of fact that is what actually happened when seduced by the subtlety of Satan. But immediately following the fall the inevitable consequences of wrong-doing began to take effect. The tragedy of human history with all its corruption, pain and death was under way. But in the midst of all the darkness was God's promise of hope of redemption, ". . . He shall bruise your [Satan's] head, but you shall bruise his [the woman's seed] heel" (3:15). If there was ever an example of history with prophetic significance, this is it.

It would seem clear now as to why the author of Genesis stated this initial title as he did, that is, "the heavens and the earth" combined to "generate" man and the circumstances which occasioned his fall from his high estate. "The heavens and the earth" have within them also the promise of redemption. But from this point on individual human beings, guided by God, are described as progenitors of developing history.

The two sections of Genesis that directly follow "the generations of Noah" and its flood are "the generations of the sons of Noah" and then "the generations of Shem." The one on the "sons of Noah" reports a new beginning of the human race. It tells how humanity became so diversified in race and place. Then the prophet-historian concentrates on Shem. It is in Shem's descendants that God will find a man in whom he may intensify his plan of redemption. The final link in Shem's chain of descent is Terah, father of Abraham and his brothers Nahor and Haran.

Of the five remaining segments of Genesis two of them are minor in terms of content and contribution to the principal theme. They are "the generations of Ishmael" (25:12-18) and "the generations of Esau" (26:1-8). One should keep in mind that the importance of any person, event or institution is determined by his or its relation to God, particularly his redemptive purpose threading its way through

157

the book. Ishmael and that which he generated finds its significance because of his relationship to and influence on Abraham. He was definitely a part of the struggle of Abraham to honor faithfully the promise of God. Besides, Ishmael was also promised a heritage in history because he was Abraham's son. Thus the author of Genesis made a place in his book of genealogies for Ishmael. But he follows his line only on a limited scale.

The author treats Esau and that which he generated in a similar fashion. Chapter 36 encompasses the "generations of Esau." That's about 1/16th of the amount of material given to "the generations of Jacob." Though Esau was Jacob's twin brother, though he was the older of the twins, though he was more aggressively active in his life style, yet he was not the one selected by God to transmit His promised redemptive heritage. Nevertheless, Esau's conflict with his brother helped to shape and mold both the man, Jacob, and the form the promise took. In addition, what Esau generated, namely the people of Edom, became a continuing pressure on Israel's historical development. So the author of Genesis felt constrained to give the "generations of Esau" a place in his history suitable to Esau's relationship to Jacob. The purpose of any material introduced into the history is to throw into sharper relief the purpose of God as it develops through the chosen line.

Three component parts of Genesis remain that may help in determining that which it proposes about itself. They are "the generations of Terah" (11:27—25:11), "the generations of Isaac" (25:19—35:29), and "the generations of Jacob" (37:2—50:26). These three furnish by far the most material for the entire book. Slightly over one page records the creation of the world including sun and stars.

This forms the stage on which the human drama is to present its triumph and tragedy. Approximately ten pages recount seven of the ten "generations of _____." That leaves about 43 pages in which is recorded the "generations" of Terah, Isaac, and Jacob. The very massive amount of material clues the reader into the fact that in these three the message of Genesis shines the clearest.

First comes Terah. Immediately a question rises. Why Terah rather than Abraham? It is Abraham, not Terah, to whom the tribes of Israel have always looked as their patriarchal progenitor. Three religions extending into modern times call Abraham "father" — Judaism, Christianity, and Islam. John the Baptist, Jesus and Paul all remind that Abraham was the prime example and father of faith! Yet it's Terah, not Abraham, who is incorporated into the title of this important segment of Genesis. Why?

No question exists but that Abraham provides the most prominent and most important person beginning at 11:27. In fact before this section scarcely starts Terah's death is disclosed. From 12:1 through the whole of the "generations of Terah" the name of Terah is never mentioned. It is Abraham who occupies center stage and around whom the entire saga revolves.

True, it is Abraham who stands in the spotlight. But Terah is mentioned as the one who generates. That is because Abraham's brothers, other sons of Terah, play vital and imposing roles in the ongoing of Abraham's part in the divine plot. Terah's son, Haran, "begat Lot." And Lot took no little place in shaping Abraham's experiences at a crucial time in the patriarch's life. The other son of Terah was Nahor, who married his niece, Milcah. Nahor and Milcah became the parents of Bethuel, the father of Rebekah. Like a mountain stream contributes to the width, depth and quality of a broad river Rebekah entered into Abraham's plans in passing on his heritage to Isaac. Besides, Rebekah became a mighty force in the direction Isaac's place in God's plan took. So, "the generations of Terah" encompassed not only Abraham but other tributary streams that entered into the channel of God's ongoing river of redemption. Without question, McBeth is the main character in the Shakesperian play of the same name. But there are other characters in the play, not to mention time, place, and historical setting in which the tragedy occurred. But each prop, each scene, each character even down to the witches in the opening scene of the first act are all vital in developing the theme of the play. Each supplies some color that paints the development of the chief character, McBeth. Thus too the sons of Terah and their families are essential threads in the whole cloth God weaves. One thread cannot make a pattern. Many threads, woven together, create not only the cloth but the design laced into the cloth. The "generations of Terah" encompass not only the main character, Abraham, but also all the players in the drama.

God's goal in human history is plainly stated to Abraham at the time of the patriarch's call. It is God's set intent to bless "all the families of the earth." His purpose is universal. God's call of one man is only that he may reach all men (Gen. 12:4). But if God is to attain his ultimate goal, for the time being, He must concentrate his revelations of himself on one man. That man must be uprooted from his Chaldean environment, transplanted to another land, blessed with superior moral and spiritual equipment and then taught how to use his special knowledge and experiences by becoming a blessing to others. All this only that God might, through the one man, Abraham, extend the blessing to "all the families [nations] of the earth." These ideas are imbedded in Genesis 12:1-4. These verses set the tone for the entire segment of "the generations of Terah."

Taking Abraham as the premier character in "the generations of Terah" at least twenty paragraphs in Genesis 12:1 through 25:11 detail various crises that shaped the man's character. In addition they reveal both the moral nature of God and his purposes for man. Besides the brief glance above to the call and departure of Abraham to the land of promise we propose to examine a selection of three of these crises.

First, the attempt on the part of Abraham in conjunction with Sarah and her handmaiden, Hagar, to manipulate, steer, and force the promise of God (16:1-16). It had been fourteen years since Abraham had broken ties with homeland and kindred. No sooner had he set foot in the land of Canaan than the voice of God came and said, "Unto your seed I will give this land." Yet he had no seed. With Sarah still barren and long since past the age of childbearing what was to become of the promise of God? It was an experience not only to test a man's faith but to demolish it. Abraham faced what has become a common experience of many saints of God. When confronted with the impossibles in God's promises instead of waiting patiently on God to make his move men frequently step in to force the issue. At such a point men decide that it's God who needs the help rather than men.

It was Sarah, the wife, who suggested the plan. "Go in, I pray you, unto my handmaid; it may be that I shall obtain children by her" (Gen. 16:2). In those times in that culture no moral issue was involved. Such a method for getting

161

children on the part of barren parents was in keeping with accepted social standards. Besides, it was logical. They might even rationalize that this was *the* method God had in mind anyway. After all, God had promised but that did not mean Abraham was to dismantle his mind and refuse to do all he could to bring the promise to fruition. Whatever the reasons, Abraham had no hesitation for "he hearkened unto the voice of Sarah." Thus it was *they* got *their* child. But the fatal flaw in their plan was that it was not the child of *God's* promise.

There are times when in order to trust God man must obey, that is, he must act. At other times he must wait. Both the acting and the waiting have one thing in common; they both testify to a man's trust in the promise of God. God honors a man's personal trust whether it be in positive obedience or in passive waiting.

What does this attempt at manipulating the promise of God have to say? How did God use it? What contribution does it make to the theme of Genesis? In the first place, God respects insuppressible faith. While no doubt it was a faltering of Abraham's faith, it still represented faith. So much did he believe in the promise he would go to any length to see it ripen to full fruit. Though it was a running before God rather than a following, God honored even that faith. God not only gave to Abraham a son in Ishmael but reassured Abraham of Ishmael's place in history. "And also of the son of the handmaid will I make a nation, because he is your seed" (Gen. 21:13).

In the second place, this experience introduced into Abraham's life a discordant note. It would have continuing effect on Abraham, his family, and the purpose of God in the patriarch. Another fourteen years would pass. It's reasonable to suppose that Abraham was reluctant to give up his notion that in Ishmael should the "seed" of God's redemption be passed along. But when God's promise took shape in Sarah's womb at the age of 89, of necessity he realized the heritage of his faith was to be deposited in Isaac. Nevertheless, Ishmael was a fact of life and must still be reckoned with. There would be jealousy between the two mothers, there would be conflict between the half-brothers, there would be perpetual harassment of Israel by Ishmaelites through the centuries. It is reported of Ishmael that "he abode over against all his brethren" (Gen. 16:12). Ishmaelites would not hesitate to turn a profit if they could buy a Hebrew and sell him into slavery for gain. It was Ishmaelites who purchased Joseph from jealous brothers. Yet, in spite of it all, God's original promise had envisioned his blessing on "all the families of the earth." And Ishmael was the progenitor of at least one of the "families of the earth." Oh! the grandeur of the mercy and grace and wisdom of God! This was a part of God's reinforcement in the mind of Abraham of his revelation about himself and his purposes with men. No man, no race of men, has ever been abandoned by God. It's men who abandon God, not God men. God did not *begin* being gracious in the New Testament. Man's comprehension of God may be larger in the mind of Paul and more directly revealed on the pages of the New Testament. But God is not any more gracious.

Finally, this experience taught Abraham—and through him all succeeding generations—the nature of real faith. Faith must rest absolutely on the promised word of God, not on the manipulations of man. There are to be no reservations, no secret attempts to withhold any portion of the heart. To have faith man must abandon himself in the simplicity of childlike trust to the promised will of God. The patriarch's faith survived his self-initiated juggling of the promise. When it came down to the actual getting of the child of promise from an eighty-nine year old womb "he did not weaken in faith when he considered his own body, which was as good as dead. . . . No distrust made him waver concerning the promise of God, but he grew strong in his faith . . . fully convinced that God was able to do what he had promised" (Romans 4:19-21).

Another important turning point in the life of Abraham came when God's judgment fell on the "cities of the plain." Lot had chosen to live in the fertile valley of the Jordan. He had built his home and was raising his family in the corrupt city of Sodom. But these cities of the plain had descended to such a moral depth God could no longer delay judgment. God had revealed to Abraham that his redemptive blessing was destined for "all" the families of the earth. But love in order to be love must be righteous. The judgment of love against sin is destruction. Abraham must be made to see that the God who seeks to bless "all" nations cannot bless any nation who turns from righteousness to sin. Love in the presence of sin shows itself as judgmental wrath. The iniquity of Sodom was full and running over. If God is to be God, if God is to reveal his basic nature of love for "all" nations, he must rain judgment on that people who reject his righteous love. It is crucial that Abraham understand that the blessing of all nations comes from a moral, living God, not from a mechanical, dead deity. "Shall I hide from Abraham that which I do; seeing that Abraham shall surely become a great and mighty nation, and all the nations of the earth shall be blessed in him?" (Gen. 18:17, 18). Abraham must be able to reconcile in his own mind the destruction of the "cities of the plain" in view of God's universal purpose. And to make plain the point that his righteous judgment is not opposed to his redemptive love God agrees when Abraham prays not to "consume the righteous with the wicked." And that, even if only ten righteous be found in the entire city of Sodom. God said, "I will not destroy it [the city] for the ten's sake. [That is, if I can find ten]" (Gen. 18:23-32). Such is the revelation to Abraham of the nature and purpose of God in the episode of the destruction of the "cities of the plain."

The most momentous revelation in the entire life experiences of Abraham came in the trial of faith when he was told to offer Isaac in human sacrifice. God said, "Take now your son, your only son, whom you love, Isaac, and get you into the land of Moriah; and offer him there for a burnt offering . . ." (22:2). The custom of human sacrifice by surrounding Canaanitish clans was the background. The living God who called Abraham was life-giving, not life-taking; he was life-redeeming, not life-sacrificing. Yet here were neighbors who served their heathen non-entities enough to dedicate their very children in adoration to their gods. Would Abraham have that kind of faith? Was Abraham's God that kind of God?

Besides these questions of religion and faith it simply did not appear to be logical to take the *only* son of promise and eliminate him by death. What then would become of the promise? It was in Isaac that the seed was to come! Beyond that, the instincts of parenthood fought against such a sacrifice. The customs of the country and his desire to obey God said "Yes" to Abraham. But logic, the nature of God, plus the moral love of a father dictated "no." It would seem that the war of feelings going on inside Abraham lies beyond description until one himself has the experience.

165

How much do I love God? What is the nature of the God whom I love? What is my particular place in the unfolding work of God? These and other questions lie at the base of Abraham's heart in the struggle of faith he endured. And though his heart would break he stood the test. "He offered up Isaac . . . accounting that God is able to raise up, even from the dead; from whence he did also in a figure receive him back" (Heb. 11:17, 19).

From this trial of faith the "father of the faithful" learned two lessons. He learned that God calls for a faith that leads to absolute, unquestioning, total obedience. Furthermore, such obedience will be reimbursed in kind. That is to say, a mutual trust between God and the one believing will henceforth become a personal, rewarding fellowship. God honors and trusts him who obeys — absolutely! And he also learned that the living God does not demand nor does he take delight in human sacrifice in the form of death as a victim of worship. From this point on the Old Testament never recognizes human sacrifice as part of the program of God. If a human being's life is taken because of his worship and service to God, it is sin, not God, who demands and executes the sacrificial victim. Human sacrifice comes from the worship of Satan. The worship of God leads to life. Even when *the* supreme human sacrifice, the death of Jesus took place it was the reality of sin that made such a sacrificial death necessary in the plan of God.

The revelations to Abraham were to be transferred to the next generation in the person of Isaac, the son of promise. But it's not enough to hear of God's purpose. One must confront God himself, personally. Nothing is real to *me* until *I* experience it. So it became essential that God and Isaac come face to face in personal confrontation. Were it not for these personal encounters of Abraham, Isaac and Jacob with God the book of Genesis would be of limited value to us. But these face-offs between God and man form links in a chain of events that slowly uncover God's eternal plan for man. With such links present then details of daily life take on far-reaching significance. Marriage, birth, watering wells, famine or fortune, friend and foe, — these and more take on meaning because they are so important in refining the human instruments of God's purpose for the whole world. Hence, the promise to Abraham must be transferred to Isaac in face to face encounter.

Of the trio of patriarchs, Abraham, Isaac, and Jacob, the second, Isaac, plays out his life on a much lower key than the other two. He appears more passive in personality, less aggressive in life style than the others. Even his individual legacy to the developing purpose of God is but an extension of Abraham's. And his chief endowment to that ongoing purpose finds more fulfillment in his son, Jacob, than in himself. As the author of Genesis tells the story of Isaac it follows a course obviously patterned after Abraham. Blessed because of Abraham he did little more than be the agent of transmission of Abraham's blessing. He too experienced a wife who endured a long period of barrenness as did Abraham. He deceived Abimelech about his wife calling her his "sister" as did his father with the Pharaoh. Even as his father, Isaac too experienced domestic turmoil due to two incompatible sons. Famine and the threat of famine, in other words, economic opportunities or lack of them shaped much of his movements in life. He was a carbon copy of Abraham on a small scale. Even the wells of water he opened were those of his father's that had been plugged up by Philistines.

One parallel to Abraham that Isaac tasted was personal appearances by God. On at least two occasions it is said that God "appeared to him" (26:2, 24). Such personal encounters gave Isaac much more than a mere intellectual knowledge of God's legacy. It left him with a feel for God that only can come through experience. Knowledge is more than thought! To know God includes to think correctly, feel purely, and obey conscientiously. This Isaac was privileged to do no matter how passive, withdrawn, or low-key he was.

Famine occasioned Isaac's initial encounter with God. As frequently happened in ancient times many people gravitated toward Egypt in famine times. "And Isaac went to Gerar, to Abimelech, king of the Philistines" (Gen. 26:1). Apparently he had decided to emigrate to Egypt. There was always the possibility that such a change in residence might become permanent. Judging by what God enjoined on Isaac, the patriarch definitely was planning on seeking relief in Egypt from the famine. "The Lord appeared to him and said, 'Do not go down to Egypt; dwell in the land; stay in the land in which I tell you to live. Stay in this land and I will bless you; for to you and your descendants I will give these lands . . .'" (26:2, 3a). Egypt was to have its place, a vital place, in the Lord's unwinding plan. Egypt would house God's people in their formative years as a people of destiny. But the time was not yet. "This land" was to be Israel's ultimate home, whereas Egypt would only be a temporary school of discipline. So it was that Gerar on the borders of entrance toward Egypt and its king, Abimelech, became his haven of refuge for a time.

Besides, this experience with God broadened Isaac's view of God and God's concern for him. It clearly revealed the reason for God's special interest and providential care for him. God took advantage of this famine confrontation with Isaac to expand the patriarch's outlook on the divine plan. In pointing out the necessity to stay in "this land" God renewed the covenant made to Abraham. "I will fulfill the oath which I swore to Abraham your father. And I will multiply your seed as the stars of heaven, and I will give unto your seed these lands; and in your seed shall all the nations of the earth be blessed" (Gen. 26:3b, 4). God was interested in Isaac and where he moved, where he lived, whose his associates were — why? because Isaac was a necessary coupling tying together Abraham to Jacob. Maybe Isaac did not have the talent, ability or strength of character as the other two. Maybe he was a weaker link. But a chain cannot do its work at all without its weakest link. This too was a revelation of how God concerns himself with men, the weakest of men. Bricks may give strength, warmth and beauty to a house but they cannot perform their function without mortar to hold them together. God used Isaac as a brickmason uses mortar. God's appearance to Isaac helped build the man's self-esteem. Besides, it was one more highlight of the portrait of God and his purpose and plan.

The second reported appearance of the Lord to Isaac followed a series of disheartening conflicts with "the herdsmen of Gerar." In such a parched land as was Palestine water was more precious than gold, more necessary than banks, as essential to life as air, food or land. Life was tenuous at best; if one was to live at all he, his family, his cattle must have access to an unfailing supply of water. Thus it was that when Isaac "encamped in the valley of Gerar" he "dug again the wells of water which had been dug in the days of Abraham his father" (Gen. 26:17, 18). But no sooner had the well been reopened and the security of his family insured than "the herdsmen of Gerar quarreled with Isaac's herdsmen, saying, 'The water is ours.'" Instead of standing his ground and contesting by arms for his rights Isaac abandoned the well and withdrew to another site to open another well. This was repeated several times. Finally he settled in Beersheba. Frustration, fear, uncertainty seemed to be the building blocks of human life! Then it was that God appeared to Isaac again, reminded him of his heritage, and then offered these reassuring words, "Fear not, for I am with you and will bless you and multiply your descendants . . ." (Gen. 26:24).

It has been suggested that Isaac was the *least* of the triad of patriarchs that appear as prominent mountain peaks on the horizon of Old Testament history. And this is true! But that very fact is part of what God reveals in Isaac. To be "number one" in God's program does not mean to be tallest in terms of feet and inches. It means rather to stand up to the height of one's own personal capacity. Isaac was not supposed to be tall in comparison to others. He is to be measured only in terms of his own potential. A six-foot man is not to be called least in a land of seven-foot giants. He must only be gauged by how he performs on a team of six-foot men. *Everyone* is called to be "number one" and each can actually be "number one" as God arranges history. God appeared to Isaac at every point in life when Isaac needed God to appear. God is always available to all at whatever place each occupies in God's ongoing plan. A weak link is not weak when it is as strong as *it* can be!

As hinted earlier Isaac's real contribution is not to be discovered in him as much as in his passing on to his son, Jacob, the heritage of God's spiritual values. "The generations of Isaac" extend from Genesis 25:8 through 35:29.

But most of the material deals with crucial points in the life of Jacob. The "generations of Isaac" fall into three sections. First, the birth of his twin sons to the flight of Jacob to Haran (25:21—28:9). The disposition of the family birthright is the chief concern of this section.

The struggle of the twins while yet in the mother's womb foreshadows God's basic revelation to Isaac as well as Isaac's basic need for understanding God's ways. The sovereignty of God amid the conflicts between men is the truth revealed in the rivalry between the twins. That the "elder should serve the younger" was not the normal pattern according to human law or custom. In answer to the confusion and pain of Rebekah's pregnancy God's sovereignty in guiding or even overruling man's ways was affirmed (25:23).

The rest of Jacob's life up to his hasty retreat from the land of promise to the ancestral home in Haran was a continuation of how God maneuvered His sovereign will amid the vagaries of human deceits. Esau's voracious hunger, Jacob's conniving duplicity, the parents' overt favoritism between the boys, the faulty eyesight of Isaac, jealousy and hatred between the brothers, these and other factors were the threads in God's hands with which he could weave his sovereign will. The foibles, mistakes, and sins of human freedom were not barriers to God's engineering his will. They were tools within his grasp with which he built his will in men's affairs.

The second section in the "generations of Isaac" extends from the dream at Bethel of the heavenly ladder to Jacob's departure from Haran back to his homeland of promise (28:10—31:55). Here again the sovereignty of God amid human treachery is a basic element in God's revelation to Jacob. But over and above that, God's willingness and ability to press into service the very faulty human material with which he has to work is an important part of that which God reveals. Little in Jacob's natural constitution would mark him as ever being an instrument of God's purpose. Yet God was set on using this selfish, crafty deceiver. The heart and core of what Jacob was to learn in the next twenty years' experience came on his first night away from the warmth of his parental home. In the open country with a stone for a pillow,

> He dreamed that there was a ladder set up on the earth, and the top of it reached to heaven; and behold the angels of God were ascending and descending on it! And behold, the Lord stood above it and said, "I am the Lord, the God of Abraham your father and the God of Isaac; the land on which you lie I will give to you and to your descendants; they shall be like the dust of the earth, and you shall spread abroad . . . in you and in your descendants shall all the families of the earth be blessed. Behold, I am with you and will keep you wherever you go, and will bring you back to this land; for I will not leave you until I have done that of which I have spoken to you" (Gen. 28:12-15).

Once again the reason for God's special interest in Jacob and his family is voiced: "In you and your seed shall all families of the earth be blessed." Amid all the demoralizing effects of his own double-dealing, scheming nature he would be sustained by the knowledge that he was useful as an apprentice in the hands of God. He also learned that God is not limited to one place or family but is true God in any place and among all peoples. "I am with you and will keep you wherever you go" became his beacon light through all his wanderings. The low places of earth are touched by the angels of heaven in spite of — maybe even because of —

the guiles of men. But of the brightest stars in that lonely night of Jacob's dream no revelation surpassed the word "I will not leave you until I have done that of which I have spoken to you." The skulduggery and perfidy of the human material with which God has had to work has been his handicap. But still he assured perfidious Jacob "I will not leave you." God's promise to stick with him through all the devious crooks and turns (he foists on others and others foist on him) would be the sturdy rudder to guide Jacob through all storms. Nor would that guidance be taken away "until I have done that which I have spoken to you." A man's own evil can be surmounted when he lives with the knowledge that God has designated him for a specific task.

Nevertheless, evil must be purged, motives must be purified if God's servant is to get to God's goal in him! Thus we arrive at the third stage of the "generations of Isaac." Isaac's son, Jacob, was such a stubborn fraud that a vision of God's purpose was not enough. If a man is ever to learn the limitations of his own strength he must be pitted against God in mortal combat person to person. Thus came Jacob to Mahanaim and Peniel (Gen. 32:2 and 32:22-32).

All the skill of Jacob's guileful nature rose up in selfish fear when he heard that his brother, Esau, was approaching with a band of 400 men. As so often, Jacob plotted his own protection, although now at the cost of his wealth and family. Flocks of sheep, herds of cattle, even his wives, maids and his children he sent across the Jabbok's flowing waters. "And Jacob was left alone." As at Bethel years before, once again he was alone here at Peniel. His thoughts recaptured the words of God at Bethel, "I will do you good, and make your descendants as the sand of the sea. . . ." But what kind of a man does God have to claim this place in the flow of God's eternal purpose? He must be depolluted of his evil and purified in his motives. This provides the necessity for Jacob's "wrestling" with God at the fords of the Jabbok.

In every man's life span there comes that hour in which in some life and death struggle he must gaze without evasion in the mirror of reality. Jacob's wrestling with the heavenly visitor that night by Jabbok's waters was his hour of combat with God. The question at issue was not his place in God's scheme. Rather it was the reshaping of his own personal character. In Jacob's existence it was something similar to that of which Jesus spoke, "You must be begotten again." Jacob must fight with *facts,* not illusions, about *himself.* Deceit was the root of all his troubles; the seed of guile was harvesting in self-destruction. Shall he remain Jacob, the deceiver? Or shall he become Israel, the soldier of God? This was the issue of his warfare that night when he wrestled God by Jabbok's babbling brook.

After the battle of Jacob by the brook Jabbok one element of importance must yet be experienced. "God appeared to Jacob again" at Bethel. God confirmed Jacob's change of character by affirming his new name, Israel. God identified himself again to Jacob by name, "I am God Almighty." Furthermore, God renewed his pledge concerning the future both as to the land and as to Jacob's descendants in that land. "A company of nations shall come from you . . . I will give the land to your descendants after you" (35:11, 12). It was the time and place for a renewal. Jacob's heart was in a condition for renewal, so renewal expressed itself fittingly in worship. "Jacob set up . . . a pillar of stone; and he poured out a drink offering on it . . . So Jacob called the name of the place where God had spoken with him, Bethel." That is, "house of God."

Thus Isaac's generations incorporated three stages in Jacob's developing trek with God through life. Isaac's place in God's scheme stretched itself through the developing, growing of Jacob's consciousness of God at work in him. David could feel the need for a temple but it was Solomon who would have to build it. So, Isaac passed on the heritage he received through Abraham but it was in Jacob that it flowered. The planting of Abraham, the cultivating of Isaac ripened to its harvest in Jacob whose twelve sons became the patriarchal precursors of the people of God.

The final of the ten sections of Genesis tells the story of the "generations of Jacob." As the "generations of Isaac" covered mostly the life experiences of Jacob, so the "generations of Jacob" deal largely with Joseph and his brothers. Is there any story in Old or New Testament which demonstrates more clearly the providence of God working itself out through the life of one individual human being than that of Joseph? Or for that matter, working itself out into an embryonic people in the persons of the twelve sons of Jacob, the brothers of Joseph?

The theme of Genesis is gathered up and magnified as the author focuses his camera on those scenes which took Israel to Egypt. At seventeen Joseph is pictured as an enthusiastic, innocent, idealistic youth with a sense of destiny — maybe with a slight touch of arrogance. Betrayed by his brothers, duped by his Egyptian master's wife, forgotten by his fellow-prisoner, there was nothing at the age of thirty-four that gave hint of any remembrance by God, much less of a significant place in his ongoing purpose. Yet after years of disappointment and suffering, during the peak of his useful years of responsible power, he would say to his conscience-stricken brothers, "Fear not, for am I in the place of God? As for you, you meant evil against me, but God meant it for good, to bring it about that many people should be kept alive, as they are today" (50:19, 20). Modern proverbial wisdom says, "Hindsight is better than foresight." But there are times when hindsight gives insight! In the case of Joseph and his brothers after the years of tragic betrayal, disappointment, heartache and anxiety the cloud of selfishness was removed. They were able at last to trace the guiding hand of God moving through all their various experiences. God was at work weaving "all things together for good," the good of his unchanging purpose to "bless all the families of the earth." Such is the meaning of "the generations of Jacob."

By the time the author of Genesis reaches chapter fifty the ten "generations" have accomplished their task. Through ten genealogical movements the will and purpose of God has been gradually and repeatedly revealed. One thread running through various episodes of separate lives transforms these different jewels into one united necklace of sparkling divine beauty. And it declares that God is interested in, works with and plans for individual people. But more than that, through these people he is moving onward toward his goal of redeeming "all the families of the earth." Genesis is a book of beginnings as the name indicates. Not only is it the beginnings of the creation but most especially the beginnings of God's redemptive movement for man after he forfeited his right to life in the garden of Eden.

What does the book of Genesis say about the book of Genesis? As a part of the Judeo-Christian scriptures what does it say about itself? As observed above, Genesis is a part of the Jewish books of law. As a part of the Pentateuch Genesis might lay claim to share in the more direct statements about the law as having come from God. But in and of itself Genesis really makes no direct pronouncement about itself. It lacks even a formal title unless the first verse be viewed as one, "In the beginning God created the heavens and the earth." However, the context would seem to suggest that this is more of a title to 1:2 — 2:4 than of the entire book. So in the absence of any comprehensive title or direct statements we are reduced to the author's device of incorporating his claim in his ten "generations of _____." These ten generations as subordinate titles followed by the narrative material make perfectly plain that the author is declaring, "I am writing history as His-Story!"

By the content and arrangement of the material in the book the author makes transparent his belief that he is recording the word of the God who invests himself in the affairs and hopes of mankind. What does the book say about itself? In answer let's paraphrase the words of Joseph to his brothers after the death of Jacob. "As for you, you meant it for evil against me. But God turned it into good, to bring about the redemption of many" (Gen. 50:20).

By its content the book claims to contain the beginning of God's redemptive movement in history. It leaves the reader prepared to follow that movement as it broadens from the limited channels of individuals into the more deeply cut channel of national corporate flow. That becomes the theme of Exodus and the rest of the books of the law. Genesis initiates the speaking of God to men by means of the written word.

Chapter Ten

THE PROPHETS

That portion of the threefold Hebrew dividing of the Old Testament called "The Prophets" offers the most candid statements of scriptures about themselves. The prophets claim inspiration much more than the law or poetical books. This should be no surprise since the very nature of their work often required them to claim a "thus saith the Lord." The prophets all labored under the conviction that they were called by divine imperative to deliver the word of God. Furthermore, that message was directed toward a particular, local, never-to-be-repeated situation. They had a conscious awareness of the divine urgency of what they were declaring.

Typical of this sense of inspired call is that which befell Isaiah in "the year that king Uzziah died." A moral and spiritual cancer had been eating at the vitals of God's people for more than two centuries. It had brought them to a national crisis. "The whole head is sick, and the whole heart faint . . . there is no soundness in it . . ." (Isa. 1:5, 6). The Assyrian juggernaut was casting its threatening shadow over the king-doms of Palestine. On a day of worship when the man, Isaiah, was musing in the temple he caught a vision of God "sitting upon a throne, high and lifted up." Angels were filling the temple with songs praising the holiness of the Lord. Sight of the holy God jolted Isaiah into a realization of his guilty sinfulness — and of the total corruption of the society of which he was a part. "Woe is me! For I am lost; for I am a man of unclean lips, and I dwell in the midst of a people of unclean lips . . ." (Isa. 6:5). How could such a consciously sinful person become convinced that *he* would be a spokesman of God's word in the impending crisis? At the same moment in which he became so alive to his own guilt an angel took a "burning coal" from the altar of God and "touched my mouth." The prophet never forgot the angel's words, "Behold, this has touched your lips; your guilt is taken away, and your sin is forgiven" (6:7). After Isaiah envisioned the holiness of God, felt the guilt of his own soul, experienced the relief of forgiveness, he was in a position, spiritually and psychologically, to dedicate himself to God's service. He was emotionally ready for a challenge. Then it was that he heard the voice of God calling, "Whom shall I send, and who will go for us?" A person in Isaiah's condition could scarcely keep from responding, "Here am I! Send me" (6:8). Such a singular experience carved a permanent gash into his sensitive heart. Henceforth the sense of the urgency of God's word in the moral and political disorders of his time became rooted in his soul. And that *he* was the one to deliver *that* message settled on him as a deathless conviction.

The prophets of God were neither philosophers, theologians, nor social reformers. They did not advocate a particular school of thought nor did they come before the people as men of religion. And they certainly were not activists espousing political rebellion or overthrow of the government. (Without question their messages, if heeded, would shake up government, alter social patterns and change religious forms and standards of life. And true, some of the classical prophets stemmed from the ranks of religious officials. Jeremiah was of a priestly family. Others were thinkers with literary and poetic bent. Habakkuk was certainly a pundit of philosophic quality. And numbers of these writing prophets inveighed against the immoralities and social abuses of society around them.) But the fact remains that they did not speak as religious officials, social rebels, or philosophic theorists. They came as men with a message. They spoke

179

for God! They spoke to men in personal or national crises! As such no honest man would dare present himself as a man with a message from God without a definite sense of a call. In fact many of these men were reluctant and resisted God's urgent hand prodding them into their life's calling. Jeremiah protested arguing "I do not know how to speak, for I am only a youth" (Jer. 1:6). Amos never intended to perform as a prophet. "I am no prophet, nor a prophet's son; but I am a herdsman, and a dresser of sycamore trees, and the Lord took me . . . and said, 'Go prophesy . . .'" (Amos 7:14).

God's entrance into the prophet's life in a call could not but engraft into each man's soul a sense of urgency. He may not have liked his work but it had to be done and it was imperative that *he* do it. Thus, as in the case of Isaiah, all the prophets reflect such a sense of driving compulsion. No two calls were exactly alike. That fact is clear because no two persons were precisely alike. Nor were the circumstances that demanded the need for a prophet ever strictly the same. God's call of each man suited the circumstances and the person called. But regardless of who, or how, or in what situation, the urgency was to be the life-long burden of the prophet. "The Lord has spoken; who can but prophesy?" (Amos 3:4b). "If I say, 'I will not mention him, or speak any more in his name,' there is in my heart as it were a burning fire shut up in my bones, and I am weary of holding it in, and I cannot" (Jer. 20:9). The logic of Amos became the experience of Jeremiah. If and when God calls one to deliver his word, "who can but prophesy?" And when, like Jeremiah, he who is called tries to "hold it in" it won't stay in. It's too urgent! One *must* speak for God!

The "call" is a common denominator but the shape of the call differs with each prophet. Isaiah, city bred, of noble blood, educated, cultured, was in the temple at worship. As we have described above it was a highly dramatic moment. Emotionally stirring, it shaped the direction of his ministry. Ezekiel's call was equally emotional, equally dramatic yet so different. Ezekiel was one of the early captives "in the land of the Chaldeans by the river Chebar" when the "hand of the Lord came upon him there" (Ezek. 1:3). He saw a storm rising in the north filled with symbolic visions of fire, living winged-creatures, wheels with wheels, "full of eyes round about." He saw in his visions a crystal firmament, the "sound of many waters" and a throne above the firmament. "Such" says Ezekiel, "was the appearance of the likeness of the glory of the Lord." God appeared and spoke and the young prophet said, ". . . when he spoke, the Spirit entered into me and set me upon my feet; and I heard him speaking. And he said to me, 'Son of man, I send you to the people of Israel . . .'" (Ezek. 2:2, 3).

Isaiah caught his vision of God in the holy land in the sacred temple in an hour of personal worship. Ezekiel was a captive in a heathen land and saw the symbols of God amidst the violence of a storm filled with dark clouds, flashing lightning, crashing thunder. And in this rumbling storm appeared unnatural combinations of feathered creatures inhabiting moving wheels. Ezekiel lived as a captive in a land far away from home securities. On the immediate horizon was the imminent fall of Jerusalem linked with the total destruction of the temple. Here was a young man, an alien in a foreign land, hostage to a barbarian government and its pagan gods. He had no sanctuary to house the symbols of his God, no shrine as a holy place of refuge. Of necessity God came to Ezekiel to call him in the forms most available —the fury of nature's storm and the wheels of commerce in his current environment. Both city and temple, though threatened, were still standing when God called Isaiah. More than a century later Ezekiel lived amidst the crashing fall of both city and temple. He was forced to envision a reconstructed temple within his own imagination; to create a renewed temple from the building blocks of his own faith. It was the same God who called both men to speak His word suited to different times, places and persons!

For some of the classical prophets there is no detailed record of their call. That they each experienced their own particular summons there is no doubt. What they each endured as men, what each said as spokesmen for God, what each claimed for his message — these things combine to remove any doubt that God invaded their lives to give special direction to them. A Nahum became haunted by one obsession — a city as ruthlessly violent and wicked as Nineveh would inevitably be wiped from the face of the earth. That is, if God be just, then the unjust must fall! So, when Nahum inveighs against Nineveh for three unrelenting chapters of prophetic doom it is God anathematizing the criminal city. Nahum looked upon his book as "An oracle concerning Ninevah" (1:1). An "oracle" is what God says, not man. "Behold I am against you, says the Lord of hosts, and I will burn your chariots in smoke, and the sword shall devour your young lions; I will cut off your prey from the earth, and the voice of your messengers shall no more be heard" (Nahum 2:13). Nahum's hostility toward the scourge of Nineveh was captured by God to reveal that he (God) *is* just, that he *does* bring the proud, militant, arrogant despoiler to justice. The call of Nahum is not recorded. It is revealed in his message and ministry.

As with Nahum so with all the prophets for which no description of their special call appears. Obadiah concerned himself with his loathing of Edom. As Nahum anticipated the justice of God falling on Nineveh, so Obadiah could not see a righteous God allowing Edom to continue its arrogant pride living "in the clefts of the rock, whose dwelling is high . . ." (Obadiah 3). One fact all these prophets declared: the living God rules over the peoples of this world. And that rule is even exercised in the ethical, moral, and spiritual rudiments woven into the fabric of all life, human and divine, natural and supernatural. One can as well escape from the law of gravity as he can rid himself of God and God's rule in human nature. If God be righteous love then those people who violate the image of God in them can only inherit judgment. The prophets were "doomsters" only in the sense they announced the inevitable harvest of doom. Those who sow unethical, immoral, unspiritual seeds must expect to harvest that kind of a crop. The herdsman-farmer Amos observed the corruption of the citizenry of Bethel in Israel. As a spokesman of a God of absolute purity in the presence of a people of ingrained immorality he fearlessly proclaimed, "Thus says the Lord. . . ." The rugged honesty of his mountain background in Tekoa, the unentangled simplicity of his life, the uncomplicated line of his thought processes left his soul open to hear God. "Thus the Lord showed me . . . he was forming locusts . . ." (Amos 7:1) and "I saw the Lord standing beside the altar, and he said, 'Smite the capitals until the thresholds shake . . . and shatter them on the heads of all the people . . .'" (9:1).

What do the prophets say about themselves? What do their writings disclose about themselves? Those men make claim that they have been called, set aside and guided into special service to God. They avow that the messages which they proclaim are God's word to their special problem — God's answer to their generation's predicament. God's word is quite frequently a message of wrath and judgment. But imbedded in the word of judgment there breaks through a shaft of light and hope. Even a doom-filled message like Obadiah can close with a vision of a hopeful future. "Saviours will go up on Mount Zion to govern the mountains of Esau. And the kingdom will be the Lord's" (Obadiah 21). No matter how dark the valleys the mountain peak eventually will be climbed. And in the bright light of the mountaintop "the kingdom will be the Lord's." But whether judgment or hope each of the prophets believe and say that "This is what God says!"

This belief of the prophets about themselves and their messages is echoed by the books that bear their names. Besides the direct statements about their date, situation and authorship they have written on every page and between all the lines a conviction that "Thus says the Lord." Sometimes they openly claim that their word is God's word. Sometimes they imply it. But they always are laboring under the conviction that they speak God's word addressed to man's need.

The prophet is conscious of himself as a spokesman for God. He views himself as being on intimate, personal terms in his relationship to God. He has dialogues with God in which he, the man, suggests, proposes and persuades God to do or not do possible options. Amos provides a good example. In the opening words of chapter seven the prophet says, "The Lord God showed me." This is positive claim that God made a specific revelation of what follows. "Behold, he [God] was forming locusts in the beginning of the shooting up of the latter growth; and lo, it was the latter growth after the king's mowings" (Amos 7:1). According to this verse Amos was vouchsafed a preview of threatened

184

crop failures due to swarming locusts which would destroy the crops before the farmers could harvest. Amos himself was a herdsman familiar with the tenuous, border-line existence of rural life. Failure of a single harvest in the dry, rocky soil of that land was a harbinger of disease, starvation, misery and death. When he saw what God was planning as judgment against the people the devastation was so vividly real that he was emboldened to dissuade God from such destruction. "O Lord God, forgive, I pray! How can Jacob stand? He is so small!" Then the book of Amos reports, "The Lord repented concerning this; 'It shall not be,' said the Lord" (Amos 7:2, 3).

Twice more in chapter seven (vs. 4-9) the prophet repeats the "Lord showed me." In one vision "the Lord God was calling for a judgment by fire, and it devoured the great deep and was eating up the land." Again the prophet valiantly protests the judgment. "Then I said, 'O Lord God, cease, I beseech you! How can Jacob stand? He is so small!'" Then once again the Lord responds to the prophet's plea, "This also shall not be!"

The dialogue continues through a third vision. Amos saw "the Lord standing beside a wall built with a plumbline, with a plumbline in his hand. And the Lord said, 'Amos, what do you see?' And I said, 'A plumbline.' Then the Lord said, 'Behold, I am setting a plumbline in the midst of my people Israel; . . . I will rise against the house of Jeroboam with the sword.'" On this occasion no report is given as to whether the prophet argued the point or not. It would seem that after the prophet had persuaded God to soften his judgment twice God's final decision was that the judgment must fall on hapless Israel.

The point of chief concern here is what the book of Amos has to declare about itself. This verbal exchange in 7:1-9 reveals the self-consciousness of Amos as to his access to God and God's word for the people. God showed Amos divine counsels. God spoke something to the prophet and the man spoke something back to God in response. And a point of particular import is that the prophet clearly distinguishes between that which "I said," and that which "the Lord said." There seems to be no doubt in the mind and heart of Amos that God talked to him and that he talked to God. And that what God said was of vital concern to all the people of Israel. This awareness of all the prophets that they were transmitters of "oracles" from God is itself testimony that their persons and their writings stand apart from just ordinary books. They have in them the very "breath of God." In this respect Amos is an example of all the prophets' attitude toward themselves and their writings. Furthermore, though occasions and forms do differ he is *typical* of them all.

To all this is added the timeless quality of the prophets' messages to ancient Israel. The books of the prophets are as pertinent to today's political, social, economic, moral, ethical and spiritual problems as they were when first delivered to an obscure nation of antiquity. Too often it is assumed that because Christ fulfills the Old Testament expectations they have been outmoded as to their authority. That cannot be true. No matter in what form or which stage truth appears, by its very nature it cannot ever be outmoded. Advanced mathematics does not outmode the multiplication table. No piece of English literature can get so classic in style or message that it can dispense with the alphabet. And all advanced physics is confined to a very few basic principles. Truth is truth whether told at the kindergarten level to a child's mind or discussed in advanced abstract terms at the PhD level. Jesus said, "Don't think that I came to destroy the law and the prophets; I didn't come to destroy but to fulfill" (Matt. 5:17). When one fulfills the law against murder by not even wishing, thinking, or feeling murder against a neighbor, then in no way has he lessened the obligation of the law which asserts, "Thou shalt not murder." Christ is the fruit; the law and prophets are the root of the tree of God's revelation. But cut the roots off and the fruit withers. Christ brings power to fulfill the law and the prophets; he does not abolish the truth of either law or prophets.

Now all this becomes plain when one catches the profound insight of the prophets into God's nature as revealed in their books. How a holy God governs the nations of men is written on every page, between each line, and on all the margins of the prophets of the Old Testament. Moreover God's moral, ethical, spiritual qualities express themselves in every nation, every age, every climate, and every system of government known to history. The context in which Jeremiah delivered his message presupposes the escape of Israel from Egypt under Moses. It assumes his hearers are familiar with the turbulent centuries of Israel's rebellious nature through these centuries. The prophet reminds the people of seventh century Israel, "I brought you into a plentiful land to enjoy its fruits and its good things. But when you came in you defiled my land, and made my heritage an abomination. The priests did not say, 'Where is the Lord?' Those who handle the law did not know me; the rulers transgressed against me; the prophets prophesied by Baal, and went after things that do not profit" (Jer. 2:7-8). Kings and commoners, lawyers, priests and preachers violated every law of the covenant given on Sinai. Under the protection and forms of religion and morality they transgressed and ignored both real religion and practical morality. In

187

view of that Jeremiah delivered God's message, "There-fore," says the Lord, "I contend with you, and with your children's children I will contend" (Jer. 2:9). "Shall I not punish them for these things?" says the Lord, "and shall I not avenge myself on a nation such as this?" (Jer. 5:29). Though the context makes plain that Jeremiah addressed a never-to-be-repeated historical circumstance in Israel, the moral and spiritual realities that fired his heart are constantly repeating themselves in every generation. If one can read Jeremiah with sensitive perception he will be prepared for the overthrow of the Bourbon dynasty in France at the coming of the French revolution of the 18th century. Or the rapid rise and meteoric fall of the third Reich under Adolph Hitler. There is no way to remove God's moral and spiritual attributes from the processes of human history. One could as easily remove the law of gravity from physics! Given a holy Creator who is immanent within his own creation, given an immoral people who ignore, defy, and run rough-shod over the absolutes of God's morality, the outcome is obvious.

It is this delicate sensitivity to the moral nature of God that gives to the prophetic books their timeless quality. The keen awareness of the prophets to the consequences of corrupt social conditions emerges in their writings as time-less truth. The overwhelming tide of Assyria's invading armies furnished the background on which Habakkuk painted his portrait of faith and trust. His observation, ". . . the righteous shall live by his faith" (2:4), has become classic by means of Paul's use of it. But it also embodies a universal fact; in any time of terror, personal or national, it is univer-sally true that "the righteous *do* live by faith." The genius of the Old Testament prophet is that he clothes immutable truth in local, temporal, fleeting fashions. The fact of the timelessness of their truth in the face of the fading character of their moment in history is witness to the prophets' self-consciousness that they spoke God's word. And in addition it clinches the fact that Christ, his teachings, his church "fulfills" without destroying the law and prophets. Jesus Christ is the embodiment of the deepest *meaning* of the Old Testament.

Merely to quote statements from all the Old Testment prophets as to what they say or imply about themselves would extend beyond any practical length for a book. We prefer to confine the remainder of this study to a single prophetic book. That seems more practical. One book, typical in a general way of all the books, will afford us a view of how the prophets viewed themselves and their works. A number of prophets have been quoted to show a variety of principles. In general they thought of themselves as heralding a message from God to a particular crisis. We now propose to concentrate on a single volume of one prophetical writing to illustrate "What the prophets say about the prophets."

The opening words of the book of Jeremiah state, "The words of Jeremiah, the son of Hilkiah of the priests who were in Anathoth. . . ." This is an obvious claim that this prophetic book contains "the words of Jeremiah. . . ." But it does not claim that Jeremiah actually penned the book. As a matter of fact it is certain that at least a part of the work was authored by Jeremiah but not penned by him. It is said in 36:32, "Then Jeremiah took another scroll and gave it to Baruch the scribe, the son of Neriah, who wrote on it at the dictation of Jeremiah all the words of the scroll which Jehoiakim king of Judah had burned in the fire; and many similar words were added to them." On many occasions the prophet proclaimed his messages extemporaneously, as it

189

were. He spoke impromptu to meet the demands of the moment. But when the need demanded a permanent record in written form, according to 36:32, the prophet dictated what he had to say. The particular dictation referred to in 36:32 was most probably his major messages delivered from his call in 627 B.C. until "the fourth year of Jehoiakim ben Josiah, king of Judah." It was in that year that "word came to Jeremiah from Yahweh" that he should preserve in writing "everything that I [Yahweh] have said to you concerning Israel and Judah, and all the nations, since I first spoke to you . . ." (Jer. 36:2). At that time Jeremiah employed his friend Baruch as a secretary to record the message as he dictated it. When the king burned the book the prophet redictated it to Baruch as told in 36:32.

A word of explanation concerning the term "book" when referring to Jeremiah is needed. It is not a book in the modern use of the word. It is an amassing of a lot of material the source of which was the preaching of Jeremiah from 627 B.C. until some years after the fall of Jerusalem in 586 B.C. In the passages quoted above (Jer. 36:2 and 32) two expressions ought be noted. Verse 32 contains, "and many similar words were added to them." Besides the messages delivered by Jeremiah from his call in 627 B.C. until the fourth year of Johoiakim in 605 B.C. "many similar words" were appended. But there was no narrative background or continued story to follow. There was no particular orderly arrangement of the material, either of the basic discourses or the "added" words. The "book" is really a collection of Jeremiah's sermons plus some "added words."

In verse two God directed the prophet to write "everything I have said" not only about Israel and Judah but also "all the nations." In this collection of prophetic sayings words of God to and about "all nations" were included. The arrangement of this material is chiefly characterized by its lack of arrangement. So we do not think of Jeremiah (or Baruch) sitting down with a coherent, well-designed outline in front of him with which to form an orderly book. They were discourses, scattered over many years of political and personal turmoil and delivered as strictures against a sinful nation.

Nevertheless, in the book we do have reliable statements of the prophet about himself and his words. Chapter 1:4-19 place together a number of episodes in Jeremiah's early experience. One theme joins them together in a literary unit — that is, the call and commission of the prophet. The call itself occupies verses 4-10 in which three ideas unfold. Furthermore, the prophet disclaims that the three ideas were his. They are "the word of the Lord" which "came to me saying . . ." (Jer. 1:4a). In other words, God reveals; the prophet receives. God is the origin; the prophet is the instrument of revelation. This is Jeremiah's view of God's involvement in his call. However, it sets the tone and reflects his understanding of his message to Israel as reported in the rest of his book.

Three words may summarize the three ideas of the call. They are: predetermine, reluctance and reassurance. The call came "in the thirteenth year of" king Josiah's reign (627 B.C.) when Jeremiah was in his late teens. It was a decided shock, to say the least, when the Lord disclosed that in the eternal counsels of God three important features in Jeremiah's career were predetermined: "I knew you . . . I consecrated you . . . I appointed you. . . ." He was a preconceived idea, for a preconceived task to which he was preappointed by God.

In spite of this startling revelation that he was high in the plans of God even before birth the young man was reluctant to accept his divinely-ordained task. He resisted the call by citing his extreme youth with his obvious lack of maturity. His youthfulness was a fact; he had not as yet "found himself." The revelation that God had such lofty plans for him was overwhelming to such a young man. Lack of experience breeds lack of self-confidence in anyone. There is no need to question the honesty of his aversion to God's call.

In his dialogue with the young man God respected the young man's right to resist although he insisted that the young seer would go: ". . . to all whom I send you, you shall go. . . ." However, God reassures him and builds up his self-confidence in three ways. First, "I am with you." The lad may be yet in his teens but he has at his side one who doesn't count the years. The strength of the Eternal buttresses the frailty of flesh. In the second place, "The Lord put forth his hand and touched my mouth and said, 'I have put my words in your mouth. . . .'" God would give the message. Fear of a poorly prepared word, stagefright, anxiety about whether he could or how to articulate God's message was not to fret the prophet's heart. "I have put my words in your mouth" was to be his rhetorical reservoir from which he could draw in any crisis. In the third place God gave him a well-defined job description. Nothing can be more demoralizing than not to know what the boss expects on a job. And while the task may be difficult at least it's reassuring to know precisely what is expected of the laborer. "I have set you this day over nations and over kingdoms, to pluck up and to break down, to destroy and to overthrow, to build and to plant" (Jer. 1:10). The southern kingdom of Judah was to be the people to whom he would deliver his major message. But by no means was this to be the limit of his field of work. In point of fact, as his ministry developed he published messages to and about Egypt, the

192

Philistines, Moab, Ammon, Edom, the Arab tribes, and Babylon (Jer. 46-50). Judah and these nations were the objects of his prophetic calling.

But even more important in job-description was the texture of his messages to these peoples. His work, as described before it happened, was to be both negative and positive in results. He was "to pluck up . . . break down . . . destroy . . . overthrow." After that he could "build and plant." If one wants to plant a garden or build a new structure on a field that is occupied with stubble of former plantings or the frame and rubble of previous buildings he must first tear down before he can begin to "build up." It was a difficult assignment to the youthful prophet but the clarity and honesty of the job description was part of the reassurance God gave. God did not minimize the harshness of the commission. In fact, later in chapter one when the call is expanded in more detail he seemed to expose more fully the abusive opposition the prophet would be called upon to endure.

> But you, gird up your loins; arise, and say to them everything that I command you. Be not dismayed by them, lest I dismay you before them. And I, behold, I make you this day a fortified city, an iron pillar, and bronze walls, against the whole land, against the kings of Judah, its princes, its priests, and the people of the land. They will fight against you; but they shall not prevail against you, for I am with you, says the Lord, to deliver you (Jer. 1:17-19).

So, in redefining the severity of the task ahead for the prophet God gave encouragement by reaffirming the promise "I am with you."

Two visions that came to Jeremiah appear in 1:11, 12 and 1:13-16. Without doubt they happened early in the ministry of the prophet while yet a youth. And so far as the

book of Jeremiah is concerned they are placed here in connection with the original call because they reinforce the call.
They clarify certain aspects of his task.

The vision of verses 11, 12 makes its point through a
play on words, lost in our English translations. The word
almond (*saqed*) only has a slight change in vowel points
from *watching* (*soqed*). That kind of tree was the herald
of spring for by its profusion of blossoms it was the first to
announce the stirring of life from winter's somber death. It
awakened first. We may envision the young Jeremiah seated
on the flat roofed patio of his home. The word of the Lord
came to him saying, "What do you see, Jeremiah?" His
eyes turned from the jumble of sand-packed hills to the
southeast toward the Dead Sea twenty miles distant to the
broken stalk of an almond tree in his front yard. It was
springtime and from the stump of the almond tree struggled
colorful blossoms announcing the new life of coming spring.
The almond tree was the watch tree! Then he answered,
"I see an almond rod [a "watch" rod]." And the Lord said,
"You see quite well! For I am watching over my word to
perform it." To Jeremiah this was a clarifying experience.
It interpreted anew the meaning of his call to the prophetic
function. It was added reassurance that he was not dependent on his own unaided resources. God's word, working
in him, would bring full bloom to the prophet's work.

On another day from that same roof top the prophet
heard the voice of God, "What do you see?" Looking down
he noticed the family washing pot, filled with the week's
washing, boiling over in the back yard. He answered, "What
I see is a boiling pot, and it is tipped from the north." The
voice of God interpreted the significance of the bubbling
pot. "Out of the north evil shall break forth upon all the

inhabitants of the land . . . I am calling the kings of the north
. . . and each will set his throne in front of Jerusalem's gates
. . . and all the cities of Judah. And I will utter my judgments against them . . ." (Jer. 1:14-16). Here again, early
in his ministry, Jeremiah gained an intimation about a "foe
from the north" that would shape his message to Israel. Not
only would God watch over his word but his judgmental
word would find its instrument of fulfillment in "the kingdoms of the north."

Even the commonplace corruptions of men are a part of
God's vocabulary in his speech through his prophets. Jeremiah 13:12-14 supplies an example.

> You will repeat to them this saying, "Every jug should be
> filled with wine." They will reply, "Ah, don't we know it!
> Indeed every jug should be filled with wine!" Then you will
> say to them, "This is what Yahweh has said: Believe me, I
> am going to fill all the inhabitants of this land—the kings
> who sit on David's throne, the priests, the prophets, and
> all the citizens of Jerusalem—with drunkenness; and I will
> smash them one against another, old and young alike. No
> pity, no mercy, no compassion will deter me from destroying
> them (The Anchor Bible).

According to this passage the Lord instructed the prophet
to go before a representative cross section of the leaders
and people with a familiar, oft-quoted proverb, "Every jug
shall be filled with wine." This was a witticism circulating
in the debauched revelries of the social circles of the age.
This particular message was delivered by the prophet shortly
before 597 B.C. when a first group of captives were exiled
to Babylon. Suddenly Jeremiah appeared at one of their
revelries and shouted aloud the proverb! The staggering,
half-drunken party-goers taunted and heckled the prophet

195

as they guzzled another jug of wine. "Ah, don't we know it!" Then, mocking the seer, they alluded to themselves as "jugs" that "should be filled with wine." Then the man of God pronouced the word of judgment which he had been commissioned to declare. "I am going to fill all the inhabitants of this land . . . with drunkenness . . . I will smash them. . . . No compassion will deter me from destroying them." The nation had descended so far down the scale of moral values that God was obliged to speak to them through the social depravities of the people.

Innumerable are the ways in which God unmasked his message to the people in the work of the prophet. The skill of the craftsman was one of them. God prodded Jeremiah to "Go down to the potter's house, and there I will tell you what I have to say." As the narrative develops in Jeremiah 18:1-12 the ultimate word that God gives to the nation is: "Look, I am shaping evil against you. . . . Turn, every one of you from his wicked way and reform the whole pattern of your conduct" (Jer. 18:11). It would seem that God might more easily have divulged that message without detouring it through a potter's shop. Why not articulate directly to the prophet? Why send him to the potter at his wheel there to understand the meaning of the divine revelation? In fact, the introduction to the story openly claims that "the word came to Jeremiah from Yahweh: 'Go . . . to the potter's house.'" Since the word could come so plainly to Jeremiah, why not give him the primary message without going through the secondary medium of a potter?

Whether the question can be answered for certain or not the fact remains God *did* so choose. And since He did so we have every right to conclude that it was wise and good for the end in view. The times in which Jeremiah

196

prophesied demanded judgment. God's love will redeem if it can but it will condemn if it must. The message of the potter's shop was a warning of judgment. Yet it contained a word of hope because of the sovereignty of God. It is possible for God to rechannel his redemptive will if the clay in his hand responds properly. To deliver such a message in the abstract would require the hearer to think in the abstract. That which is seen with the eye, touched with the hand, heard with the ear, is easier for the mind to grasp than that which comes only in pure thought. To *teach* the doctrine of the sovereignty of God, the need of repentance for man, the hope of redemption for rebels is a troublesome task for the best of teachers. And as for learners, relatively few people think in theoretical terms. The thought patterns of the mass of people are in terms of objective, concrete, tangible solids that may be touched, tasted, smelled, seen and heard. In other words God often chose to speak to mankind in simple experiences or objects verifiable by the five senses. The Greeks were the abstract thinkers of history; the Hebrews were the "picture" thinkers whose ideas were framed in concrete, corporal terms. The human mind is capable of boundless abstractions but the soul feels the easiest and responds the quickest to bona fide, true-to-life specifics.

It is for these reasons that Jeremiah, not to mention all the prophets, incorporated in the prophecies vast ideas with visual aids. Not a home in the land was without a vessel shaped by a potter's skill. Even growing children fed lively imaginations with hours at the potter's house watching him shape and reshape earthen vessels. How much easier to embed an abstract truth in an experience so familiar to all the people.

To call attention to just a few of Jeremiah's messages objectified in familiar figures will demonstrate how frequent and how effective is this method of divine revelation.

1. The linen waistcloth (Jer. 13:1-27).

> The figure: Yahweh spoke to me thus: "Go buy yourself a linen waistcloth and put it about your middle. . . . Take the waist-cloth . . . which you have on and go to the Euphrates and hide it in a cleft of the rock." . . . After a considerable lapse of time Yahweh said, "Go back . . . get the waistcloth." So I went back back . . . the waistcloth was ruined, unfit for use.

> The message: "Just so will I ruin the pride of Judah . . . til it resembles this utterly worth-less waistcloth. . . ."

2. The broken bottle (Jer. 19:1, 2 and 10, 11)

> The figure: "Go buy a potter's earthen bottle and, taking with you some of the elders. . . . Then, smash the bottle in the presence of the men. . . ."

> The message: "Just so will I [Yahweh] smash this people and this city, like a man smash-ing a potter's vessel so that it can never be mended again."

3. The good figs and the bad (Jer. 24:1-10).

> The figure: "Yahweh pointed out to me . . . ar-ranged in front of the temple were two baskets of figs. . . . In one basket the figs

were excellent, like early ripening figs. In the other basket the figs were extremely bad, so bad, as to be inedible."

The message: "Like these good figs I [Yahweh] will favor the exiles . . . I will keep watch over them . . . will restore them to this land . . . will give them a will to know me. . . ."

"Like the figs too rotten to eat . . . so will I treat Zedekiah, his nobles, what is left of the people of Jerusalem. . . . I will make them a sight to horrify . . . an insult, a taunt, a curse . . . and send upon them sword and famine and disease. . . ."

4. The ox-yoke (Jer. 27:1—28:17).

The figure: "Make yourself thongs and yoke-bars and put them on your neck . . . send word to the kings of Edom, Moab, Ammon, Tyre, and Sidon. . . ."

The message: "As for the people of the kingdom that will not place its neck under the yoke of the king of Babylon, by sword, by famine and plague I will harass that people . . . until I have delivered them into his power.

"To Zedekiah . . . Bring your neck under the yoke of the king of Babylon . . . that you may live."

Besides such extended mimicries which pantomime the truth more than preach it are numberless allusions that frame the truth in concrete figures. Why weight down a whole paragraph in stolid, heavy style when three poetic lines can paint a picture? "Can a male give birth? Why then do I see every man clutching his loins?" (Jer. 30:6). "Your hurt is mortal, your wound past cure, No salve for your sore, no healing for you" (Jer. 30:12, 13). The preaching of the prophets is characterized by this kind of a vivid, picturesque style. It objectifies truth more than argumentation. It's true that the prophets pronounce judgmental preachments but they more often do it by painting pictures than by abstract logic.

All the scriptures, both Old and New Testaments, breathe out the breath of God. Like gentle breezes in the morning herald the coming day, like winds from the ocean waves sing of distant life, like gusting eddies announce tidings of a coming storm, so all scriptures exhibit in one way or another the Spirit of God in their making. Sometimes the Spirit of God appears as tranquil as the gentle breeze: "I thank thee, Father, Lord of heaven and earth, that thou hast hidden these things from the wise and understanding and revealed them unto babes; yea, Father, for such was thy gracious will" (Luke 10:21). ". . . They who wait for the Lord shall renew their strength, they shall mount up with wings like eagles, they shall run and not be weary, they shall walk and not faint" (Isa. 40:31). Other times the scripture sounds like waves washed ashore from far-away lands, a serenade of music from heavenly shores. "With a love everlasting I love you, So with grace I draw you to me. Once again I will build you securely . . . Once again you'll set out vineyards . . . For soon comes the day when the watchmen will shout . . . 'Up! Let us go to Zion, To Yahweh our God'" (Jer. 31:3-6). "Did not our hearts burn within us while he talked to us on the road, while he opened to us the scriptures?"

200

"The Lord is risen indeed . . ." (Luke 24:32, 34). Still again some scriptures warn and rumble like gathering storms. "Spread the news 'round about Jerusalem! Enemies come from a land far away, raising the shout against Judah's towns. Like watchmen at a field they have ringed her round about. . . . Your ways and your deeds have brought all this upon you. It's this sin of yours that's bitter, that has stabbed you to the heart" (Jer. 4:16-18). "You brood of vipers! Who warned you to flee from the wrath to come? . . . Even now the ax is laid to the root of the tree; every tree therefore that does not bear good fruit is cut down and thrown into the fire" (Matt. 3:7, 10). But whether it be the gentle breeze, the distant carol, or the dark storm cloud all the Judeo-Christian scriptures bear the stamp of the Spirit of God. It is true that "all scripture is God-breathed" (II Tim. 3:16).

Our theme calls for an answer to the question, "What Does the Scripture Say About the Scripture?" A few New Testament texts make some references to various parts of the Old Testament scriptures. These texts reveal a reverence and respect for the literature of the older covenant. In fact, the apostolic writings candidly stated the Old Testament to be "God-breathed" (inspired). They saw the fulfillment of the Old in the events and records of the New! But of all the kinds of literature in the Bible, the prophets stand the highest in both direct claims to possession of the Spirit of God as well as allusions, implications, assumptions and such like. "Thus saith the Lord" is the constant refrain of the prophets. "The word of the Lord came to me" is their badge of divine service.

The prophetical books of the Old Testament not only offer frequent direct claims of "thus saith the Lord" etc. but they also excel in the moral quality, spiritual depth, and loftly insight in unchanging truth. Other books of the Bible may equal but none surpass the prophets in the immutable timelessness of their teachings. "Let justice roll down like waters, and righteousness like an everlasting stream" (Amos 5:24). When can that ever be out of date? It was true before it erupted from the mouth of Amos! It was appropriate for humanity when the shepherd of Tekoa spoke it to Israel. It fits the needs in the twentieth century A.D. in Moscow or Washington. And will be up-to-date throughout all eternity to come. And by what logic can it be denied that the Spirit of God was involved in its first utterance and in its continued aptness? For such a text one does not need a stated "thus saith the Lord." The idea itself speaks louder than a voiced claim. It says so much about itself by just being transparently true! The proverb that says, "the proof of the pudding is in the eating" finds no greater confirmation than the Old Testament prophets. What they say about themselves is best seen in the content, beauty and truth of what they say!!!

Chapter Eleven

THE WRITINGS

The third division of the Hebrew Bible was the Writings, the Hagiographa. The books of the Writings we are considering are Job, Psalms, Proverbs, Ecclesiastes and the Song of Solomon.

In the previous chapter the *Prophets* came under scrutiny as to what they say about themselves. No set of biblical books have more direct references to themselves than the prophets. But the opposite is true of these books of the Hagiographa, the Writings. What these books say about themselves is almost exclusively determined by the content of their message rather than direct declaration. The prophets' "thus saith the Lord" is conspicuous by its absence. This is not to say that the Lord's voice is not heard in these books. On the contrary, it is loud and clearly heard. But it is the purpose and quality of each book's message by which the Lord's voice can be determined. Who speaks is recognized by what he says! It is more so in these books possibly than in the others.

What does the book of Job say about itself? In the search for an answer an overall survey of the content will be helpful. The drama divides into five segments of unequal lengths.

I. *The Prologue* occupies the first two chapters. It sets the stage and introduces the chief actors who must face a perennial problem of human beings. Is there any meaning to suffering? Can human life have meaning? What is the ultimate loyalty for man?

II. *The Dialogue* forms the heart of the book extending from 3:1 through 31:40. The "friends" of Job challenge his integrity in a series of arguments to which

203

Job responds with equally strong feeling. He maintains his innocence and defies both friends and God to prove his guilt of wrong-doing.

III. *The Elihu speeches* cover chapters 32:1—37:24. The arguments of Elihu represent a replay of an old tune; they are a reworking of the arguments of Job's earlier three friends. No new insights are given and little comfort to the agony of Job.

IV. *The Theophany* is in 38:1—42:6, though no answer to the mind relieves the soul of the sufferer. Where God cannot be traced he can be trusted. Faith may not satisfy the intellect but it can assuage the feverish heart. The mysteries of the physical universe lie beyond the ken of man; how much more the moral and spiritual universe of God?

V. *The Epilogue* reports the repentance and return of health and happiness to the afflicted, Job. 42:7-17.

The reader of the book of Job may liken himself to a climber who, after a laborious hike up, stands atop the mountain. From that vantage point he can see the resultant view while overlooking the tangled details. Many knotty problems, too intricate for our limited space, reside in the book of Job. They merit a separate, extended study. But whatever the details would disclose they cannot blot out the truth and beauty of the spacious view. The message of Job is as enduring as the human race in this world of mortal pain. How can a man trust such a God who permits such extremes of unjust torment human beings are called on to endure? The problem of human pain is accentuated when so many times it is the innocent who suffer while the guilty go free. The insights of the book of Job into the problem of suffering are astounding.

In view of the meaninglessness, the heartlessness of gnawing human hurt why should one seek to go on living? When life comes tumbling down and nothing but rubble and debris lie all around—physical, mental, moral, emotional—why not seek refuge in death? This is particularly a valid question when the suffering comes through no fault of one's own. Life can become so terribly meaningless! Moral absolutes become blurred, spiritual values become defaced under the despair born of stabbing torment. Life is a burden; death becomes inviting!

The book of Job probes the meaning of human life in the light of so much pain and suffering—unjust suffering! As the book pictures Job he "was the greatest man among all the peoples of the East." He was a Semite by race being of Uz. Racially he was of the best. He was a devoted family man who encouraged his ten children to keep alive family traditions through reunions, birthday feasts, and warm community forms of fellowship. The robust individual character of his children found its roots in the strong home which he as patriarch developed. His wealth was renowned; his property included thousands of sheep, camels, oxen, asses—so much wealth that he became the envy of the peoples of the East and the object of violent, thieving bands of Chaldeans. He was a deeply religious man who was concerned about an active, open relationship to God for himself and also for his children. "Early in the morning he would sacrifice a burnt offering for each of them, thinking, 'Perhaps my children have sinned and cursed God in their hearts'" (Job 1:5). The moral and spiritual excellence of such a human being was exemplary. If justice rewards righteousness and condemns iniquity surely this man would enjoy the favor of God free of pain and death, the consequences of sin!

But *why* is a righteous man righteous? "Does Job fear God for nothing?" is the Satanic question. What's his motive for conforming to goodness? If a man is hedged about with good health, immense wealth, universal fame, and a happy home *because* he is righteous, then his righteousness is essentially selfish. Remove the hedge and he will cease being saintly. If he's pure because he's paid then remove the pay and he will quit being pure. This is the view of a cynical world that has enrolled in the school of Satan.

God is willing that Job be put to the test of such a censorious accusation. It is not that God doubts Job's righteousness. On the contrary, it is because he believes in Job's strength of character that God allows a testing. God believes in man as much as he expects man to believe and trust him. Humanity is capable of being righteous for righteousness' sake; not for selfish rewards. At least this is what God believes about man whom he has created in his image. And Job was an exemplary man!

The devastation wrought on the family and property of Job was the work of one day. Sabean vandals plundered his oxen and asses; raiding parties of Chaldeans robbed him of his wealth of camels besides "putting his servants to the sword." Volcanic eruption burned up his flocks of sheep along with their shepherds. As if that weren't enough, while his ten children were assembled in the oldest son's house celebrating a festive meal, a tornado from the desert struck and destroyed house and family all in one blow. In less than a twenty-four hour period Job and his wife were left without wealth, family and property. For a man to raise questions and wonder why such reverses of large proportions came so quickly is to be expected. No doubt Job entertained such questions. But if he did the only report that the book makes is about the triumph of his faith over any doubts. "Naked came I from my mother's womb, and naked will I depart. The Lord gave and the Lord has taken away; blessed be the name of the Lord" (Job 1:21).

But doubt is persistent. Satan always is unyielding in his attack on the vulnerable pride of man. In extremity man will sell his soul to gain personal security. A man may give up property and even family and retain his honesty. But he won't give up his life for personal integrity. "All that a man has he will give for his life" (Job 2:4). To save his own skin a man will repudiate God. Self-preservation is the first law of life! This is the Satanic conceit! It's also the persuasion of those who have matriculated in the school of Satan.

However, this kind of scurrilous skepticism is not a part of the divine certitude. God *believes* in man! So again God granted a testing of Job, this time an invasion of his person though not to the point of death. Immediately "Satan went out from the presence of the Lord and afflicted Job with loathsome sores from the sole of his feet to the top of his head" (Job 2:7). Whatever medical relief was available didn't prove of any value to Job's malady. So he "took a potsherd with which to scrape himself, and sat among the ashes" (2:8). That he was shocked from center to circumference is obvious from his increasing ill-humored fractiousness in the dialogue with his friends. But up to this point he did not waver. Even his wife's acrimonious hostility toward God's apparent injustice did not ruffle his basic trust. "Shall we receive good at the hand of God and not evil?" (2:10).

Up to this stage in the book, Job says that a cosmic conflict is being waged between God and Satan, good versus evil. The prize to be gained is the mind, heart, and soul of man. The area of conflict is the conscience, the tug of right against the pull of wrong! The instruments of warfare on the side of Satan are family, house, home, nation, race, sex, wealth, fame, health, suffering and the threat of death. On the other side God depends on the fundamental nature of man as He, God, created man to be. Man was made to be in the image of God and God believes that man can and will live up to that quality in His creation. He allows "no temptation but such as man can bear" (I Cor. 10:13). But one of the chief disclosures of the book of Job is that trust in God is not achieved without moral wrestling and spiritual anguish. He who never doubts never has a vigorous faith; he who doesn't question God is afraid to trust God; when one probes with the keen scalpel of doubt he will thereby gain the health of faith. Doubt properly dealt with breeds faith. Judged by the first two chapters, the prologue, this is the testimony of Job.

When we turn from the prologue to the dialogue of Job and his friends we discover the stormy waters through which Job had to steer before reaching his haven of faith. Trust did not come without trouble! The horror of Job's condition gagged the three friends when first they laid eyes on the suffering saint. They sat in silence a whole week so great was their grief. "No one spoke a word to him, for they saw that his suffering was very great" (Job 2:13).

Job was the first to break the silence. Every angle of his distressing plight he had turned over and over in mind. The integrity of his heart was as clean as the cloudless Syrian sky. Neither man nor angel could convict him of substantial wickedness. So *why*? Why must he suffer so?

Like a boiling cauldron within a long-silent volcano Job erupted with a paroxysm of passion. He cursed the day of his birth, cried for death, conceded life to be irrational in

the face of pointless pain. "May the day of my birth perish
. . . Why did I not perish at birth, and die as I came from
the womb?" (Job 3:3a, 11). "Why is light given . . . to those
who long for death that does not come . . .?" (3:20, 21).
"Why is life given to a man whose way is hidden, whom
God has hedged in?" (3:23). In other words, life has no
purpose. Why be born, or, being born, why go on living?

Eliphaz the Temanite, staggered at the apparent irreverent complaint of Job, replied with growing fervor. "Your
words have supported others . . . who stumbled . . . But
now trouble comes to you . . . and you're dismayed" (Job
4:4f.). In other words, "You dished it out but you can't take
it!" And Eliphaz continued his "comforting" words, "Who,
being innocent ever perished?" (4:7). In a word, retribution
is for the guilty, not the innocent. Besides, "If God . . .
charges his angels with error, how much more those who
live in houses of clay?" (4:18, 19). You're mortal, Job,
you are bound to be guilty. Furthermore, only a fool loses
family and fortune in one blow. "I myself have seen a fool
taking root, but suddenly his house was cursed" (5:3).
Finally in a lengthy blast (5:7-27) Eliphaz concludes that
since "man is born to be trouble . . . if it were I, I would appeal
to God; . . . do not despise the discipline of the Almighty.
. . . he injures but he also heals" (5:7, 8, 17, 18). Job, you've
got a great future if you'll just turn yourself and your sin
over to God's corrective punishment.

Job's retort to Eliphaz reflects a rising resentment at his
friend's unfeeling orthodoxy. Anger is in Job's voice; disappointment in friendship in his heart as he spews forth his
hurt. "If only my anguish could be weighed and all my misery
be placed on the scales! . . . no wonder my words have
been impetuous" (Job 6:2, 3b). Indeed, the severity of his

209

affliction warrants his harsh complaint. Moreover, the arguments of Eliphaz are repugnant: "Is there flavor in the white of an egg?" (6:6b). The pain, not only of his physical ailments but also of the heartlessness of his friend sharpens again his desire for death. "Oh, that I might have my request . . . that God would be willing to crush me, to let loose his hand and cut me off!" (6:8). His "friends" prove to be as false as wadies "that cease to flow in the dry season" (6:12). Man, made to be god-like, lives like a slave longing "for the evening shadows" whose "days are swifter than a weaver's shuttle" that "come to an end without hope" (7:2, 6). Job grumbles, "My days have no meaning" so why can't you "let me alone" you "watcher of men"? The anger in his voice is shifting toward God! (7:11-21).

The "comfort" offered by Bildad the Shuhite outdid that of Eliphaz in sarcasm and his orthodoxy was as correct and cold, accurate but helpless to relieve the pain in the soul. His first word in effect was, "You're a big bag of wind, Job!" (Job 8:1). That was as painless a remark as jabbing a splinter in an already festering, puss-filled infection. It was followed by the orthodox doctrine, "Does God pervert justice?" It was a remark that revealed Bildad's knowledge of creedal truth without knowing how to use it to save a suffering soul. Truth can destroy when used in the hands of a self-righteous, creed-bound "friend." "Surely God doesn't reject a blameless man" (8:20). So the rejection of Job by virtue of his misfortunes proved blame on the part of the sufferer! Furthermore, "When your children sinned against him, he gave them over to the penalty of their sin" (8:4). They made their house; they should live in it; they got their just deserts! Bildad's verbalizing was about as reassuring as a doctor who steps into the patient's hospital room and finds fault with his terminally ill client for getting sick. Or as helpful as the friend who says to the sick, "My mother died of the very disease with which you suffer!" Bildad's appeal to the experience of past generations showed neither tact, sympathy or practical understanding of how to be supportive. "Ask the former generations and find out what their fathers learned. . . . Will they not instruct you and tell you?" (Job 8:8, 10). "Can reeds thrive without water? While still growing and uncut, they wither more quickly than grass. Such is the destiny of all who foget God; so perishes the hope of the godless" (8:11b-13). Thus far in the argumentative exchanges Job's friends can hardly be accused of using a surgeon's scalpel for healing. On the contrary, while their motives may have been good the result was that of double-dealing traitors. Theirs was like the dagger of a Brutus in the back of a Caesar. Their statements of doctrines were true but their use of them did not heal. The medicine was good but it didn't fit the disease at hand.

Job's response to Bildad's speech covers two basic ideas. He concedes that a man cannot "be just before God." "If one wished to contend with him, one could not answer him once in a thousand . . ." (Job 9:2b-3). Yet it's because of God's vast power. The end result is that the innocent and guilty are both subject to destruction, for wickedness prevails in the earth. Blind are the ways of justice! "The earth is given into the hand of the wicked; he blindfolds its judges. If it is not he, then who is it?" (9:24). So! A man cannot be just before God! And God is responsible for the injustice in the world! If he is not, who is?

Zophar the Naamathite can contain himself no longer. He questions the motive of Job's claim of innocence, "Will your babble silence men?" (Job 11:3a). In other words, your claims for piety are merely a hypocritical design to divert the attention of men away from your real guilt! The greatness of God guarantees that "he recognizes deceitful men; and when he sees evil, does he not take note?" (11:11). My advice to you, Job, is that "you devote your heart to him." "If you put away the sin that is in your hand . . . then you will lift up your face without shame" (11:13b, 14).

As a drama of movement and action Job as literature does not merit a high grade. As a probing of the problem of human suffering no literature known to man surpassess it. But any movement is in the increase of the inflamed feelings of the contestants, not in their dramatic actions. The cycle of speeches of Job, Eliphaz, Bildad and Zophar go over and over the same ground with variations in intensity of irritation. But no real solution to the problem ever emerges. The three friends are set in their orthodox theology; they are as firm as concrete reinforced by steel. And Job is as confident in his innocence as they are in their flawless logic. Even a younger friend, Elihu, who has listened with heightening impatience, invades the contest with his polemics (Job 32:1—37:24). But his new contributions are but a rehashing of the traditional views expressed by the others.

Through all the argument Job had consistently maintained his virtue. Friends could not shake his impeccability. Before God Job insisted on his faultlessness. He silenced his "friends" and challenged God with a closing series of denials of wrongdoing! He never lusted after women, never got wealth by cheating, never exploited land or man, never abused servants, the poor, widows, orphans, nor committed adultery. He had not worshipped the heavenly bodies nor rejoiced at a foe's misfortune. "Oh, that I had someone to hear me! I sign now my defense—let the Almighty answer me; let my accuser put his indictment in writing" (Job 31:35). With these imprecations and challenge, "The words of Job are ended" (31:40b).

Thus far the only attempts to resolve the problem of why the innocent suffer have followed along the familiar road of orthodox traditional ideas. In fact, orthodoxy has insisted that the presence of suffering is prima facie evidence that guilt is present, not innocence. No one in the book casts doubt on the truth of traditional dogma. And it is well and beautifully stated by all who came to sympathize with Job. But however true, the truth as stated simply did not deal with the problem. So, up through 39:30 the book of Job doesn't really have any answer to the problem of human suffering. If there is an answer God must give it!

At this point in the book God takes up the task of addressing the predicament. He speaks from out of a storm. And yet what God says ignores the issue at hand. It does not deal with suffering in general or Job's in particular. In the speech from the storm God doesn't even inform Job that all along He, God, knew that Job was righteous. In fact it was God who at the first called to Satan's attention the strength of character which the saint had. "Have you considered Job? There is no one on earth like him; he is blameless and upright, a man who fears God and shuns evil" (Job 1:8). All through his suffering and the arguments with his false friends Job was unaware that God believed in his (Job's) righteousness. And now that God speaks to Job he still doesn't say a word about the righteousness of the man. And if there is any reason as to why Job had to suffer, God doesn't tell why! The book never answers the question of why the innocent suffer — or for that matter, why suffering of any kind occurs!

213

God addresses Job with a series of questions that relate to the created order: the "foundation of the earth," the sea, the dawn, the light, snow and hail, the constellations, clouds, lightning, the lioness and her cubs, mountain goats or bears, wild donkey and ox, the ostrich, the war horse, the hawk and eagle, the hippopotamus or leviathan. What do these matters have to do with the question troubling Job's heart? The issue as Job was facing it seems to be completely ignored by God's reaction. The fact that God evades the issue itself says something. It would say that there is no answer that can satisfy man. Furthermore, where there is no answer faith must take over.

Midway through God's speaking, "The Lord said to Job: 'Will the one who contends with the Almighty correct him? Let him who accuses God answer him!' Then Job answered the Lord: 'I am unworthy—how can I reply to you? I put my hand over my mouth. I spoke once but I have no answer —twice but I will say no more'" (Job 40:1-5). And it is to be noted that in the Epilogue Job said, "Therefore I despise myself and repent in dust and ashes" (42:6). We have already observed that in the prologue God had expressed his confidence in Job's righteousness, "a man who fears God and shuns evil" (1:8). We have also noted with what firm consistency through all his pain and arguments with friends he had insisted on his integrity of soul. Nor did God ever brush him aside or put him down with accusations of guilt. If all this be so, then for what did he "repent"? Nothing in the whole book (except the false accusations of friends who obviously spoke out of ignorance of Job's real soul condition) is charged against Job's character. Was there anything for which he needed to repent?

In seeking an answer to the question of Job's need for repentance it is helpful to make some basic observations.

First, the opinions of Eliphaz, Bildad, Zophar, and Elihu represent well-established, well-known, generally accepted viewpoints.

A second observation is that doctrinal soundness, no matter how plainly perceived or clearly stated, is absolutely true in the abstract but not necessarily right in living, personal situations. The skill of the surgeon enables him to perform miracles of open-heart operations, delicate brain surgery, or the removal of kidney stones. But if the doctor performs an appendectomy when it is a tumor on the brain that is causing the trouble then his knowledge is useless and his skill misdirected. Truth memorized, repeated by rote, and applied to every ailment of human sin won't save. On the contrary, it may destroy. Redeeming truth is not an abstract dogma; it's a concrete cure in a living, particular human situation in which thought, feelings, deeds have all become entangled in one living human being.

A young mother, abandoned by her husband, faced with caring for an infant child, and alone in a forbidding world sought counsel from a minister of a small church alien to her experience. Baffled, confused, seeking guidance in thought, support in emotional needs, not to mention the practical matter of food and clothing, she ventured the question, "What and where is God?" The easy answer is to quote scripture. That would be giving her the "truth" would it not? Would it not give the young mother a lift to hear I John 4:8, 10, "God is love." But as a matter of fact, with full knowledge of what I John says, the minister avoided confusing the mother further with biblical quotations. Instead, he secured the cooperation of a number of families within his congregation. They surrounded this perplexed child of God with love. They saw that the mother and baby

215

were fed, clothed and warmly housed. And more important they offered warm emotional support by enfolding her in friendly embrace, extending social pleasantries, accepting her as a vital part of their personal, family and congregational life. In other words they gave the woman an experience of being loved. After thirty days of sharing such love the minister felt he was ready to answer her original query, "What and where is God?" He approached her in the security of her own room, at a time when she felt her own baby nestled in her own arms and with a thirty day demonstration of God's love behind her. Reminding the mother of her question a month before he said, "What would you think if I would tell you that 'God is love!'" Her reply was, "That makes sense."

Had the preacher recited orthodox truth "God is love" when her experience testified to the contrary it would have been a crushing weight. She could not have reconciled the truth of the statement with the facts of her ordeal. But once having encountered love in tangible forms of life, to trust God as love made sense. Such was the problem of Job. He had "friends" who cited dogmatic "truth" to him. Job knew the doctrinal statements of truth as well as his comforters. He believed them in the abstract. But he also knew his own innocence was a truth. Yet the two truths didn't reconcile each with the other. The prescription didn't fit his malady. Something lay beyond the traditions; something also lay beyond the fact of his innocence. And *he was ignorant of that something!* Job must be brought to the point in life at which he does not rest on his innocence. He must be shocked into the fact that the usual values which bolster man's security at a given point along the highway of life become but foundations of sand.

216

Job, in theory, knew that man as creature is limited when compared to the greatness of the power, knowledge, wisdom, and person of God the Creator. Nor did it take guesswork to know that he himself, as an individual man was circumscribed and insignificant when measured by the Eternal One. But in personal relationships there is no such thing as "theory." There are just persons acting and reacting intellectually, emotionally, morally, physically, spiritually. It was not moral evil of which Job needed to repent. As far as the attributes of God as known by men Job was not ignorant. He was physically healthy, financially wealthy, emotionally stable and spiritually pure. But there are mysteries about God, human life, and divine purposes that lie beyond the ken of human kind. God's speech in the storm reminded Job of this very fact—that in some areas even of this creation he, as man, did not have knowledge. And no amount of suffering certifies a man to criticize God's wisdom or justice in his government of human life. There's too much that we *don't know* to be able to judge God to be unjust! And it is of *this* that Job repents. "My ears have heard of you but now my eyes have seen you. Therefore I despise myself and repent in dust and ashes" (Job 42:5, 6). It's not lack of knowledge of true doctrine about God that Job had—not what he *did* know but what he *didn't* know that led him to think of God as unjust.

God did not answer Job's puzzling heart about why he as an innocent man must suffer. Why? Because there is no answer, satisfactory to man in his present limitations. God, and hence the book of Job, offers no real solution to the problem of suffering. That sin brings suffering and eventually death is true. But some suffering cannot be so easily dismissed as due to sin when innocent people suffer. "Who

sinned, this man or his parents, that he was born blind?"
(John 9:2). To the disciples of Jesus there didn't appear
to be any other alternative. In their thinking suffering was
the insignia for sin but in the case of the blind man they
weren't sure *whose* sin! It was either the blind man's or his
parents'. It didn't occur to them that it might be from some
other cause, or from *NO* moral cause! At any rate Jesus
replied, "Neither this man nor his parents sinned." There
is another reason which you are not in a position to appreciate right now. There are factors that lie beyond the horizon
of your human view. You're just going to have to leave the
whole of the government of the world to God. Where you
cannot trace God you have to trust him.

Thus it was in the case of Job. No question but that the
orthodox doctrine was true but it can't explain *all* suffering.
Furthermore, if your human knowledge — or from another
point of view — your human ignorance — cannot fathom the
mysteries of the natural creation around in this world — the
denizens of the sea, forest, or heavens, then how can you
sit in judgment on the Creator of these creations? Suffering,
even extreme suffering, does not qualify man to pass judgment on God and how he conducts the affairs of men. God's
answer to Job is at bottom an invitation to faith. Man is like
a child trudging through a dangerous swampland holding
on to his father's hand. When the foot doesn't fall on solid
soil and begins to sink in the mush of the marsh the child
just tightens his hold on his father's hand and walks on.
That's the ultimate answer to the problem of pain, particularly the pain of the innocent.

But there is much more in God's answer to Job than an
invitation to faith. In fact it seems quite likely that this *more*
is the real reason lying back of the entire drama of Job.

218

This is what the book of Job really says about itself. From the innocent sufferer's point of view God appears as an enemy. To Job God was one who shoots poison arrows into his flesh, who sends terrifying dreams in the loneliness of the night, who "mocks the despair of the innocent" and "blindfolds judges" so they are unjust, who throws men into "the clutches of the wicked" to be their plaything, who "tears me down" and "uproots my hope like a tree" whose "anger burns against me." How can a man ever place his trust in such a God who is the "Watcher" and "Slayer" of men?

The message of the book of Job—what the book of Job says—is how God leads men from despair to hope, from God as foe to God as friend. Hostility must be displaced by fellowship; fear must become faith; hate must become love; despair must become hope. Such is the pilgrimage of every human being who discovers the meaning of life. But the supreme question is: How is this accomplished? If God is involved in every man's redemption what are the means at his command to lead man from hate to faith?

It is precisely this that Job teaches. God must lead a man into a situation in which he surrenders absolutely and unreservedly reliance on all concerns lesser than God. He who possesses and enjoys the best life can offer is subject to the enchantment that "the best life can offer" *is the best!* There is no such thing as best if it's less than God!

To have the best life can offer and to think that by having it one has God is delusion. Job possessed the best of life in a palatial home, a good and happy family, broad fields, extensive commercial interests, charitable causes to which he gave himself and his wealth generously, the respect and admiration of his peers and community. He was religiously orthodox and sincere in the practice of his religion. He believed in God and shunned evil. But did any one of these, singly or all together collectively, have a greater hold on Job than God? Where did Job's security lie? What was the ultimate to Job, the indispensable, the nitty-gritty, the bottom line, the final loyalty? Was it these things or was it God?

A word of caution!! None of these things were wrong, sinful, corrupting or in any way evil. It's not a question of sin. It's a question of what is the ultimate. Every one of the best things life can offer enumerated above will terminate. They all, one by one, will slip out of our grasp. But man, as created by God, is eternal by design and he is made for him who does not pass away. The Eternal One made man to be eternal. To be fastened tightly to anything lesser than the Eternal One is to miss the point of living. In the pilgrimage of life God must bring each man to a practical, working, experiential knowledge of this fact. God is the sacred ultimate; things are temporal tools — means by which God gets us into a vital fellowship with Himself.

Without exception each person must have a staggering shock that will lead him to a distinction between good things and God. A broken heart, a disappointed marriage, a fire that consumes house and treasured possessions, betrayal of friend, death of loved one, earthquake, storm, disease, murder, rape, robbery, prison, poverty, self-destruction of a son, daughter, or parent — and how much more! These can act as penetrating oil on rusty bolts to loosen up the soul for God. And it's not theoretical, intellectual perception that God wants; it's experiential, practice of fellowship with God on a one-on-one basis. Man must be brought to a realization of the predicament in which he lives in this world. What he possesses are filthy rags until he is possessed of

220

God. There is no record in all sacred literature in which a person or a people chosen by God have not been called upon to suffer some shock of disappointment. But the shock has always stripped them of all their false securities. The book of Job is the very highest classic containing this message.

Before the calamities visited upon Job he had heard with the ear of sense. But after being stripped of the best of life and having endured the worst that life can offer he was in a position to see with the eye of the spirit. After listening to the voice of God in the storm, after being reminded that he was in no position in this world to pass judgment on God's justice, now he surrenders his claim to righteousness *as a means of contention with God.* Not that Job denied his innocence. But he no longer claimed it as a basis for accusation against God. He has no claim; only trust in God. God is his only and ultimate claim. What does Job say about Job? "I had heard of you by the hearing of the ear, but now my eye sees you" (Job 42:5).

Epilogue

A final word must be added! And the final word was the first word. "In the beginning was the Word, and the Word was with God, and the Word was God. . . . And the Word became flesh . . . we beheld his glory . . . And of his fulness we all received" (John 1:14, 16).

At the outset we noted that God spoke through people. He also spoke through God-breathed writings.

The doctrine of inspiration should not be a mere literary statement. It must be related to our vital experience with the living God. The doctrines emerging from the Bible arose out of the living experiences of men and women bathed in the Spirit of God. The doctrine of the deity of Christ is expressed in the written word, the Bible, because twelve men lived in Christ's presence, experienced His teaching, saw His mighty works and were inspired by His Person. They experienced the deity of Christ. Therefore they wrote about Christ as deity.

The doctrine, however, of the deity of Christ is not to be left in the words of the Bible. It doesn't become vital until once again it is experienced in the life of a struggling human being. The power of Christ as God's Son must be transposed from the written record into performance in the life of a human.

The truth of the Bible needs to be preached and practiced. When we accept the inspiration of the Bible we submit to God's speaking—both to the ancients and to us today. God spoke through the prophets and He spoke with finality and fulness in His Son. He spoke to prophets and apostles who recorded His word in written form that all His later children might hear Him speaking in their own lives. Jesus pointed out to his generation, "You search the scriptures, because you think that in them you have eternal life, and

222

it is they that bear witness of me; yet you refuse to come to me that you may have life" (John 5:39, 40). The written word must lead to the living Person of God. It is HE who gives me life!

So we come to the end of our story. What does the Bible say about the Bible? Because of the nature of the Bible containing many books written over a period of several hundred years and how it was written book-by-book in a variety of situations, it really could say nothing about itself as a completed book. On the other hand, the individual writers left no doubt that they believed that they were delivering a word from God. Sometimes it was a positive "thus saith the Lord." Often it was what they said, the way they said it and the result on their first readers or hearers that engraved upon it the signature of God. So when I read the Bible I read with confidence that this is what God is saying. As a tuning fork puts me on key, so what the Bible says sets my soul in tune with the harmony of God all around me. I can hear Him today in my life because they heard Him so well then. The Bible says, "God having spoken . . . has spoken!"

Appendix I

HOW WE GOT OUR BIBLE

By Seth Wilson[1]

INTRODUCTION: The importance of knowing. The Bible is not just a book of ideas to try out, but a definite guide to eternal life. Everything depends upon its authority and truth. If it is not from God, man has no light in the darkness. If it has not come to us unchanged and correctly preserved, we cannot know the will of God or His plan for us.

I. We got the Bible by revelation, by inspiration from God. Inspiration means that the Spirit of God put the messages in the mind of men. God controlled the writers so that what they wrote was free from error and was a true record of what God wanted to have written.

A. The people to whom it was first given were convinced that it was from God, and was greater than other books in authority, truthfulness and importance.

1. The testimony of the Jewish nation to the Old Testament.

2. The testimony of the church to the New Testament.

B. The Bible claims to be the word of God.

1. Old Testament - Deut. 6:1-8; 31:24-28; Jer. 36: 1-4; Amos 7:14, 15. These are mere samples. There are hundreds more.

2. New Testament claims for the Old Testament - Matt. 5:17-19; John 10:35; II Pet. 1:21; II Tim. 3:16; Heb. 1:1-4; I Pet. 1:11; and many others.

---

1. Seth Wilson is Dean Emeritus of Ozark Bible College, Joplin, Mo., where he has served for forty years.

    3. New Testament claims for itself - I Cor. 2:9-13; Gal. 1:11, 12; I Thess. 2:13; I Cor. 14:37; II Pet. 3:15; Rev. 1:10, 11 and many others.

    4. These great, insistent claims cannot be innocent mistakes. They must be divinely true or monstrously false. The Bible is either a book of God or a batch of lies.

C. The Bible is a true record. No other book has been so examined and tested. It has always proved to be more reliable than any other.

D. The Bible has supernatural characteristics which support its claims.

    1. Prophecies in it are fufilled in detail centuries later.

    2. Its unity of purpose and plan, though written by 35 or 40 writers over 1600 years.

    3. Its accuracy, fairness, impartiality.

    4. It is wonderfully complete, but brief.

    5. It fits all people and is always up to date.

    6. Its standard of morals surpasses all that men can devise.

    7. Its purpose, its overall plan, and its motives are those of God, not of men.

    8. Its perfect understanding of man, his nature and needs.

    9. It contains the soundest psychology, sicence and philosophy; and avoids the erros of men in these departments of study.

II. We got the Bible progressively, over a period of about 1600 years.

A. The Old Testament from about 1500 to 450 B.C. From Moses to Malachi.

225

B. The New Testament from about A.D. 50 to 100.

C. The Old Testament was collected into one book by about 400 B.C., perhaps it was done by Ezra the scribe and his helpers.

D. The New Testament was gradually collected as the books became available. Complete lists of the New Testament as we have it are known from the period of A.D. 170 to 200. By that time it has been widely published in many nations, fully examined, and proved to be the inspired word of God, accepted by the churches everywhere.

III. We got the Bible by preservation and publication through the centuries.

A. Moses had the book of the law preserved in the tabernacle (Deut. 31:24-26).

B. It was to be read to the people in general assembly at least every seven years (Deut. 31:10-13).

C. It was to be copied especially for the use of kings (Deut. 17:18).

D. Ezra found copies of Old Testament books even in captivity in Persia (Ezra 7:14).

E. It was copied by hand until A.D. 1454 when printing was invented.

1. Handmade copies are called manuscripts. They were made on skins of calves, sheep, goats, or antelopes; or on a kind of paper made from the soft core of the stalk of a very large grass-like plant called papyrus. Our word paper is derived from the word papyrus.

2. Early copies were in the form of a roll, or scroll, made of many pieces pasted or sewed together.

226

3. Later books with leaves were made. This kind of book was called a codex.

4. The copyists were called scribes. They took great care to avoid mistakes.

5. Copies were very expensive because of the scarcity of materials, and because of the large amount of work required to make one. Still many were made. Many copies were destroyed by persecutors. Many wore out. Others were destroyed by wars, fires, and other accidental causes. Weather and age rotted many away, but in some places like Egypt they did not rot because of the very dry climate. Still more than 5,000 manuscripts of the New Testament and parts of the New Testament in the original language (Greek) are known and are used today in determining the exact original wording of the New Testament.

6. All the original copies have been lost or destroyed. We know what they contained by using copies, translations and quotations from them.

F. The Bible has been translated into many languages. A translation is the same thing in another language. Usually they are called versions.

1. The Old Testament was written in Hebrew, and was translated into Greek, about 280 B.C. for Jews living in Egypt and speaking Greek. This is called the Septuagint Version and is the one used by the apostles (LXX).

2. The New Testament was written in Greek, and was translated by about A.D. 150 into Latin, Syriac and two Coptic (Egyptian) dialects. Many other translations followed in later centuries.

3. By December 1980
   the whole Bible had been translated into 275
   languages, the New Testament into 479 more
   languages, at least one whole book into 1710
   more languages.[2]

   There are many more languages which still have
   no part of the Bible published in them, but they
   are the languages of small tribes or nations having
   only a few thousand people using each language.

4. The Bible was first translated into English in A.D.
   1384 by John Wycliffe and his associates. Some
   parts had been translated into Anglo-Saxon before that.

G. The translations have been often revised.

   1. The Latin Vulgate was a revised Latin Bible, done
      by Jerome, about A.D. 400. It became the most
      common Bible for about a thousand years, and
      and was made the official Bible of the Roman
      Catholic Church in A.D. 1550.

   2. Many English versions and revisions. The New
      Testament has been translated or revised more
      than 100 times in English. The King James Version
      was revised in 1611. Revisions are made, not to
      rewrite the Bible or change it, but to improve the
      wording of the former translators or to correct
      their mistakes and to represent more exactly the
      meaning of the Bible as it was in the beginning.

---

2. According to the Bible Society of London.

Appendix II

HOW DID THE BOOKS BECOME THE BOOK?

A Brief Study of the Formation of the Canon of Scripture

by Seth Wilson

The Bible is composed of sixty-six books written by about forty authors during a period of nearly sixteen hundred years. How, then, did it become one Book—the Bible?

This collection is called the canon, and books included in it are called canonical while other books are non-canonical, though they may be very ancient, very religious or even historically true.

Moses did not write the first books ever written, but he did write what God told him to write. His books had the special quality of being written by divine direction and inspiration so that what he wrote was the word of God, "Jehovah said unto Moses. 'Write this for a memorial in a book . . .'" (Exodus 17:14). "And Moses wrote all the words of Jehovah . . ." (Exodus 24:4). "And Jehovah said unto Moses, 'Write thou these words; for after the tenor of these words I have made a covenant with thee and with Israel'" (Exodus 34:27). "And Moses wrote their goings out according to their journeys by the commandment of Jehovah" (Numbers 33:2). Many times the books of Exodus, Leviticus, and Numbers record that God spoke to Moses and tell of Moses' special position as God's prophet or spokesman to give God's will to the people.

In Deuteronomy Moses' speeches are regarded as God's word, saying, "Ye shall not add unto the word which I command you, neither shall ye diminish from it, that ye may keep the commandments of Jehovah your God . . ." (Deut. 4:2).

Several passages indicate the special respect and preservation for these books from the very beginning. Deuteronomy

229

31:9-13 and 24-27 tell that Moses wrote the law that God had given and commanded it to be kept by the priests, even beside the ark of the covenant, and to be read to all the people every seven years. Deuteronomy 17:18-20 orders that when Israel would have a king over them, he would make a copy of the book of the law, out of that which was kept by the priests, and read it all the days of his life to keep all the words of this law. (See also Joshua 1:8.)

According to the uniform testimony of all the sacred historians, the law of Moses, thus carefully guarded and made obligatory upon the people and their rulers, was ever after regarded as canonical and divinely authoritative, and that even in the most degenerate times. The punctilious obedience rendered to it by Joshua is repeatedly noticed in the course of his life (e.g., Joshua 11:15). Canaanites were left in the land to prove Israel "whether they would hearken unto the commandments of Jehovah, which he commanded their fathers by the hand of Moses" (Judges 3:4). Saul forfeited his kingdom by failing to comply with a requirement of the law, which Samuel had charged him to execute (I Sam. 15). David charged Solomon to obey the law of Moses (I Kings 2:3). David is repeatedly commended for keeping the law (I Kings 3:14; 9:4; 11:34, 38). Solomon's compliance with the law of Moses in the worship instituted in the temple is noted (II Chron. 8:13); and he impressed upon the people their obligation to obey it (I Kings 8:56-58, 61). The prophet Ahijah denounced Jeroboam for his disobedience to the commandments of Jehovah (I Kings 14:7-16). King Asa commanded the people to keep the Law (II Chron. 14:4). Jehoshaphat sent a deputation throughout all the cities of Judah to teach the people the book of the law (II Chron. 17:9). The law of Moses was observed under Joash (II Chron. 23:18; 24:6). Amaziah is said to have acted in accordance with the law of Moses (II Kings 14:6; II Chron.

25:4). Hezekiah kept the commandments which Jehovah commanded Moses (II Kings 18:6; II Chron. 30:16). Manasseh's gross transgressions of the law of Moses were denounced by the prophets (II Kings 21:2-16). Josiah bound the people in solemn covenant to obey the law of Moses (II Kings 23:3, 24, 25; II Chron. 34:14, 30-32). The exile of both Israel and Judah is attributed to their infractions of the law of Moses (II Kings 17:7-23; 18:12; II Chron. 33:8; Dan. 9:11, 13; Neh. 1:7-9; 9:14-30). The first colony of returned exiles recognized the authority of the law of Moses (Ezra 3:2; 6:16-18). The book of the law was read and expounded to the people by Ezra and the Levites (Neh. 8:1-8), and all solemnly pledged themselves to obey it (Neh. 1:28, 29; 13: 1-3)[1]

Joshua was guided by God in his work as leader of Israel. He spoke the words of the Lord by inspiration and then he wrote them and added them to the law of the Lord (Joshua 1:1; 24:2, 25, 26).

Samuel was chosen by God to be a prophet, and all the people of Israel knew that he spoke and wrote the words of the Lord (I Samuel 3:19-21; 4:1a).

Whenever a book was written by a man, known to be a prophet, that book was part of the body of holy Scripture so far as it was known at that time. Thus the Old Testament canon (list of authoritative books) was formed piece by piece. The books came with the inherent authority of God's inspired message and were accepted at once by those who knew of them. There is no indication that any council of men decided for the nation what books to regard as authoritative.

Making the one Bible out of numerous books was not a matter of selecting a bunch of books out of many others.

---

1. William Henry Green, *General Introduction to the Old Testament* (New York: Scribners, 1898), pp. 12, 13.

It was simply a matter of recognizing God's Word as each portion was written.

Neither the finding of the law by Josiah's men (II Kings 22:8—23:8) nor the reading of the law by Ezra (Nehemiah 8:1—9:38) was a process of canonizing or gathering the Scriptures, but in both cases the people and their leaders recognized the law as having been authoritative from its origin centuries before.

The decision to place a book in the Bible was not based on the authority of men who collected them, but on the authority evident in the book itself.

From the very start one thing held the Bible books together as soon as they were produced: the fact that they were God's Word. Their divine origin made them unique and separate from the books of mere men.

The books belong together, because they fit together into one master design. They are parts of the whole plan of God. They belong to each other because together they declare the whole counsel of God.

Christ appointed the twelve apostles to be His emissaries, and He gave them His message to the world (John 14:26; 15:26; 16:13; 20:21-23; Luke 24:46-49; Acts 1:18; Matthew 10:40; 28:18-20). From its beginning the church continued steadfastly in the apostles' doctrine.

Paul became an apostle later, but his apostleship is fully attested (Acts 26:6-21; 26:16-18; Galatians 1:11—2:10). As soon as any books were written by any apostles they had the authority of apostles' doctrine. Because they were received as authoritative they were copies, circulated, and collected together.

Peter's second letter (about A.D. 68) speaks of "all his [Paul's] epistles" as Scriptures misused by some, as if they had wide circulation and were probably published together in one collection.

In collecting and preserving the apostolic writings the church was not creating a canonical body of literature, it was merely continuing steadfastly in the apostles' doctrine, the same true revelation of God that gave rise to the church. The church never knew anything else as its foundation and its faith than this same divine message guaranteed by the fact that Jesus appointed the apostles to be His spokesmen and promised to them the power of the Holy Spirit to guide them into all truth. Read I Thessalonians 2:13; II Thessalonians 2:15; 3:6, 14; and I Corinthians 14:37.

Appendix III

THE GROUND OF OUR FAITH

by Seth Wilson

The Gospel records of the life of Jesus are the focal center of the entire Bible; and they are the chief foundation of our assurance that the Bible is from God. If these accounts are true, they confirm the Old Testament and guarantee the divine inspiration of the New Testament. If Jesus actually said what these report He said, then indeed He spoke as never man spoke. If He did what they say He did, His works bear witness of Him that He is from God, for no one could do these things except God be with Him. If He died for us and rose again as they testify, He is the Conqueror of death and the Lord of all. If what they say is true, He came forth from God, was born of a virgin, and ascended back to God's throne; then the Son of God has visited us, and we can know whom we have believed, and can trust Him completely to do whatever He has promised.

According to these accounts, Jesus has all authority in heaven and on earth; He will raise all the dead and judge all men; He is the Way, the Truth, and the Life, and no one can come to God except through Him (John 14:6): no one knows God unless he learns of Him from Jesus Christ (Matt. 11:27); if we do not believe in Jesus, we walk in darkness, we will die in our sins, the wrath of God abides upon us, and we will be condemned (John 8:12, 24; 3:18, 36; 12:46-48; Mark 16:16); if we do believe in Him and obey Him, we will have eternal life with Him in glory. Our eternal destiny depends upon what these records say. They had better be right. It is of utmost importance for us to know whether or not they are true and reliable.

234

Truthfulness and Trustworthiness of the Gospel Accounts

Some men say the important thing is that the story of Jesus inspires us to nobler attitudes and better deeds, whether it is historically true or not. There are religious leaders who insist that we should simply take the samples and sentiments of the New Testament as a pattern for our lives, and not believe the supernatural claims and events recorded in the Gospels. They even claim that the Gospels present sublime principles in an oriental style of personifying and illustrating ideals in the form of exaggerated accounts of real events or stories of imaginary incidents. They say it does not have to be true history to be great religion. *But that is not true.* Beware of such a delusion! Christianity is not mere sentiment stirred by fiction. It is not noble feelings and ideals based on the psychological effect of examples, real or imaginary. Christianity is living under a contract with God, faithfully following His definitely revealed will for us.

The Gospel is not primarily a set of ideals for conduct. It is first a message of facts—real, true, unique facts of what God has done for us and made known to us. It is, of course, a message to be believed, and that faith is to be genuine and deep enough to control our lives. We are to know these things so that we may act accordingly. But the gospel story cannot adequately affect our lives unless we are convinced that it is true.

Furthermore, it certainly cannot bring us the gifts and helps from God which it promises, unless it is true. We cannot change the basic nature of our sinful hearts, or bear the fruit of a divine spirit of righteousness, without regeneration and the coming of the Spirit of God to dwell within us. The righteousness taught in the New Testament is not something that can be embodied in a set of impersonal rules or described

235

in abstract principles, but it is a personal relationship with the living Christ. (See Rom. 8:1-17; II Cor. 5:14-17; Gal. 2:20, 5:6; Phil. 3:8-11; Col. 1:27, 2:6-23, 3:1-17; Rom. 14:17; I Cor. 16:22). The person of Christ the Son of God must be real, must be known, must be relied upon with complete trust, must be loved. Any religion that could exist without faith in the truth of the New Testament message is not the Christianity described in the New Testament—that is sure!

There is nothing the world needs as much as a clear, decisive faith in the Christ of the New Testament. We need the kind of firm conviction that makes us eager to follow wherever He leads, obey whatever He commands, and trust Him whatever befalls us. Faith is not holding to an idea regardless of the evidence, but it is trusting the reliability of the Lord regardless of the consequences. We need a solid foundation of facts and good reasons to show that the New Testament is the Word of Him whom we can trust for all of life and eternity.

The Gospel accounts of the life of Jesus furnish that foundation. John stated the purpose of His writing, and it fits all four Gospels: "These are written that ye might believe that Jesus is the Christ, the Son of God; and that believing ye might have life through His name" (John 20:31). "*Believing*" means being convinced that it is true, so that we act upon it, with our consciousness, desires, and will controlled by it.

There is plenty of evidence to convince any reasonable person that the Gospels are true—evidence both within the books themselves, and outside the books concerning them and their contents.

We Have In The Gospels the Surest Kind of History

1. *The Credibility of the witnesses.* Here are enough good witnesses to establish any fact. They tell their story with serious purpose, factual details and steadfast consistency. Their writings show that they were intelligent men. They were prepared by extensive and close association with the things of which they speak. Early Christian writers declare, without a dissenting voice, that our four Gospels were written by Matthew and John, who were apostles of Jesus, and by Mark and Luke, who were companions of the apostles. Many direct testimonies and incidental references in numerous writings of the first three centuries unite to show that these four Gospels were written in the apostolic age, were handed down to the succeeding generations as authoritative Scriptures, and were in widespread general and public use at least from the beginning of the second century. Thus our four records are the work of men who were qualified as eyewitnesses and close associates of eyewitnesses who were constantly engaged in proclaiming these facts. And the facts which were written by them did not originate at the writing, but had been preached for several years by other eyewitnesses, and had been accepted by vast multitudes of people of whom many had opportunity to know personally or to inquire directly concerning the circumstances involved. These witnesses were men of good character, having reverence for God, love for the truth, and zeal for righteousness. They lived as believers in their own testimony, and spent years in labors and hardships to propagate this message, which meant no gain to them unless it was true. Their sincerity is sealed by their martyrdom and the persecutions which they were willing to bear for the sake of the truth and their love for the Lord.

237

2. *Agreement of the Testimony.* The accounts in the four Gospels are so similar that they have been accused of copying. Yet they are so independent and different in telling many details that they are sometimes accused of contradicting one another. They make no attempt to explain the differences or to prove agreement, in what they say. On close study they are seen to agree perfectly, but not with the kind of surface agreement that would appear if they were made up to agree. R. A. Torrey observed concerning their testimony of the resurrection of Jesus:

> These accounts must be either a record of facts that actually occurred or else fictions. If fictions, they must have been fabricated in one of two ways—either independently of one another, or in collusion with one another. They could not have been fabricated independently of one another; the agreements are too marked and too many. It is absolutely incredible that four persons sitting down to write an account of what never occurred independently of one another should have made their stories agree to the extent that these do. On the other hand, they cannot have been made up, as we have already seen, in collusion with one another; the apparent discrepancies are too numerous and too noticeable. It is proven that they were not made up independently of one another; it is proven they were not made up in collusion with one another, so we are driven to the conclusion that they were not made up at all, that they are a true relation of facts as they actually occurred.[1]

3. *Support of Archaeology, Geography, and History.* The Gospel testimony is confirmed by agreement, not only

---

1. R. A. Torrey, "The Certainty and Importance of the Resurrection of Jesus Christ" in *The Fundamentals,* Vol. II, ed. by R. A. Torrey, A. C. Dixon, and others (Grand Rapids, Michigan: Baker Book House, reprint 1972 [1917]), pp. 301, 302.

with one another, but also with many other writings and with all available facts of the land of Palestine, the rulers, the parties, coins, customs, etc. Gospel writers have been accused of error, but they have never been proved false. When the facts have been brought to light, in every instance the Gospels have been shown to be accurate history: e.g., the account of Quirinius (Cyrenius) and the enrollment in Luke 2:2. Everywhere their testimony can be checked it proves to be sound.

4. *Support of Old Testament Prophecies.* By far the most important outside information to confirm the Gospels is found in dozens of passages in the Old Testament which give many scores of items of information about the Christ, His life, character and work. Matthew makes many references to the testimony of the prophets; and all the Gospels quote Jesus' appeal to the prophets in support of His claims and for explanations of His life and sufferings. This testimony from the Old Testament has special quality and value, because obviously it reports not things as seen understood by men, but truths as known and revealed by God.

5. *Evidence of Miracles.* Miracles wrought by the apostles confirmed their testimony to the hearers who saw and knew them, and their confirmation has been relayed to us by many witnesses, both Biblical and traditional. Their miracles are not mere unexplained wonders, but are given clear meaning as credentials of their message (Heb. 2:4). They tell plainly that Jesus gave them the miracle-working power to support the message, and that He also gave them inspiration of the Holy Spirit to aid them in remembering what He taught and to guide them in revealing the truth. Miracles were a reasonable accompaniment to their message, for it was all concerned with the facts of God's revelation to man and His supernatural intervention in the affairs of the world.

239

6. *Claims of Divine Inspiration.* An integral and indelible part of the apostles' testimony is found in their repeated claims of supernatural aid and inspiration from God to guarantee the accuracy and Divine authority of their message. This claim extends to some who were their co-workers like Mark and Luke (See Matt. 10:1-20, 40; 16:19; Mark 13:11; 16:20; Luke 24:45-49; John 14:26; 15:26; 16:13-15; 20: 21-23; Acts 1:4-8; 2:1-4, 16, 17, 33; 4:8; 5:12-26; 8:6, 13-18; 13:1-4; 15:6-12, 28; I Cor. 2:6-16; 12:8-11; 14: 37; Gal. 1:8-12; Eph. 3:2-5; I Thess. 2:13; II Tim. 1:6; I Pet. 1:12; II Pet. 3:15, 16). If they are men of truth, these claims are true. In any case, such claims demand from us a strong and decisive verdict either for or against them. Such claims are either very significantly true or they are monstrously false. They mean that the apostles cannot be treated indifferently, but must be considered either deliberate liars, deluded maniacs, or completely dependable messengers of God. There can be no middle ground, no supposition of general good intentions, partial reliability, and innocent mistakes. If they are not the worst of frauds, they are the truest of witnesses, and vice versa.

7. *Incredibility of Fraud.* The charge of fraud is answered by their consistent and extended witnessing, by the agreement of their lives with their testimony, by the success of their proclamation among people to whom many of the facts were known, by their endurance of persecution and death for the Gospel. Furthermore, it is absolutely incredible that the matchless life and character of Jesus could have been invented by deliberate liars, or dreamed up by lunatics, or formed in the popular imagination over any period of time. It is almost as incredible that anyone who invented such a character could have made other men to believe him

240

to be real and to join in the proclamation of the fraud without having any evidences of His reality. The almost irreverent words of Theodore Parker have a strong element of truth in them: "It would have taken a Jesus to forge a Jesus." Another has said, "If Jesus is not the living Lord, then the man who invented Jesus deserves our worship." It is a shocking and repulsive thought; but it is true—if the Bible is not true, then there is no true God known to man, and we have nothing more admirable and helpful to man than the lies about Jesus. Just try to imagine how fiction, forgery, and fraud could produce the teachings of Christ, the converting power of the Gospel, and the actual establishment and spread of Christianity—just think of the magnitude of the imposture, the difficulty of contriving the mighty features and the many details of such a system, the sharply contradictory types of skills and cunning and character that would be required in the fabricators—and you will see how anyone who faces the facts must believe that the Gospels are true. It is necessary for any normal mind to believe that every effect has an adequate cause.

We do not have to prove all the facts of the record, if we can be sure of reliability of the author. If the Gospel record is not only good and honest human testimony, but also written by men inspired of the Holy Spirit, then we can and must believe it whether we can verify it or not. It becomes more than a collection of ideas to be tested; it is a source of truth to be trusted. It is also the solid ground on which we rest a faith that is reasonable, helpful and honest—a faith that knows whom it believes and why he is deemed trustworthy. After we know the evidence that Jesus is the Son of God, we can quite reasonably say, "If Jesus says it, I believe it, and that settles it." When we know the facts of

His life which manifest His love and goodness, as well as His wisdom and power, we follow Him with loving confidence and are content to say:

And so I go on not knowing: I would not know if I might.
I would rather walk with Him by faith, than to walk alone by sight;
I would rather walk with Christ in the dark, than to walk alone in the light.

Appendix IV

"MEN SPOKE FROM GOD"[1]

by John T. Willis

The biblical writers state repeatedly that they are writing God's words to men. For example, Paul writes to Chrisitans at Corinth: "If any one thinks that he is a prophet, or spiritual, he should acknowledge that *what I am writing* to you is *a command of the Lord*" (I Cor. 14:37—The italics in Bible quotations in this essay are added by the author.). Again he writes very clearly to the Ephesians: "For this reason I, Paul, a prisoner for Christ Jesus on behalf of you Gentiles —assuming that you have heard of the stewardship of God's grace that was given to me for you, how the mystery was made known to me by revelation, *as I have written* briefly. *When you read this* you can perceive my insight into the mystery of Christ, which was not made known to the sons of men in other generations as it has now been revealed to his holy apostles and prophets in the Spirit" (Eph. 3:1-5). Thus the biblical authors were quite aware of the fact that they were writing God's word to their audiences.

Biblical writers also refer to scriptures written before their own works as God's words to men. A classic example is found in Paul's letter to Timothy: "But as for you, continue in what you have learned and have firmly believed, knowing from whom you learned it and how from childhood you have been acquainted with *the sacred writings* which are able to instruct you for salvation through faith in Christ Jesus.

---

1. John T. Willis is professor of Old Testament at Abilene Christian University. This material was originally presented in a series of weekly meetings of Bible majors at Abilene Christian University. It was then published in four parts in *Firm Foundation* (Dec. 2, 1980-Dec. 23, 1980). College Press Publishing Company has secured permission to include this essay in this volume.

All scripture is inspired by God and profitable for teaching, for reproof, for correction, and for training in righteousness, that the man of God may be complete, equipped for every good work" (II Tim. 3:14-17). Further, Peter writes: "And count the forbearance of our Lord as salvation. So also our beloved brother Paul *wrote* to you according to the wisdom *given* him, speaking of this as he does in all his *letters.* There are some things in them hard to understand, which the ignorant and unstable twist to their own destruction as they do *the other scriptures"* (II Pet. 3:15, 16). Here Peter refers to Paul's letters as scripture and as given by divine wisdom.

Now if these statements of the authors of the books of the Bible were not true, there would be every reason to suspect other statements they make about matters which lie outside the realm of human experience, such as life after death, the existence of angels or the devil or demons, the existence of and conditions for God's forgiveness of man's sin, and the like. Similarly, there would be then no objective means of determining with certainty the truthfulness of anything they say outside the realm of observable natural and historical phenomena.

There are strong evidences which support the claim of the biblical writers that the Bible was produced under divine inspiration. The staunchest advocates of plenary (full) verbal inspiration of scripture, however, freely acknowledge that this evidence does not belong to the same realm as "scientific proof," and in the final analysis is to be accepted by faith. For example, B. B. Warfield affirms,

> We . . . adopt the doctrine of the plenary inspiration of Scripture . . . because it is taught us as truth by Christ and His apostles, in the Scriptural record of their teaching, and the evidence for its truth is, therefore, . . . precisely that

evidence in weight and amount, which vindicates for us the trustworthiness of Christ and His apostles as teachers of doctrine. Of course, this evidence is not in the strict logical sense "demonstrative"; it is "probable" evidence.[2]

And J. D. Thomas says: "Christianity will never be removed from the realm of faith by 'proving' its basic tenets to be final, absolute truth, but it need not be. It was meant for man to 'walk by faith, and not by sight' (II Cor. 5:7)."[3]

Characteristics of the Biblical Writings

At least five specific characteristics of the biblical writings give strong support to their claim to be divinely inspired. First, the Old Testament prophets, Jesus, and the apostles all speak with authority. There is no doubt in their mind that they are uttering the message of God to man. The Old Testament prophets repeatedly introduce their oracles with "Thus says the Lord." Speaking of these prophets, Peter writes: "First of all you must understand this, that no prophecy of *scripture* [thus referring to prophetic oracles which have been preserved *in writing*] is a matter of one's own interpretation, because no prophecy ever came by the impulse of man, but *men* moved by the Holy Spirit *spoke from God*" (II Pet. 1:20, 21). Jesus says: "I have not spoken on my own authority; the Father who sent me has himself given me commandment what to say and what to speak" (John 12:49). And Paul writes to the Thessalonians: "And we also thank God constantly for this, that when you received

---

2. B. B. Warfield, *The Inspiration and Authority of the Bible* (Philadelphia: Presbyterian and Reformed Publishing Co., 1948), p. 218.

3. J. D. Thomas, *Facts and Faith*, vol. II (Abilene: Biblical Research Press, 1980), p. 35.

the word of God which you heard from us, you accepted it not as the word of men but as *what it really is, the word of God,* which is at work in you believers" (I Thess. 2:13).

Second, men of God uttered many predictions of the future which were fulfilled. Several passages in Isaiah 40-55 emphasize that only the one true God can predict the future and cause what he predicts to come to pass. The Lord cries out to the false gods of the nations:

> Tell us what is to come hereafter, that we may know that you are gods (Isa. 41:23).

Again, the Lord describes himself in this way:

> I am God, and there is no other; I am God, and there is none like me, declaring the end from the beginning and from ancient times things not yet done (Is. 46:9, 10).

A specific example of prediction which was fulfilled appears in Joshua 6:26. After the Israelites destroy the city of Jericho, Joshua pronounces this curse: "Cursed before the Lord be the man that rises up and rebuilds this city, Jericho.

> At the cost of his first-born shall he lay its foundation, and at the cost of his youngest son shall he set up its gates.

Several hundreds years later, during the reign of Ahab in North Israel, Hiel of Bethel built Jericho; he laid its foundation at the cost of Abiram his first-born, and set up its gates at the cost of his youngest son Segub, *according to the word of the Lord, which he spoke by Joshua* the son of Nun" (I Kings 16:34). Other cases of fulfilled prophetic predictions include the prediction of the suffering servant in Isaiah 52: 13—53:12 fulfilled in Christ (see Acts 8:30-35), the predictions concerning Tyre in Ezekiel 26-28, and concerning Babylon in Isaiah 13-14.

246

Third, the message of the Bible is harmonious and consistent throughout, in spite of the fact that it was written over a span of several centuries by a number of writers in three different languages: Hebrew, Aramaic, and Greek. Because of the needs of the various audiences addressed, one book or section may emphasize one aspect of truth and another book or section another, but when these various parts are compared, there is no contradiction but a well-balanced unity.

Fourth, the biblical writers present an unbiased view of their heroes in light of the divinely-guided purposes which they had in mind in writing. For example, the author or authors of I and II Samuel relate how David spared Saul's life on two occasions when he had an excellent opportunity to kill him (I Sam. 24; 26), but they also record his adultery with Bathsheba and the plot to have Uriah killed (II Sam. 11).

Fifth, the Bible contains incredible insights into the nature of man, the created world, and the character of life on earth. He who lives according to the biblical teachings soon realizes that both life itself and the scriptures are the product of one and the same personality.

These five arguments provide weighty evidence to support the biblical claim that all scripture is inspired by God. The present writer subscribes to this claim in full.

Definition of Inspiration and Revelation

A proper understanding of the biblical teaching on the inspiration of scripture requires an attempt to define the term inspiration in light of biblical statements made about it and the many phenomena which exist in the Bible. On this point, one must be very cautious not to elevate a human

247

definition of this word to the level of divine authority. C. H. Pinnock says, "Inspiration . . . is the miracle of conservation whereby the truths of divine revelation have been *preserved* in an authentic and sufficient form."[4] Harry Rimmer states that inspiration "is the process by which the Spirit of God kept his word free from error or fallacy, and preserved it from contradiction or mistake"; it is "the supervision of the writing by the Holy Ghost, Who alone could have operated over the centuries as the editor of all parts of the Book."[5] B. B. Warfield defines inspiration as "a supernatural influence exerted on the sacred writers by the Spirit of God, by virtue of which their writings are given Divine trustworthiness."[6] Further, he points out that inspiration has to do with the final act of producing scripture.[7] H. S. Miller affirms:

> Inspiration . . . is the inbreathing of God into men, thus qualifying them to receive and communicate divine truth. It is God speaking through the Holy Spirit through men to men. It is the work of God through the Spirit, in men, enabling them to receive and give forth divine truth without error. It makes the speaker and writer infallible in the communication of this truth, whether this truth was previously known or not.[8]

J. D. Thomas states that II Timothy 3:16 means that

> God supernaturally controlled the production of the books of the Bible by means of the Holy Spirit's influence upon the

---

4. C. H. Pinnock, "Inspiration," *Wycliffe Bible Encyclopedia*, vol. I, (Chicago: Moody Press, 1975), p. 847.

5. Harry Rimmer, *Inspiration Plus Revelation Equals the Bible* (Grand Rapids: Wm. B. Eerdmans, 1944), p. 17.

6. B. B. Warfield, *op. cit.*, p. 131.

7. *Ibid.*, p. 160.

8. H. S. Miller, *General Biblical Introduction*, 8th ed. (Houghton, N.Y.: Wordbearer Press, 1954), p. 17.

writers so that the words of the original manuscripts are exactly what God wanted them to be. The men were so inspired or controlled that the end product was precisely what was desired, yet it is well-known that the writers of Scriptures used their own vocabularies and their own knowledge of history, geography, and other such matters.[9]

All these authors were well-known conservative scholars who hold a very high view of inspiration. Summarizing their statements, it should be noted that they define inspiration as a "supernatural influence, inbreathing, supervision, or control" by the Holy Spirit over certain writers to "preserve or conserve" truths which God wanted preserved in a "trustworthy, authentic, and sufficient" manner. It should also be noted that all these writers agree that inspiration is "plenary" (i.e., full, complete; it pertains to every portion of scripture equally) and "verbal" (i.e., and not merely the concepts or ideas, were inspired; this is not to be confused with mechanical dictation), and that the Bible does not state *how* God inspired the various authors but only *that* he did so. J.D. Thomas writes:

Plenary inspiration is the name commonly used to indicate the view of a definite and sufficient inspiration to insure that the end product has the precise and exact words, yet without committing oneself to any exact plan of how the Holy Spirit actually functioned in inspiration. It holds that the Bible is inspired so that there is no error in a real sense (though there may be apparent discrepancies), and that the person who depends upon the Bible can do so, because the writings in the original manuscripts were written accurately and they say exactly what God wanted said. In this way plenary inspiration is "verbal" in its end results, though it is not what

---

9. J. D. Thomas, *op. cit.*, p. 19.

what is called "passive dictation." As to method, the Holy Spirit did what ever was necessary to have absolute control of the end product, though he may well have used different methods for different portions of Scripture, and in different contextual situations.[10]

But it is also necessary to understand the difference between *inspiration and revelation.* B. B. Warfield[11] and those influenced by him, including, for example, C. H. Pinnock,[12] regard inspiration as a type of revelation. The point these scholars make is a valid one, namely, that the same God who reveals himself in nature also reveals himself in his words, and the two are compatible and harmonious. However, it is equally valid and important to see that inspiration can be understood as the much larger entity of which revelation is a part. For example, Harry Rimmer defines revelation as "the supernatural impartation to man of knowledge and information he could not derive from his own observation or research." In light of this, he goes on to state that in the process of inspiration "the Holy Spirit is . . . quite free to use natural methods to achieve his purpose, such as the testimony of eyewitnesses, the accumulation of reliable historical documents, or the experiences of chosen men."[13]

In view of all this, the following observations of H. S. Miller are of utmost importance in attempting to understand the nature of inspiration.

Inspiration extends to the whole of the Scriptures, although the subject matter is of two kinds: (1) revelation, (2) known facts.

---

10. *Ibid.*, p. 20.
11. B. B. Warfield, *op. cit.*, pp. 74, 75.
12. C. H. Pinnock, *op. cit.*, p. 847.
13. Harry Rimmer, *op. cit.*, p. 55 and p. 66.

Revelation is the work of God by which he communicates facts and truths which were not known before. . . .

Known Facts may come either (1) from personal observation, or (2) from existing documents. . . . It did not require revelation for Moses to write the journey of Israel from Egypt to Sinai and the Plains of Moab, but it did require inspiration to let him know what to include and what to omit, and to secure accuracy.

Revelation discovers new truth to men (see I Cor. 2:10, 11); *Inspiration* guides and controls the giving out of the truth (see I Cor. 2:13). Not all of the Bible was *revealed* by God to the writers, nor did it need to be; but the entire Bible is *inspired* by God. The Bible *contains* revelation; it *is* inspired.[14]

Claims and Phenomena in the Scriptures

It is very important that one's view of the inspiration of the Bible be biblical. In other words, it must agree with the *claims* made by the inspired authors of the various biblical books, and with the *phenomena which* appear in these books. The present article makes no claim to be exhaustive in calling attention to some of these claims and phenomena, but simply to offer certain thoughts to point in the right direction.

1. Certain inspired writers of the Bible *claim* to preserve only portions of written and oral material available to them, and the basis on which they preserve this is *to meet the needs of the audiences* they are addressing. For example, John writes: "Now Jesus did many other signs in the presence of the disciples, *which are not written in this book*; but these

---

14. H. S. Miller, *op. cit.,* p. 17.

are written *that you may believe that* Jesus is the Christ, the Son of God, *and that* believing *you may have life* in his name" (John 20:30, 31; see also 21:25). This brings out two important principles which must be kept in mind in attempting to understand the Bible. First, in the Bible one can expect to encounter many gaps in the flow of historical events, a record of only certain parts of events which are preserved, and even apparent contradictions in the text. One searching to discover the minute details of various events can expect to be greatly disappointed and frequently perplexed. For example, he will be troubled about the presence of large numbers of people in the days of Cain, since Cain says to the Lord, "Whoever finds me will slay me," and since "the Lord put a mark on Cain, lest any who came upon him should kill him" (Gen. 4:14, 15). Or he will be disturbed by the fact that Mark says Jesus rode a colt into Jerusalem when he made his triumphal entry (Mark 11:1-9), while Matthew says he rode a colt and an ass (Matt. 21:1-9). But the purpose of the biblical writers is not to supply the kind of information which would be necessary to explain such situations or to harmonize such passages. But by faith one can be assured that if all the historical details were known, such problems would not exist.

Second, since the different inspired writers wrote what they did under divine guidance to meet specific needs of the people to whom they wrote, the only proper way to apply the Bible to man's needs in any generation is (a) to discover the needs of contemporay men, and then (b) to apply to this situation those biblical texts which were intended for a similar situation when a given biblical book was originally written. It is not sufficient to know the needs of a contemporary person or church, or to know the teachings of the Bible.

One must bring the two together in a real situation. Then and only then can God speak satisfactorily through his word to meet man's needs.

2. Certain inspired authors of the Bible *claim* they used written sources and got information from eye-witnesses and others in personal conversation in the course of writing their books. For example, Luke says that "eye-witnesses and ministers of the word" "delivered to us" (note he includes himself in the "us") information concerning the life and teachings of Jesus, and refers to the fact that "many have undertaken to compile a narrative of the things which have been accomplished among us." Further, he states that before he wrote his gospel he "followed all things closely for some time past" (Luke 1:1-3). Apparently Luke used oral and written sources in the production of his gospel, and checked carefully the information handed down to him to assure its accuracy. Of course, he did all this under the superintendence and control of the Holy Spirit.

This same phenomenon occurs frequently throughout the Bible. After his account of the life of David, the author of the books of Chronicles says, "Now the acts of King David, from first to last, are *written* in the Chronicles of Samuel the seer, and in the Chronicles of Nathan the prophet, and in the Chronicles of Gad the seer, with *accounts* of all his rule and his might and of the circumstances that came upon him and upon Israel, and upon all the kingdoms of the countries" (I Chron. 29:29, 30; see further II Chron. 9:29; 12:15; 13:22; 16:11; etc.). A very instructive example is found in Proverbs 31:1: "The words of Lemuel, king of Massa, which his mother taught him." The mother of Lemuel taught him the proverbs now recorded in Proverbs 31:2ff. orally, later he wrote them down, and now they are preserved in the last chapter of the book of Proverbs.

Some of the sources used by the biblical writers may have been inspired when they were first written because they became a part of the Bible, but some were not. For example, Ezra 4:11-16 preserves a letter written by Rehum, Shimshai, and their associates to Artaxerxes king of Persia, urging him to stop the Jews from building the walls and city of Jerusalem, then verses 17-22 contain the letter Artaxerxes sent back. Neither of these letters was originally inspired but the inspired writer of the book of Ezra decided to include them in his book as he was borne along by the Holy Spirit, so now they become inspired by the fact of their inclusion.

3. The Bible is a record of the words and deeds of many people, such as Adam and Eve, Abraham, David, Peter, the devil, Simon the Pharisee, and many others. It is also a record of the words and deeds of God. When God or one of his authorized spokesmen speaks, it is the word of God. But when, for example, Peter rebukes Jesus for announcing his death, burial, and resurrection (Matt. 16:22), this was not the word of God, because Jesus himself reproves Peter for saying this in the very next verse. The later *recording* of what Peter said is true—and makes it inspired in that sense; but *what Peter said* was not at the time inspired—in fact, it was the opposite of God's will. Accordingly, the entire Bible *is* inspired of God and is true, but only portions of it are specifically God's message to man. In other words, the Bible *is* the word or message of God, but inasmuch as it includes the words of unbelievers and not all of it is a word of God, it is spoken of as *containing* the words of God.

This is an important point, because it emphasizes the importance of determining the *speaker*, the *audience*, the *occasion*, the *problem* or *need*, and many other things when interpreting a biblical passage. Failure to do this can lead to misundertandings of the real message of the Bible. An example of such misunderstanding may be helpful. John 9:31 is sometimes cited to prove that God does not answer the prayers of an alien sinner or one who is not a Christian. It says: "We know that God does not listen to sinners, but if any one is a worshiper of God and does his will, God listens to him." However, when one examines the context, he discovers the following facts: (1) the speaker here is the blind man Jesus had healed (cf. vs. 30); (2) he is speaking to the Jews, who are seeking to show that Jesus had not really performed a miracle, causing the blind man to see (cf. vss. 18, 22); (3) since the Jews had called him a "sinner" in verse 24, the "sinner" under consideration here is Jesus (of course, this does not mean Jesus was really a sinner, but only that the Jews so labelled him); (4) the point the blind man was making in verse 31 was that Jesus could not be a sinner, because he had called on God the Father to work through him to heal the blind man, and the Father had answered his prayer and had healed him. The accounts of the conversions of Cornelius (Acts 10:1-4) and Saul (Acts 9:11) indicate God does answer the prayers of honest truth-seekers who are not yet Christians as they attempt to learn his will and obey it.

The point being made here is obviously distinctively different from the view of inspiration or revelation which affirms that the Bible *is not* the word of God, but through the operation of the Holy Spirit *becomes* the word of God to one studying it, if and when God chooses that it shall. This view is that the Bible *contains* the word of God, but not objectively or absolutely as it is ordinarily read.

4. A comparison of duplicate accounts of the same event or of two records of the same song or poetic piece shows

that the inspired writers were often not concerned to quote the *exact words* of speakers (whether God or man), but only to preserve faithfully the *meaning* of what they said. When one compares Matthew, Mark, and Luke in the original Greek, he discovers that there is not a single verse which reads exactly the same in all three Gospels.

An illustration of this point may be found in the record of the words God spoke when Jesus was baptized. Matthew 3:17 quotes him as saying, "*This is* my beloved Son, *with whom* I am well pleased." However, the parallel accounts in Mark 1:11 and Luke 3:22 quote him as saying, "*Thou art* my beloved Son; *with thee* I am well pleased." Now did *God actually* say, "*This is* my beloved Son," or "*Thou art* my beloved Son?" It is impossible to know on the basis of the biblical evidence. But this does not matter, because it is obvious that the inspired biblical writers do not always claim or intend to quote the words of their speakers verbatim. Of course, they may have done so at times, but the only criterion modern man has to know this is the occurrence of duplicate passages in the Bible, and these indicate they did not quote the exact words.

5. A study of the Bible shows that the records of historical events it contains may or may not be in chronological order. Accordingly, one's belief in the inspiration of the Bible does not depend on its being in chronological order. Two examples may be cited to illustrate this point. II Samuel 5, 6 relate this order of events: David's conquest of Jerusalem (5:6-10), Hiram's building him a palace (5:11, 12), the children David had by several wives and concubines in Jerusalem (5:13-16), David's two victories over the Philistines in the Valley of Rephaim (5:17-25), and David's bringing the ark to Jerusalem (6:1-23). However, the parallel account in I Chronicles

11:4-9; 13-15 record this order: David's conquest of Jerusalem (11:4-9), David's bringing the ark toward Jerusalem as far as the house of Obed-edom (13), Hiram's building him a palace (14:1-2), the children David had by several wives and concubines in Jerusalem (14:3-7). David's two victories over the Philistines in the Valley of Rephaim (14:8-17), and David's bringing the ark from the house of Obededom to Jerusalem (15). From these two records, one can only conjecture as to the precise order in which these events occurred. But this offers no problem for one's belief in the inspiration of the Bible, because there is no claim that the biblical authors intended to present the events they record in chronological order, nor is there any reason why they should.

A New Testament example of the same phenomenon is the account of the temptations of Christ. Matthew 4:1-11 records the temptations as (a) turning the stones to bread, (b) jumping off the wing of the temple, and (c) worshipping the devil to receive all the kingdoms of the world. However, Luke 4:1-13 relates them as (a) turning the stones to bread, (b) worshipping the devil to receive all the kingdoms of the world, and (c) jumping off the wing of the temple. In what chronological order did the three temptations occur? From the biblical evidence, it is impossible to know with certainty. But there is nothing which demands that inspired writers record events in the exact order in which they actually occurred.

6. The Bible contains various kinds of literature, including parables (Luke 15), allegories (Gal. 4:21—5:1), fables (Judges 9:7-15), mythological language (Job 26:12-13; Isa. 14:12-14; 27:1; Ps. 74:13-14), figurative language (Ps. 42:1; James 4:14), and the like. Therefore, it is a mistake to suppose everything in the Bible is intended to be

257

historical. Indeed, God can and does teach through history, but he can teach in other ways as well. If Jesus fairly represents God's teaching method, God must love parables.

7. The authors of some biblical books are named, but the authors of others are not. For example, the Bible makes no claim as to who wrote Joshua, I and II Kings, Job, Hebrews, and so forth. The Christian is under no obligation to take a position on this issue where the Bible does not speak. Ancient writers sometimes made claims concerning this matter. For example, early Jewish rabbis said Moses wrote the book of Job, and early Church Fathers claimed Paul wrote the book of Hebrews. But these rabbis and Church Fathers were not inspired by God, and thus the Christian is not bound to defend their claims. The only *biblical* view, compatible with the Bible itself, would be, "We do not know who wrote the books of Job and Hebrews."

Further, in order to be biblical, sometimes it is necessary to distinguish between the "moving force" behind a book and the person who actually wrote it. For example, Jeremiah 36:32 states that Baruch wrote at least part of the book of Jeremiah at the dictation of Jeremiah, Isaiah 8:16 indicates Isaiah entrusted the oracles he delivered during the Syro-Ephraimitic War to his "disciples," and logic would suggest they in turn wrote them down, Romans 16:22 demonstrates that Tertius actually wrote the book of Romans although it was in reality an epistle of Paul, and I Peter 5:12 suggests Peter dictated the book of I Peter to Silvanus. However, this action in no way removes these sections from the claim that the Bible is inspired by God.

8. There are many passages in the Bible which are difficult to understand historically, theologically, or otherwise. The inspired writers themselves acknowledged the difficulty

of understanding portions of the Bible. For example, Peter says concerning Paul's letters, "There are some things in them hard to understand" (II Pet. 3:16). Accordingly, it is not necessary to understand everything in the scriptures to accept them by faith as inspired. In fact, the Christian's attitude often must be a humble admission of ignorance. Paul told the Corinthians: "If any one imagines that he knows something, he does not yet know as he ought to know" (I Cor. 8:2). Although it is important for the Christian to know all he can about God, man, salvation, and the like, his knowledge will necessarily be limited. It is important for him to love God (I Cor. 8:3), since ultimately his salvation depends on God's grace and mercy.

Summarizing, the weight of evidence supports the biblical claim that every scripture is inspired by God. One's belief in the inspiration of the Bible must be in harmony with what the Bible itself says about its composition, and with phenomena which appear in the various biblical books.

In conclusion, it is important to be reminded that belief in the inspiration of the Bible pertains only to the autograph (original) copies of the various books. No autograph of any biblical book has survived, but only copies and ancient translations. Therefore, careful detailed study of the manuscripts is necessary; so it is vital for one concerned about determining the original text to learn the tools, techniques, and languages necessary to work in the area of textual criticism. Those who have done so generally agree we can be assured that no significant biblical teaching has been effected by the variant readings which appear in the ancient manuscripts and versions. H. S. Miller says:

> Only the Bible in its original languages . . . is inspired . . .
> By the process of textual criticism and the comparison of the

259

many existing manuscript copies, versions, and patristic quotations, we have good reason for believing that we have a
text which is substantially the same as the original. No claim
is made for the inspiration of a translation, yet our English
translations are quite true to the Hebrew and Greek.[15]

---

15. *Ibid.*, p. 27.

Appendix V

GROUNDS ON WHICH WE RECEIVE THE BIBLE AS THE WORD OF GOD, AND THE ONLY RULE OF FAITH AND PRACTICE[1]

by J. W. McGarvey

Definitions

In saying that we receive the Bible as the word of God, we distinguish between the word of God and the words of God. We do not mean that all of its words are words of God; for some of them are recorded as the words of angels, some as the words of men, some as those of demons, and some as those of Satan. We mean that it is God's word in the sense that God, by the inspiration of its writers, caused to be written this record of things that were said and done by Himself and certain of His creatures.

In saying that we receive this book as the only rule of faith, we mean, first, that we receive all of its utterances as true in the sense which properly belongs to them, and therefore as objects of belief; and second, that nothing else, as a matter of religious belief, is to be required of us. Of course this does not bind us to any book now printed in the Bible which may prove to have been improperly inserted, or to any passage in any book which may prove to be an uninspired interpolation. In receiving it as the only rule of practice, we bind ourselves in conscience to observe all that it appoints for us to do, distinguishing what it appoints for

---

1. J. W. McGarvey taught at College of the Bible, Lexington, Kentucky. This essay was published in *The Old Faith Restated*, vol. I, edited by J. H. Garrison (St. Louis: Christian Publishing Co., 1891.) This essay sets forth in summary form the evidence for Christianity presented in McGarvey's *Evidences of Christianity*.

us from what it appointed for others in former dispensations; and we refuse to be bound by anything which it does not thus appoint.

By the "we" in our proposition, is meant, not the writer of this essay, nor the particular body of disciples with which this writer is identified; but all, everywhere who do thus receive the Bible. Many, it is true, receive the Bible as the word of God who do not receive it as the only rule of faith and practice; and we shall accordingly divide the question, discussing first the grounds on which the book is received in the former sense, and afterward the grounds on which it is received in the latter sense.

There is still another distinction which must be noted before we enter upon our principal theme. While the "we" whose grounds of belief are to be stated, includes all believers, all do not receive it on the same grounds. There is a great diversity in this respect. In order that all may be properly represented in the statements which are to be made, it is necessary to present these various grounds, and to consider them separately. Believers may be divided, in reference to their grounds of belief, into three classes; first the uneducated, who have never made a study of the evidences of Christianity; second, the more intelligent class, who have paid more or less attention to the subject, but have never studied it systematically; and third, those who have investigated the subject exhaustively. This classification of believers shall guide us in marking divisions in this part of our essay.

The Narrowest Ground of Belief

A large majority of the believers of this age, and of every age except the earliest, have received the Bible as the word of God on the one and only ground that they have been so educated. They have been trained from their earliest childhood to look upon the Bible as a sacred book; to reverence it as a most precious gift from God; to abhor unbelief in reference to it as a deadly sin, and to tremble when the least shadow of doubt concerning it passes across their minds. They have learned to estimate the truth of all other writings by their agreement or disagreement with this; and they fully expect to be judged by it in the day of final accounts. If they are called upon to give a reason for this implicit faith, they seldom go farther than to answer, "We have been brought up to believe the Bible; our fathers and mothers before us have believed it; and we have never thought of doubting it."

This ground of faith has not received the respectful consideration to which it is entitled. It is often stigmatized as purely traditional and unreasoning; and so it appears to be. But is it any the less valuable on this account? On what depends the value of faith in anything that is of a practical nature? On the reasons which the believer can give for his faith? or on the firmness with which he maintains his faith, and the exactness with which he puts it into practice? Faith in the genuineness of medicines, in the skill of physicians, in the honesty of men of business, in the accuracy of interest tables and of logarithms, in the constancy of friendship and of marital vows, in everything on which life and well-being depend, derives its value from the latter consideration, and not at all from the former. If the religion taught in the Bible is true, the blessings which it offers to men are bestowed on those who believe, and who live in accordance with their faith, without the slightest regard to the reasons or the causes which induced them to believe. This is true

263

not only of the blessings which it offers as the special gifts of God, but also of those noble traits of character which this faith brings forth as its natural fruits. Not one of these is dependent on the reasons which induce men to believe. This fact cannot be emphasized too strongly.

This ground of faith has been pronounced not only traditional and unreasoning, but insufficient for the trials to which faith must be subjected. For some persons it has proved insufficient; and these have either abandoned the faith, or found better ground for believing; but it has proved sufficient for the majority of believers in ages past, and it will for ages to come. If the good results of faith are dependent, not on the causes of it, but on its steadfastness and its fruits, it follows that a faith which does not waver, and which brings forth these fruits to the end of life, has a sufficient basis in which to rest. The faith of the class now under consideration does remain steadfast to the end, and it does bring forth the required fruits. Myriads of them are now living, and myriads more have gone to rest, the shield of whose faith was never pierced by a single dart of unbelief. These believers met the arguments of unbelief, so far as they encountered them, with a smile or a frown, according to the temperament of each; they pitied the unbeliever as an unfortunate and wayward man; they turned to their Bibles with greater confidence and affection in proportion as it was assailed; they walked humbly with their God, and truly with their neighbors; and in the hour of death they were not afraid. It is offered as an objection, that the same may be truly said of faith in other books, supposed to be sacred, and in other religions which are conceded to be of human origin. As respects the ground of faith, this must be admitted; but what follows? It does not follow that all books and religions thus received are equally true and equally beneficial to their adherents. The claims of each to be true depend on the evidences which can be presented in its favor; and this is supposed to be beyond the ken of the humble believers of whom we now speak. If any one of these religions is true and divine, the believer in it reaps all the good fruits of it; and if any is false, the believer in it reaps all the good that is in it, if any, and he also just as certainly tastes all the bitter fruits which a false system must necessary bear. The objection, then, is without weight; and the ground on which a countless host of God's children have rested their faith is vindicated. It has proved sufficient for them, though many of them have passed through much tribulation to the region in which they had laid up their treasures.

Broader Grounds of Belief

The preceding ground, satisfying as it is to the mass of uneducated believers, has proved insufficient for those who, either from the natural questionings of awakened thought, or from the attacks of unbelievers, have been constrained to ask whether education has guided them aright. All these inquire for the grounds on which their teachers have taught them, and they pass into the second or into the third class mentioned above, according to the extent of their subsequent investigations.

1. Most commonly, the first new ground to which these awakened minds advance, is this: they look to see who the teachers of their faith are; and they find that they constitute the overwhelming majority of the good, the wise and the learned, of this and of all past ages up to the age in which the Bible became a completed book. They see that these

men constitute the class best informed on the subject, and most likely, both on this account and on account of their goodness of heart, to decide the question correctly. They ascertain, too, that many of these men were converted from unbelief to belief, as the result of their investigations; and although they find that some have reversed this process, the number of the latter is so small in comparison as not to seriously affect the evidence.

That this is solid ground on which to stand is made more obvious when we reflect that it is the very ground on which the deductions of science are received by the mass of mankind. We accept what we are taught concerning the geography of distant lands, concerning geology, astronomy, chemistry, and the facts of all history, because we have confidence in our teachers; and if their deductions are called in question by a man here and there, it is sufficient for us that his objections amount to nothing in the estimation of the great majority of those who are competent judges. It is only the very few who are competent to investigate these sciences for themselves; and the rest of us are never reproached because we accept our faith from their hands. Scientific men who are thus credited by their less-informed neighbors, should be the last men on earth to censure Christians for receiving the Bible on similar ground.

It is said, however, that this ground of faith depends entirely on the circumstances that in the past the majority has been on the side of belief, and that should the majority at some future time turn the other way, the argument would be reversed, and would become equally strong in favor of unbelief. This is unquestionably true. The argument would be reversed, and the state of opinion among the common people would be reversed with it. This would be true on any ground of faith, for the common people always have been and always will be governed in their opinions on all subjects by the conclusions of the great majority of those who are known to be more competent judges than themselves. Should unbelief ever secure this majority, the Bible, having lost the offices of its army, would of course be deserted by the rank and file. But we need not anticipate such a day. If the Bible is from God, it can never come.

2. Others of the class now under consideration, while holding firmly to the ground of faith last mentioned, look still farther, and, considering the effects which faith in the Bible has had on all true and consistent believers, they find that these effects are good and only good continually. They find that only those believers who have not conformed their lives to the requirements of the book have failed to realize these good effects; and that those who have conformed to it most nearly have been the purest and best of men. They cannot believe that such traits are wrought into human character by the belief of a book whose writers are impostors, and whose distinctive claim for itself is a falsehood. They cannot believe this, because they have learned by their own experience, and by that of those who have gone before them, that the belief of falsehood is injurious to men, while the belief of truth alone is truly and permanently beneficial. Many eminent unbelievers have themselves admitted that the highest ideal of human life would be attained if men would live according to the requirements of this book, and thus out of their own mouths we confirm the solidity of this ground of belief.

A feeble attempt has been made to offset this argument by pointing to a very few men in heathen lands who have lived very noble lives and taught a very pure morality, though they never saw or heard of the Bible; but to this it is truly answered that the life of the noblest man who ever lived in heathen lands cannot compare to those of thousands who have believed the Bible; and that only so far as the lives and precepts of these noble heathens are in harmony with the teachings of the Bible, is there anything in them to be admired. The fact, then, instead of being an objection to our argument, only confirms it by furnishing additional proof of the ennobling effects of that which our Bible teaches.

3. A third ground for the faith of the second class of believers is one not so easily defined, but fully as substantial as either of the preceding. It is the stamp of truthfulness which is felt rather than seen as they read the Bible and reflect on its contents. They have observed that false narratives, even when most plausible, have an indefinable air or tone about them which awakens suspicion and causes us to pause and hesitate about receiving them; and that, on the other hand, there is an air or tone about truth which asserts itself and dissipates doubt. It is comparable to the ring of a sound bell, or of a piece of sound precelain, as distinguished from that of one sightly cracked. More profound thinkers may be able to analyze and define the characteristics of truth and error alluded to, but our second class of believers make no such attempt. The human mind is made for the reception of truth, and when it is uncorrupted it has a natural susceptibility to truth, analogous to that of the eye to light, and of the ear to sound, which enables it within certain limits to recognize both truth and falsehood. This instinct is no guide in matters of a purely scientific character; but in matters of history and morals it will assert itself, and its promptings are often irresistible. A juryman is often led by it to decide cases of property and life, when the explicit

testimony would have led him in the opposite direction. Now those of whom I speak feel, as they read their Bibles from day to day and year to year, that they are in mental and spiritual contact with narratives and precepts which have the ring of truth about them. They feel this so distinctly, and it impresses them so deeply, that they cannot shake it off if they would, and they cannot attempt to do so without doing violence to their moral nature.

It will be admitted that if God were in any proper sense the author of the Bible, it would bear these marks of its own truthfulness. Indeed, if He inspired its authors, He must have desired that His creatures should believe its statements and observe its precepts; and he would certainly impart this very quality to it. The fact, then, that the Bible has the identical effect on a vast multitude of its readers which its author must have designed if that author is God, is no mean proof that God is its author. This evidence can have but little effect on those who are as yet unbelievers, and who consequently do not receive the impression we refer to; but it is solid and satisfactory evidence to all those who have for this and other reasons combined received the book as true, and studied it for the good that is in it.

4. The next ground on which we plant our feet is found in the incomparable character of Him who is the central figure in the panorama which the Bible spreads out before us. Friends and foes alike admit that Jesus who is called the Christ occupies this position. He is the centre and soul of the New Testament, and, whether unbelievers will have it or not, the law and the prophets all pointed to him as their end. Now when we consider who the writers of the Bible were, what they were in their education, in their prejudices, in their hopes, and in their conceptions of humanity, we

are driven to the conclusion that it was impossible for them to either conceive or depict such a character as Jesus. This argument has been set forth by eloquent writers in whole volumes; and it has often been said that the conception and portrayal of such a character by these writers without divine inspiration would have been a greater miracle than any which Jesus is said to have wrought. Of course the word miracle is here used in its etymological sense of a mere wonder, and not in its scriptural sense of an immediate act of God. Though so often and so confidently published to the world, this argument has never met with a serious answer, so far as the present writer is informed. Until it shall be proved to be without force, we must be allowed to still believe that the Bible is the book of God, for this reason, even if we should be compelled to lay aside all others.

5. As a result of mature reflection on the last two grounds of faith, there spreads out before the believer another field of evidence, in which he beholds a wondrous adaptation of this book to the spiritual wants of our fallen race. That we are sinners before God, is the profound conviction of every thoughtful soul who realizes the existence of a divine being to whom we are responsible for our conduct. Every such person feels the need of something to impress upon him a keener sense of his unworthiness, to deliver him from the guilt which he has already incurred, and to give him ability to resist the enticements of sin. He looks in vain for deliverance and strength to all the systems of human philosophy, and to all the religions of earth except that of the Bible. In the revelations of this book he finds what he desires; or rather, he finds that which, whether consciously sought or not, meets and satisfies the longings of his soul. He finds in this book, as he thoughtfully and believingly reads it, power

to subdue his stubborn will, and to bring him in humble penitence to the foot-stool of the God whom it reveals. He finds in the tender mercy there offered to him through the atoning blood of a wondrous Redeemer, whose work is the characteristic and the glory of this religious system, the only conceivable release from the burden of his guilt; for only in forgiveness, free and final, can the guilty soul find peace. Receiving this heavenly gift, he enjoys a peace of mind which passes all understanding. Starting forward afresh in the journey of life, he finds the same good book furnishing him with hopes, and gratitude, and courage, which enable him to control himself as no other man can, by maxims of wisdom and holiness which gradually transform him into the spiritual image of his God, and fit him to dwell with God forever. With this experience, he cannot doubt that the book which has enabled him to attain it, and which claims to be the word of God, is all that it claims to be.

6. Some of the class of believers now under consideration have extended their readings into general history and the history of the church. All such have learned that the claim of the Bible to be the word of God has passed through fiery trials in the course of its history, such as would long since have brought it into contempt had it not been too well grounded to be overthrown. If the book had come down through the ages unchallenged, the continued hold which it had on the confidence of men would argue little in its favor; but instead of this, its claim has been hotly contested by men of genius and learning from the second century after Christ until the present time. All manner of literary weapons have been wielded against it, including the sneers of scoffers, the ridicule of the giddy and profligate, the criticisms of men of letters, the deductions of philosophers, and the researches

of historians. Decipherers of manuscripts and hieroglyphics, students of archaeology, delvers in the bowels of the earth, explorers of the solar system and of the stellar universe, analyzers of historical documents, and experts in comparative philology, have unitedly and separately assailed the Bible, many times proclaiming that they had put all of its friends to flight, and that soon it would have no intelligent man to uphold its claims; but through all these conflicts it has passed without loss in the number of its friends, and not only without loss, but with an ever-increasing number who insist that it is the word of God. The enemies of the book are boldly challenged to tell how this can be, if the high claim set up for it is false, or even doubtful.

This challenge is answered by the statement that the tenacious hold which the Bible has on the minds of men is the result of superstition, and of an obstinate conservatism which is natural to our race. The answer is refuted by the fact that it is not the superstitious part of our face, nor the part most given to blind conservatism, that has thus clung to the Bible. That portion of the race most given to these two weaknesses is found where the Bible is unknown, or is made subordinate to other rules of faith, as among Muslims and Buddhists. On the other hand, those nations which have shown themselves freest of all from superstition, and quickest of all to cast aside old errors and to sezie upon new truths, are the very nations which have clung most tenaciously to the Bible. Not only so, but the class of men in these nations most noted for faith in the Bible, includes in it leaders in human thought in every department of learning. To such an extent is this true, that when unbelievers of real learning and talent have for a time become leaders of great bodies of men, they have, as a rule, soon lost their leadership as a result of defeat in the conflicts which their attacks on the Bible have provoked. More than two or three might be named, who, in the memory of persons now living, have attained to such leadership and then lost it.

Now this whole series of battles has been fought over the single question, whether the Bible is the word of God, in the sense of our proposition. The proposition has thus far been so triumphantly maintained as to inspire us with the strongest conviction that it is true, and that it will continue to be maintained in the estimation of an ever increasing number of persons, until at last there shall be none to call it in question. The Bible has today an immensely wider recognition among men than at any previous period in its history. More copies of it are now annually published and sold than ever before; more, perhaps, than of any one thousand other books combined. It is printed and read as no other book ever has been or ever will be, in all the languages of the earth which have an alphabet, while many of these languages have been provided with alphabets for the very purpose that the Bible might be printed in them. It is one of the most wonderful events of this present century of wonders, that on May 1st, 1881, when the Revised Version of the English New Testament was published, more than one million copies were sold in a single day, and this among the people of all the earth who already had in hand the largest number of New Testaments. There is nothing comparable to this in the history of books. These facts guarantee that its power over the next generation will be far greater and more world-wide than it is now. Indeed, if we judge the future by the rules of ordinary foresight, the facilities which now exist for the free circulation of this book throughout the world, and the multitude of rich and powerful friends who esteem it a high privilege to expend fabulous sums of money to put it into the hands of every human being, argue a future for it which is far more glorious than its most enthusiastic friends have dreamed, or Christian poets have sung.

A book with such a history and such prospects, all due to the fact that it is believed to be the word of God, cannot be standing on a false claim, if there is any such thing as distinguishing between documents that are false and those that are true. On this ground we rest our faith; and we feel that in doing so we would be standing on a rock, if there was nothing else beneath our feet. But we stand not on this alone. We step backward and forward on the six different grounds which we have enumerated, with no uncertainty in our tread; and when we think of them all, we realize that the believer has within his reach, if he will reflect soberly, and read but a little outside of his Bible, abundant evidence to satisfy an honest soul, and to defend his faith against the assaults of unbelief.

The Broadest Grounds of Belief

The third class of believers is composed of those who have made a thorough, systematic and scientific investigation of all the grounds on which an intelligent faith can rest. They have pursued the following lines of inquiry, though not always in the order in which we name them.

1. *Preservation of the text of the Biblical books.* Knowing that all books written so long ago as the books of the Bible, were transmitted to posterity for many centuries by means of manuscript copies not always made with proper care; and that some ancient books have undergone changes

274

from this cause such as to render the latest copies extremely inaccurate; they have first inquired as to the preservation of the text of the biblical books, so as to know whether they have suffered in like manner. They are aware that even were the Bible originally the word of God, it is valueless now, if human hands have changed it to such an extent that we cannot know what parts remain as they were first written; and they also know that if any part remains unchanged, this much is still the word of God if it was so at the beginning. If this inquiry ends in proving that the books have lost their essential character in transmission, we need to proceed no farther with our investigation; but if otherwise, we then take another step, and inquire into their origin and original character.

It is perhaps impossible to copy a book of considerable size with a pen, without making some mistakes; and the more frequently it is thus copied, each copyist using the work of his predecessor, the greater the number of mistakes in the later copies. The multiplication of copies is the multiplication of errors. Not so with printing. On the contrary, when the types are once correctly set, all copies printed from them are exactly alike, and they may be multiplied to any extent without mistakes. As a consequence, the inquiry as to the preservation of the text of the Bible is limited in time to the period between its first composition and the invention of printing, or, at the latest, to the time when printing became an accurate art. This was in the early part of the sixteenth century, the first printed copy of any part of the Bible having been put to press about the middle of the century previous. Errors of copyists then came to an end, and our question is, how many and how serious were the errors introduced previous to that time?

The investigation of this question was begun in earnest about the close of the seventeenth century, and it has been prosecuted with great diligence till the present time. Many eminent men have devoted their whole lives to it, and others, the labor of many years. They have ransacked the ancient libraries of Europe, Africa and western Asia, in search of manuscript copies of the New Testament, and have found more than two thousand of them, some containing the whole New Testament, but the great majority only parts of it.[2] These they have compared with one another, word by word, and letter by letter, noting every variation. They have also taken up the ancient translations of the book, determined the Greek words from which the renderings in them were made, and compared these with the words of the manuscripts. In most instances the translations thus used were made from Greek copies of an earlier date than that of any manuscript now in existence; and thus they represent a Greek text nearer to the autographs of the biblical penmen. They have also gathered out of the writings of early Christian authors, who lived before the date of existing manuscripts, the quotations which they made from copies in use in their days, and have compared these with the same passages in versions and existing manuscripts. Having thus exhausted the sources of information as to how these books have read, in every line and word, and in every age of their existence, they have qualified themselves to state with the certainty of exact knowledge, to what extent the text of the New Testament has been preserved in its original form. The results may be briefly stated as follows:

---

2. As of 1981 over 5000 Greek manuscripts, whole or in part, have been found of the New Testament.

a. The manuscripts, versions and quotations agree to such an extent as to leave no doubt as to the original reading of seven-eighths of the whole text, in word and letter. In other words, seven-eighths of the words originally written in these books have been preserved in existing copies precisely as they were at first. This much is unquestionably the word of God now, if it ever was.

b. So large a number of the variations between copies consist in mere mistakes in spelling, which do not obscure the identity of the misspelled words, that when these are taken out of the account, as they should be, fifty-nine sixtieths of all the words are found to be unchanged.

c. The number of changes in the text which affect the meaning, and require the skill of the critic to determine the original reading, is only about one-thousandth part of the whole, and these have been so marked in printed copies by textual critics, that a scholar can put his finger on every one of them.

d. By combining the results of these investigations, and throwing out from the text known errors, textual critics have now presented us with a Greek Testament which contains the exact words written by its authors, and this without the least doubt, except in specified instances.

e. An examination of the few passages of which the readings are still doubtful, reveals the fact that if we should erase from the book all of these passages, we would lose from our New Testament not a single precept, promise, or fact, of material importance; for all such which might be affected by the erasure are found in other passages, which are undoubtedly genuine.

f. These results are accessible not to the learned alone; but they have been placed within the reach of all who can read the English language, by means of the Revised English version.[3] This version is not only translated from the corrected Greek text, but it exhibits in marginal notes, intelligible to the unlearned reader, every word in regard to the genuineness of which there remains the least doubt, and it indicates the degree of doubtfulness which attaches to each.

On the question, then, of the preservation of the original text of the New Testament, a question which was once regarded as fraught with extreme danger to the cause of the Bible, all apprehension has passed away; the enemies of the book are silenced, and its friends are satisfied. For all time to come, unless the art of printing shall be lost, the question will never be raised again. It is, indeed, one of the marvels of this marvelous age, that now, after the passage of seventeen centuries, we have a purer text of the Greek New Testament than has existed since the second century after Christ.

In regard to the original text of the Old Testament, the investigation has not been completed, and the results are not so definite. Enough has been accomplished, however, to justify the following statements:

a. From the second to the sixth century after Christ, a succession of learned Jews, some living in Palestine and some in Babylon, devoted themselves to the critical study of the text of their Bible, and brought into use such rules to govern copyists that the variations between copies made at that time are fewer and more insignificant by far than in the Greek manuscripts of the New Testament.

---

3. Published in England in 1881. The American Standard Version (1901) is an American edition of this version. The New American Standard Bible continues this tradition.

b. So far as can be judged from quotations made from the Old Testament previous to the time mentioned, and by the translations into other tongues, the text had not suffered materially before these stringent rules were adopted.

c. While this is true, it is ascertained that in some of the books there are interpolations and verbal alterations made by editors and copyists, but of such a character that they are easily separated from the text, and that they do not materially affect the meaning of the passages in which they occur. There are also mistakes in names and figures, many of which are corrected in the context.

d. It is highly probable that there are other changes of the text which have not been detected and pointed out; but it is highly improbable that these are any more serious than those mentioned above in the New Testament. We therefore feel safe in the present state of our knowledge, and can patiently await the results of further investigation.

2. *Authorship of the Biblical Books.* Having thus ascertained that the text of the Bible has been preserved to us with all the accuracy necessary to practical purposes, we have next inquired whether the several books can be traced back to the authors to whom they are ascribed.

This task has been accomplished with respect to the New Testament by evidence so incontestable that even the most hostile critics admit it in regard to the Apocalypse and four of the most important Epistles, viz., Romans, First and Second Corinthians, and Galatians. While denying the genuineness of Luke's Gospel, Acts of Apostles, Hebrews, Colossians, and Ephesians, they assign these to dates near the close of the first century; and they place all the others between the years 115 and 150, except Second Peter, which they bring down nearly to the year 200.[4] As the period within which all of the books purport to have been written is the second half of the first century, unbelief is crowded into very narrow ground by the evidence which has extorted from it these admissions. This evidence is that of ancient manuscript copies of the Greek Testament, of which we have two still existing that were written in the fourth century; that of catalogues, or lists of the books, made out by early Christians, of which we have a succession reaching back into the second century; that of translations into other tongues, of which we have two reaching to the middle of the same century, which was in the life time of men who knew the Apostles; that of quotations made from them by early writers, of which we have some from most of the books and made by men who knew some of the Apostles; and that furnished by the contents of the books themselves, which, in the case of every book, is satisfactory, and is very strong for some for which the external evidence is comparatively weak. With this evidence, so nearly overcoming the resistance of the most determined foes of the Bible, we are satisfied; and we believe that all the books in our New Testament were written in the apostolic age; and that they were written by the men whose names they bear, with the exception of the Epistle to the Hebrews, as to the authorship of which there is difference of opinion among believers.

In regard to the Old Testament, the evidence on this branch of our inquiry, like that in regard to the text, is not so complete, owing to the remoteness of the period into which the inquiry leads us, and the consequent scarcity of of documents from which to derive evidence. In the time of

---

4. As of 1981 many liberal New Testament critics are more inclined to date most or all of the New Testament books within the first century.

Christ all of these books unquestionably existed, and constituted, as they do now, the sacred Scriptures of the Jews. Furthermore, they had all been translated into Greek, and had been circulated in the version called the Septuagint, or Alexandrian version, for at least one hundred and fifty years before Christ: for it is now conceded that this version was completed not later than the year 150 B.C., and that the first part of it was made as early as 280 B.C. This is demonstrative proof that the books existed far back toward the time when the latest of them was composed. This much is universally conceded by unbelievers, and our field of inquiry, in point of time, lies back of that period.

All the historical books of the Old Testament, together with the book of Job, are anonymous: that is, they do not name their authors. So far as their authors are known at all, they are known from the testimony of other writers; and the correctness of our knowledge depends on the reliability of this testimony. The most reliable of these witnesses are unquestionably Christ and his Apostles. They ascribe the Pentateuch to Moses; the prophets, so far as they quote them, to the men whose names they bear; and some of the Psalms to David, who is represented in the book itself as the composer of about half of the collection. Concerning the other anonymous books they give no specific testimony; but they give us a general warrant for receiving all, in that all were parts of the sacred Scriptures which they in a general way cited as the word of God. This usage does not imply the certainty that no book, or part of a book, had been improperly placed in the collection; but it does imply that no large amount of that kind of work had been done—none which would render improper the general designation of the collection as the word of God.

Much controversy has existed over the genuineness [authorship] of most of these books, and the antiquity of others; and unbelievers have not hesitated to reject some which are endorsed by Jesus and the Apostles. It would require a large volume to set forth the points of argument in this controversy, and of course it cannot be attempted in this essay. It is sufficient for our present purpose to say that the principal ground on which we receive the Old Testament as the word of God is that named above, the testimony of Jesus Christ and his Apostles. This is sufficient for all the demands of the Christian faith; and if it fails to support any particular book, on that book our faith will be found not at all dependent.

3. *Historical Credibility of Biblical Books.* Next after the inquiries concerning the preservation of the text of the Bible, and the genuineness of its books, comes the question, whether the facts recorded in it are credible and its revelations reliable. If they are, we can trust the Bible implicitly as the word of God; if not, the conclusions which we have thus far reached are without value.

There are historical tests by which the credibility of historical documents is determined. We first inquire as to the sources of information accessible to the writers, and used by them. If they speak from personal observation, being honest men, or from the testimony of eyewitnesses, they have the highest degree of credibility as regards the facts recorded. If they are more remote from the facts, their credibility diminishes proportionately. As regards the New Testament writers, if all of them except the author of the Apocalypse, and the author of the four great Pauline Epistles lived after the death of the generation in which the events transpired, as is claimed by unbelievers, their knowledge

was traditional, and their records unreliable. This consideration accounts for the unanimity with which this hypothesis
is maintained by unbelievers. But if these writings were all
composed, as believers have to their own satisfaction made
out, by the men to whom they are credited, then they are historical documents of the first degree of credibility, according to
accepted rules of evidence. The latter conclusion has been
established by the evidences which we have stated above.

The second method of testing such documents is to compare them with other histories of the same period, and note
the agreements and disagreements. This comparison has
been made in two ways: first, by comparing the references
which other writers make to New Testament facts with the
New Testament accounts of them; and second, by treating
in like manner the New Testament allusions to events more
fully set forth by these other writers. In both ways the biblical
books stand the test; for although a few contradictions have
been alleged, not one has been made out. On the contrary,
a remarkable harmony has been found to exist, a harmony
which, when we remember that all these other writers were
hostile to the religion set forth in the New Testament, is
accounted for only on the supposition of the reality of the
facts involved in the comparison.

The third test is a close comparison of these documents
with one another, where they refer to the same matters, to
see whether or not their representations are harmonious.
This comparison takes into view not only the explicit statements which the writers make, but also allusions made by
one to events described by another. The enemies of the
book have gone over this ground, from side to side, and
end to end, searching as with a microscope, for inconsistencies; and they have paraded alleged inconsistencies in

such numbers as to appall the inexperienced reader when he first encounters them. So confident are they in the correctness of their specifications, that they commonly treat with supreme contempt the man who denies it. Yet believing scholars have followed them step by step, and proved in reference to every specification, that it is either a false charge, or a charge based on some illogical assumption. A contradiction exists only when two statements are made which cannot both be true. If, on any rational hypothesis whatever, both *may* be true, whether they can both be proved to be true or not, there is no proof of a contradiction. After making a fair allowance for transcriptional errors, no such contradiction has been proved between any two New Testament writers; and if none has yet been proved, it is not at all probable that one will ever be.

Not content with this merely negative result, believers have also gone through the New Testament books, both historical and epistolary, in search of internal evidences of their truthfulness; and they have found a multitude of purely incidental agreements between them, which can be accounted for only on the supposition that they all wrote with the most minute accuracy. Many of these coincidences are found in the midst of apparent discrepancies, where they lay hidden until the appearance of discrepancy was dissolved by closer scrutiny, and the unseen agreement surprisingly brought to light. The result of the whole inquiry is not only the triumphant vindication of the New Testament writers from the charge of contradiction, but the demonstration of the fact that they are the most authentic writers known to literature.

In regard to one particular class of events, the miraculous, unbelievers contest the preceding conclusion with the most desperate persistency.

It is impossible for a man to remain an unbeliever and believe the miraculous events recorded in the New Testament; consequently the acceptance or rejection of these is the crucial test of man's faith in Christ. Every argument which philosophy, history and science could suggest has been brought to bear against their credibility, but these have all been refuted again and again by believers. We shall not attempt in this essay to go over the ground of this argumentation, for the two reasons, that it is too voluminous, and that there is a shorter way. After all that has been said on both sides, the question turns finally on the evidence for a single miracle, without which all of the others would have occurred in vain, and which, if it be established as real, carries all the others with it. We mean the resurrection of Jesus. No man who believes this event cares to deny any other material fact mentioned in the New Testament; and if a man denies this, it is a small matter if he denies everything else.

The direct evidence for this event is stronger than that for any other event in ancient history. It consists primarily of the testimony of men and and women who had been intimate with Jesus before his death, and who saw him alive after his crucifixion and burial. We receive the testimony of four of these witnesses directly from their own pens; that of the Apostles Matthew and John in their Gospels, and that of John, Peter and Paul in their Epistles, and in the Apocalypse. Paul, it is true, was not familiar with the person of Jesus before his death, but his testimony has peculiar characteristics which render it not less reliable than that of any other witness. The testimony of the other witnesses also comes to us through these men, and through the writings of Mark and Luke, who were companions of all the witnesses, and had every possible opportunity to know what their testimony was. The competency of these witnesses, both with respect to their capacity for correct observation and their opportunities for correct knowledge, is so manifest to every careful reader of the accounts, that it is not too much to say that no well informed and candid reader doubts it. Their honesty in giving the testimony was subjected to the severest tests, by the losses, afflictions and persecutions which befell them on account of it; and each succeeding generation since their own, on considering these tests, declares them honest witnesses by so vast a majority, including many unbelievers, that the few who doubt it prove by the doubt that their minds are in an abnormal condition. The number of the witnesses has also been found to be sufficient, as is proved by the fact, that no believer thinks his faith would be stronger if the witnesses were more numerous, and that no unbeliever claims, that were the witnesses more numerous he would believe. Forasmuch, then, as the witnesses are sufficiently numerous, are thoroughly competent and unquestionably honest, it is impossible to have stronger testimony; and therefore it is impossible to establish any fact which depends on human testimony more firmly.

These considerations present the force of the evidence from a positive point of view. It is equally strong when viewed negatively, as when we demand of the unbeliever to account for the disappearance of the dead body of Jesus, on any other hypothesis than that of his resurrection; and when we further demand of him, to account for the unquestioning belief of these witnesses, that they saw him alive, conversed with him, and handled his person, as is recorded. To the former of these demands, some of the older unbelievers have responded, by denying that he actually died on the cross, and by affirming that he died naturally in the tomb, and disappeared by going elsewhere and remaining in retirement until he died like other men. This hypothesis encounters so many objections which readily present themselves to those acquainted with the narratives, that it has been adopted by very few, and it has been refuted by none more successfully than by later unbelievers. With almost one voice, recent unbelieving writers unite with believrs in holding that Jesus was certainly dead when he was placed in the tomb. Most of these have deliberately shunned the question, what became of the body? and Christian Baur goes so far as to declare that the question is outside of historical inquiry,[5] thus putting outside of historical inquiry the most momentous event, if it be an event, of which history speaks—an event which, whether real or not, has affected human history more profoundly than any other that ever transpired on the earth. To refuse inquiry into such a fact, and this too, while writing a history of the church, is to acknowledge that no account of it could be given which would not put to shame the man who does not believe it. Other unbelievers, notably Strauss and Renan, have attempted to account for the disappearance of the body;[6] but their attempts are so futile that Prof. Huxley repudiates them, and goes back to the old abandoned theory of a natural resuscitation. This he does in his recent controversy with Dr. Wace. The fact that nothing better than those vain and contradictory attempts have been devised by unbelievers, a succession of whom for fourteen hundred years has been tugging at this problem, is conclusive proof, almost equal to the direct

---

5. "The question as to the nature and the reality of the resurrection lies outside the sphere of historical inquiry." *Church History*, 1: 42.

6. *New Life of Jesus.* 1: 431, 432; *Apostles*, 78-80.

testimony itself, that the only way to account for the disappearance of the body is to admit that it was miraculously restored to life.

All parties, even those who deny the actual death of Jesus, admit that his disciples became convinced of his resurrection, and believed that they saw him alive repeatedly after his crucifixion. Various attempts have been made to account for this belief on the supposition that it was a delusion; but they are all so shallow and so false to the facts in the case that any tyro in discussion can answer them at sight—so shallow and unsatisfying that Christian Baur, after considering them all, and doubtless desiring, if he could, to accept some one of them, declares that no psychological analysis can account for this belief.[7] We may say, then, that it is impossible for an unbeliever to account for either the belief of the first Christians, or the disappearance of the dead body of Jesus; and as it is impossible to have stronger proof than we have in the way of direct testimony, the resurrection of Jesus shall forever stand as one of the fixed events in human history, to be believed more and more till the end of time. This fact being established, the discussion about miracles, either those said to have been wrought by Jesus, or those wrought by his Apostles, is closed; and with this question is settled the question, whether the New Testament is a part of the word of God, and its teachings a divine rule of faith; for if these men wrought miracles in attestation of the truth of their utterances, the truth of these utterances is stamped with the seal of God.

---

7. "Though we assume that an inward spiritual process was possible by which the unbelief of the disciples at the time of the death of Jesus was changed into belief in his resurrection, still no psychological analysis can show what that process was." *Church History,* 1: 42.

The credibility of the Old Testament narratives, like the genuineness of the Old Testament books, is a more difficult question, because of the greater difficulty in applying to these documents the tests of historical criticism. We know less about the authors of the books; far less about the tests of honesty and competency to which they were subjected; and the contemporary documents which remain to us are few and fragmentary. Still, we have sufficient ground, apart from the inspiration of the writers, for believing that in these books we have a record of facts.

The serious and religious character of the books indicates that the authors were aiming to tell the truth; and there are other internal evidences of honesty of purpose. So far as their statements can be tested by contemporaneous documents, such as Egyptian and Assyrian inscriptions, their accuracy is confirmed. When the same transactions are mentioned in different books, some discrepancies are found in figures and names; but these are accounted for by the known liability of transcribers to make more frequent mistakes in such matters than in others. On the other hand, a careful examination of parallel passages in the different books reveals a large number of minute and undesigned coincidences which are accounted for only by extreme accuracy of statement. The geographical and political allusions, too, in which the books abound, are all so exact as to prove not only accuracy of statement, but fullness of knowledge.

But above all, the credibility of the Old Testament narrations is proved by the testimony of Jesus Christ and the Apostles. They cite as real many of the very facts in the Old Testament record, which are pronounced by unbelievers the most incredible. We may enumerate among these, the creation of the first human pair, and the account of the origin of woman; the tempation and the fall of this pair; the destruction of human and animal life by the flood; the miraculous destruction of Sodom, together with the rescue of Lot and the fate of his wife; the call of Abraham, the promises made to him, and his trial by the call to sacrifice his son; the afflictions and the restoration of Job; the miracles in Egypt, at the Red Sea and in the wilderness; the fall of Jericho; the miraculous preservation of Jonah in the belly of the fish; the three years' drouth in the days of Elijah, begun and terminated in answer to prayer; the healing of Naaman by Elisha, and others. Now the acceptance of these events as real by Jesus and the Apostles, is sufficient ground for their acceptance by all who believe in Jesus. But the evidence reaches farther than these particular events; for unless there were reasons for accepting these which did not apply to other Old Testament events, we must conclude that the latter were accepted also, and that Jesus and the Apostles held all the Old Testament history to be authentic. No such reasons have been alleged; and certainly such a distinction cannot be based on the greater inherent credibility of the events quoted and endorsed; for with the single exception of the miracle of causing the sun to stand still in its course, nothing so wonderful as some of these is on record. Moreoever, the manner in which the Old Testament was constantly cited by these authorities precludes the supposition that they had in mind any such distinction. It follows that Jesus and the Apostles endorse the Old Testament as real history. More solid ground than this for believing we cannot have, and we do not desire.

If the contents of the Bible consisted only in facts which passed under the personal observation of the writers, evidence additional to that already presented would scarcely be called for. But much of the record has respect to past events, which could not have been witnessed by the writers; much to matters in the spiritual world which men in the flesh could not know by their unaided powers; much to the will and the thoughts of God, alike inscrutable; and much to the distant future which no mortal vision can penetrate. In order that the statements of the writers on such subjects may be taken into our creed, we must have satisfactory evidence that they enjoyed supernatural means of obtaining and imparting knowledge. If they did, this not only gives good ground for believing them on these topics, but it also imparts a new element of certainty to their statements on matters of ordinary history. Thus we reach the question of the inspiration of the Bible writers, and we see the necessity for settling this question before our survey of the grounds of faith will be complete.

4. *Inspiration of the Biblical Books.* Of the inspiration of the Apostles, those who have accepted the deduction already reached in this essay need no better proof and can have none better than the statements of the Apostles themselves; seeing they are proved to be reliable in their statements even in regard to miraculous events. Their statements show that Christ, previous to his death, promised to bestow upon the Twelve such an impartation of the Holy Spirit, that when called on to answer for themselves before earthly rulers they should not be anxious as to how or what they should speak; that they should not even premeditate; but that the Holy Spirit would give them in that hour what they should say: "For," said he, "it is not you that speak, but the Spirit of your Father who speaketh in you" [Matt. 10:19, 20]. He told them also, without special reference to their arraignment before rulers, that the Spirit would bring all things to their remembrance which he had spoken to them,

291

and guide them into all the truth [John 14:26; 16:13]. As sure as those promises were fulfilled, when we read what the Apostles said and wrote after the fulfillment, we must receive it as not coming from them alone, but from the Spirit of God, with whom there can be no falsehood or mistake. To speak of a lapse of memory in the writing is to deny the fulfillment of the promise.

That these promises were fulfilled, we are assured by the author of Acts of Apostles, who was a witness of much that he records, and a reliable reporter of all. They began to be fulfilled on the first Pentecost after the resurrection, and the process continued throughout the lives of the Apostles, the Spirit constantly giving evidence of his continued presence in them by signs and wonders which accompanied their preaching. In addition to the evidence of this writer, we have that of some of the Apostles themselves in their Epistles. Even in the four great epistles of Paul, which unbelievers acknowledge to be written by Paul, and to have been written by an honest man, there are repeated allusions to miracles which he wrought by the Holy Spirit, and a most positive declaration that he received directly from the Spirit, in words taught by it, things which he revealed to his fellowmen. These miracles were his own acts, in regard to the reality of which he could not be mistaken, and therefore he either made false representations, which would nullify the admission of his honesty, or the miracles were real, and his claim to inspiration as real as the miracles which attested it. The same is true of the other Apostles. Believers, therefore, stand on the established fact, that the writers of the New Testament, so many as were Apostles, wrote under the guidance of the Spirit of God, and that as a consequence they wrote without error on all the subjects within the range of their offical utterances. As to those writers who were not apostles, they belong to the class to which the Apostles imparted a measure of the Spirit which they themselves possessed, and we believe that they also were inspired. It is true that Luke, who is one of these, claims to have acquired knowledge of what he writes concerning Jesus by careful inquiry from the eye-witnesses; but this, instead of being a denial of his own inspiration, as some have affirmed, only shows that he employed the natural means of gaining knowledge. It does not touch the question as to his guidance by the Spirit in discriminating between the true and the false, and in writing with proper accuracy that which he had learned.

The evidence of the inspiration of the Old Testament rests on somewhat different ground. The prophets all assert in some form their own inspiration, and their assertions are abundantly supported by the fulfillment of their predictions. The historical and poetical writers, as a rule, make no such claim, though their books contain many internal evidences of inspiration, which, in an elaborate discussion of the subject, it would be proper to set forth. The most conclusive evidence, however, in reference to them all, is found in statements of the New Testament, and in this essay we shall content ourselves with presenting these:

a. Passages from nearly all the prophetic books of the Old Testament are quoted in the New as having been fulfilled by events in the career of Christ or in that of the Church. These citations were made, not to prove the inspiration of the prophets, but, being made to persons who believed the prophets, they were intended to show that the events which fulfilled them were brought about in accordance with the predetermined purpose and foreknowledge of God. But while they were made for this purpose, they also prove the inspiration of the prophets, seeing that only by direct inspiration could the latter have revealed the purpose and foreknowledge of God. So, then, these citations serve the double purpose of confirming the claims of Jesus, and proving the inspiration of the prophets. Some of them, it is true, are not predictions, but sayings of the prophets which found fulfillment as proverbs are fulfilled; but a sufficient number of them are actual predictions to answer the purpose of our argument. The fulfillments are obvious to our own understanding, and the recognition of them by Jesus and the Apostles assures us that our understanding does not mislead us.

b. As to the other books of the Old Testament, they are so quoted that their inspiration is either expressly or indirectly affirmed. Jesus quotes from Genesis the concluding verse in the account of the creation of woman, as the word of God (Matt. 19:4, 5), and this it could not have been if the writer had not been divinely inspired. He quotes from Exodus the fifth commandment of the Decalogue, as both the word of Moses and the commandment of God (Mark 7:8-10); and it could have been neither had it not been written by Moses through revelation from God. He quotes a passage from Deuteronomy as the first of all the commandments, and one from Leviticus as the second (Mark 12:28-31, *cf.* Deut. 6:4; Lev. 19:8). He affirms that the words in Exodus, represented as spoken by God to Moses at the burning bush, were the real words of God, and the book from which He quotes them He calls the book of Moses (Mark 12:26). Some of the Psalms are quoted in the same way. Jesus quotes one with the formula, "David said in the Holy Spirit" (Mark 12:35), thus affirming both its authorship by David and David's inspiration. Peter quotes another

Psalm, says that David wrote it, calls David a prophet, and says that he wrote the passage concerning the resurrection of the Christ (Acts 2:24-31); while all the Apostles unitedly declare that God spoke through the Holy Spirit by the mouth of his servant David, their father, in the second Psalm (Acts 4:24-27).

c. Besides these citations from particular books with the assertion of their inspiration, both Jesus and the Apostles make general statements of the same import concerning groups of books, and concerning the Old Testament as a whole. Jesus rebuked his disciples for not believing what the prophets had written about Himself, and, "beginning from Moses and all the prophets, he interpreted in all the Scriptures the things concerning himself" (Luke 24:25-27). He afterward said to the Twelve "All things must needs be fulfilled which are written in the law of Moses, and the prophets, and the Psalms, concerning me" (Luke 24:44). But what things could have been written in any of these books concerning him, things which were prophetic and must be fulfilled, unless their authors wrote by divine inspiration? Again, Jesus rebuked His enemies for their unbelief, and said to them, "Think not that I will accuse you to the Father; there is one that will accuse you, even Moses, on whom ye have set your hope. For if ye believed Moses ye would have believed me; for he wrote of me. But if ye believe not his writings, how shall ye believe my words?" (John 5:45-47). Here He not only recognizes certain writings as the writings of Moses, the very writings undoubtedly which his hearers ascribed to Moses; but He asserts that Moses wrote of him. But Moses could not have written of Him fifteen hundred years before He was born, unless he wrote by inspiration. Jesus probably refers in this citation more

295

particularly to the passage in Deuteronomy, which the Apostle Peter also quotes and ascribes to Moses (Acts 3:22, 23), and which inspiration alone could have enabled him to write.

Passing by other citations which might be made, we content ourselves with a single one from the Apostle Paul, the well known declaration, "Every scripture inspired of God, is also profitable for teaching, for reproof, for correction, for instruction in righteousness," etc. If this passage were isolated, it would have no special bearing on our proposition; but it is immediately preceded by the remark to Timothy, "From a child thou hast known the sacred writings, which are able to make thee wise unto salvation through faith which is in Christ Jesus" (II Tim. 3:15-17). This shows that the scriptures of which he speaks are those in which Timothy had been instructed and these were unquestionably our present Old Testament scriptures. These Paul represents as "inspired of God"; and that he believed them to be so is obvious not only from this passage, but from the way in which he cites them throughout his writings. Indeed, nothing is more certain than that Paul and all the Apostles regarded the Old Testament as a collection of inspired writings, and this alone should settle the question with all who regard the Apostles as inspired men.

In concluding this part of my argument, it may not be amiss to say, that in nothing which I have read from the pens of critics unfavorable to my conclusions, have I observed more sophistical reasoning than in their treatment of passages in the New Testament which are relied on to prove the inspiration of the Old. This is notably the case in the works of some writers who claim full faith in the infallibility of Jesus Christ.

We have now stated the grounds on which we receive the Bible as the word of God; and as we stand on the pinnacle of our last evidence, the inspiration of its writers, and look back over the field which we have traversed, every step which we have taken appears safer, and every part of the ground on which we have stood appears firmer. We can now see, as we could not so clearly see at first, why it is that a mere education in the Christian faith fixes that faith so deeply in the soul that it can seldom be eradicated. It is because the biblical books were intended by their author to have just such a power. An eminent unbeliever pours out the bitterness of a soul that has lost this faith in these mournful words: "I would gladly give away all that I am, and all I ever may become, all the years, every one of them, which may be given me to live, for but one week of my old child's faith, to go back to calm and peace again, and then to die in hope. Oh, for one look of the blue sky, as it looked then when we called it heaven."[8] Why did it not appear to the unhappy man that a faith so pure and heavenly must have come from God?

We can now see more clearly why a large majority of the more learned and wise and good of every land where the Bible has been known have believed it to be the word of God, and have so taught their children; why it is that belief in the Bible has made those who have lived consistenly with their faith the best and purest of human kind; why it is that in reading the Bible there is constantly felt by the good a sense of its truthfulness; why it is that its central figure is a character which no man or set of men could have conceived or portrayed without help from God; and why it is

---

8. *Nemesis of Faith*, J. A. Froude, 27.

that the Bible, though assailed by powerful foes in a long succession of ages, and often betrayed by those who had been its friends, has come down to our age with a constantly increasing multitude of the good and the brave who proclaim it the word of God, and who send it over land and sea to gladden the nations who have been perishing without it. We can understand why a mysterious providence, mysterious no longer, has so wonderfully preserved its text from corruption; and why it is that links of evidence, which might have been lost but for that same providence, have been preserved so that we can trace its books, so far as need be, to the very men in remote ages who wrote them, and that we can test the truthfulness of these writers to our deepest satisfaction. It is all because the Bible is God-inspired.

The Grounds on Which We Receive the Bible as the Only Rule of Faith and Practice

We now pass to the last division of our subject, the grounds on which we regard the Bible as the only rightful rule to direct the faith, and to control the conduct of men; in other words, the grounds on which we hold it to be the only rightful creed and book of discipline for the church. We receive it thus, because it was given to us by God for this very purpose. The fact that it is from God makes it our duty to believe it, even though nothing were said of this duty in the book itself; and the same fact makes it our duty to observe all the precepts in it which are addressed to us. But we are not left to inferences, however necessary, for a knowledge of this duty; it is set forth clearly in the book itself. At the close of the opening sermon of Jesus concerning his kingdom, it is declared that men stand or fall before God, as they hear and do, or hear and do not the sayings of Jesus. He declared to his apostles when sending them forth, "He that receiveth you receiveth me, and he that receiveth me receiveth him that sent me" [Matt. 10:40]. He also assured them that during the regeneration, while he should be sitting on his throne, they should sit on twelve thrones judging the twelve tribes of Israel; and consequently, we find them, from Pentecost onward, speaking as ambassadors of Christ, and requiring obedience from all the disciples. Among the last words of the chief man of the Twelve are these: "This is now, beloved, the second epistle that I write to you, and in both of them I stir up your sincere mind by putting you in remembrance that you should remember the words that were spoken before the holy prophets, and the commandment of the Lord and Savior through your apostles" [II Pet. 3:1, 2]. But why argue a proposition which is not disputed? All who receive the Bible as the word of God agree that it is a divinely appointed rule of faith and conduct. They agree that if a man denies any part of the Bible, interpolated passages excepted, he is to that extent unsound in the faith; if he refuses to obey any precept among those now binding, he is to that extent sinful; and that in both cases he is to be dealt with accordingly by the church and by individual disciples. Believers differ only as to the parts of the Scripture which should govern us now, and as to their exclusiveness as a rule of discipline.

Because the Old Testament was the God-given law of the old dispensation, and is still binding on the faith of Christians, many have concluded that it is still binding as our rule of conduct; but the New Testament makes it clear that this conclusion is erroneous. The voice of God in the scene of the transfiguration, proclaiming, in the presence of Moses

299

the lawgiver and of Elijah the prophet, "This is my beloved Son; hear ye him" [Matt. 17:5], made Jesus not only the supreme, but the only lawgiver in the new dispensation. In compliance with this proclamation, we are taught by the Apostle Paul that while the law was our tutor to bring us to Christ, now that faith is come we are no longer under the tutor; that Christ has abolished, in his flesh, the law of commandments contained in ordinances; that the first covenant, having been found defective, has vanished away and given place to the second. In this change from the old to the new, much of the old has been re-enacted, including all that was originally intended to be perpetual and universal. This part is binding now, not because it was in the old, but because it is re-enacted in the new. The New Testament is, then, the divine rule of discipline under Christ; and our final question is, whether it is the only rule, whether it excludes all rules devised by the wisdom of men.

All Protestants agree that it is the only infallible rule, but many hold that we are at liberty to frame creeds and rules of discipline based on our own fallible judgment. This question has been decided for us by Jesus in deciding for the Jews one which involved the same principle. Their wise men, in the course of ages, had concluded that in addition to the law which God has given them, some other rules were important, if not indispensable; and they adopted such rules, one by one, until they accumulated a large body of them, which they styled the tradition of the elders. These they enforced on the consciences of the people, and Jesus was himself adjudged a sinner when he neglected to observe them. He dealt with these rules in a most summary manner. He first pointed out the fact that at least one of them made void a commandment of God; and, adopting the language of one of their prophets, he indignantly repudiated the whole body of their tradition, and laid down a law to govern all such matters, in these words: "In vain do they worship me, teaching as their doctrines the precepts of men" [Matt. 15:9]. This rule peremptorily excludes from the realm of observance and faith in the church of God every precept of men; and it limits our worship and our teaching to that which God has appointed and taught. We are to stand fast in this freedom with which Christ has made us free, and not be entangled in any yoke of bondage under the rules and precepts of men. We are to repel as a usurpation any attempt, from whatever source, to bind on us any rule which our Lord has not given.

With this rule of our King agree all the deductions of human reason and experience. If we have an infallible rule which cannot mislead us, it is but a dictate of common sense to say that we have no use for a fallible rule on the same subject. Why should a merchant have two yard sticks, one of the standard length, and one a little longer or shorter? What honest man keeps two pairs of balances, one which he knows to be correct, and one which may weigh heavier or lighter? Why, then, should men who wish to please God, both in what they do themselves and in what they enforce on their brethren, make a fallible rule in addition to the infallible one which God has given?

Is it said that we need fallible rules to aid us in explaining and enforcing the one that is infallible? We answer that it argues a lack of faith in God to assume that the rule which He in His infinite wisdom has given demands any such help at our hands. It is certainly as easy to enforce a rule given by God as one given by men; and in enforcing the former, we have the consolation of knowing that we are enforcing

301

that about the lawfulness of which there can be no doubt. We cannot be misled if we follow this rule, or do injustice if we enforce it. If it fail to accomplish some results which appear to us desirable, we shall not be blamed for the consequences; the Lawgiver takes these on himself. Certainly He will not be displeased with us if we follow as best we can the rule which He has given, and if at the same time we show our faith in his wisdom by refusing to follow any other.

Finally, that unity which Christ requires His church to maintain, and for which He offered a most earnest and touching prayer, that unity which is now so sadly broken, can never be re-established on the basis of any human creed or book of discipline. The past experience of Christendom, if it has demonstrated anything, has clearly demonstrated this. The "Apostles' Creed," the shortest one ever drafted, proved insufficient for this purpose, and it was succeeded by others more elaborate. Every one of these has proved insufficient to maintain unity among even its own adherents, as appears from the fact that every sect in Christendom is more or less agitated by teachings that are heretical according to its own standards, and by acrimonious disputes as to the meaning of these standards on important points of doctrine and discipline. Dissatisfaction is everywhere springing up and avowing itself, and many of the earnest men in the creed-bound sects are urging a return to the "Apostles' Creed," forgetting, apparently, that it was tested long ago and proved a broken reed to those who leaned upon it. Surely this bitter experience of fifteen centuries ought to have taught us all that the only way out of present strife and into the unity which Christ demands and for which our own hearts cry out, is to return to the creed and book of discipline which Christ gave, and which the church maintained before its unity was broken. This is the only rule which all believers alike acknowledge, and it certainly furnishes the only basis of union which is within our reach, as it is the only one which the Lord of the church has authorized. We should return to it, not with the expectation that even by the common adoption and enforcement of it all heresy or schism will or can be avoided; for those could not be prevented even when this divine rule was being enforced by inspired apostles; they are the unavoidable results of human depravity, and they will never cease to trouble us till all men shall become subject to the law of the Spirit of Christ; but if we seek to prevent them by the enforcement, to the best of our ability, of the rule of life which God has given, and lean not to our own understanding, we shall have done our duty, and when the conflict is over the Captain of our salvation will say to us, "Well done."

Our final conclusion is, that the Bible is the only rule of faith and practice which can be rightly accepted by Christians, and that it is so because it is the word of God, and because it was given by God to serve this purpose.

A Bibliography on the Inspiration and Authority of the Bible

Prepared by Lynn Gardner
March, 1981

BIBLICAL INTRODUCTION

Archer, Gleason. *A Survey of Old Testament Introduction,* rev. ed. Chicago: Moody Press, 1974.
Scholarly, conservative work.

Bruce, F. F. *The Books and the Parchments,* 3rd ed. Westwood, N.J.: Fleming Revell Co., 1963.
Deals with languages, canon, versions, and manuscripts of the Bible.

Deal, William. *Baker's Pictorial Introduction to the Bible.* Grand Rapids: Baker Book House, 1967.
Basic introduction to every book of the Bible.

Geisler, Norman and William Nix. *A General Introduction to the Bible.* Chicago: Moody Press, 1968.
Comprehensive study dealing with inspiration, translations, and transmission of the text of the Bible. This material was condensed in a shorter book *From God to Us* (Moody, 1974).

Greenlee, Harold. *An Introduction to New Testament Textual Criticism.* Grand Rapids: Wm. B. Eerdmans, 1964.
Helpful work.

Guthrie, Donald. *New Testament Introduction,* 3rd rev. ed. Downers Grove, Il: InterVarsity Press, 1970.
Thorough, conservative work.

Lightfoot, Neil. *How We Got the Bible.* Austin, Tx.: R. B. Sweet, 1962.
Readable and reliable basic book on this topic.

Metzger, Bruce M. *The Text of the New Testament.* New York: Oxford University Press, 1964.
Best advanced work on this topic.

Miller, H. S. *General Biblical Introduction,* rev. ed. Houghton, N.Y.: The Word Bearer Press, 1940.
Deals with inspiration, canon, authorship, and authenticity of the Bible. Contains much useful information.

Schultz, Samuel. *The Old Testament Speaks.* New York: Harper and Row, 1960.
One of the best book-by-book surveys of the Old Testament.

Tenney, Merrill C. *New Testament Survey,* rev. ed. Grand Rapids: Wm. B. Eerdmans, 1961.
In many respects still the best New Testament survey.

Baillie, John. *The Idea of Revelation in Recent Thought.* New York: Columbia University Press, 1956.
Clear and concise presentation of the Neo-Orthodox view that God revealed Himself but not truths about Himself in words.

Berkouwer, G. C. *Holy Scriptures,* Jack Rogers, trans. Grand Rapids: Wm. B. Eerdmans, 1975.
Comprehensive study. Generally conservative. Does not accept inerrancy.

_____. *General Revelation.* Grand Rapids: Wm. B. Eerdmans, 1955.
Detailed treatment.

Cottrell, Jack. *The Authority of the Bible.* Grand Rapids: Baker Book House, 1979, reprint of 1978 ed.
Popular restatement of the nature of Biblical authority for today.

Harris, R. Laird. *Inspiration and Canonicity of the Bible,* rev. ed. Grand Rapids: Zondervan Publishing House, 1969, pp. 7-128.
Study of the biblical claims to inspiration.

Henry, Carl F. H. "Divine Revelation and the Bible" in *Inspiration and Interpretation,* ed. by John F. Walvoord, Grand Rapids: Wm. B. Eerdmans, 1957.
The Bible is God's Word in written revelation.
_____, ed. *Revelation and the Bible.* Grand Rapids: Baker Book House, 1958.
Good basic articles on many aspects of revelation, inspiration, and authority of the Bible by evangelicals.
_____. *God, Revelation and Authority, Vol. II: God Who Speaks and Shows: Fifteen Theses, Part One.* Waco, Tx.: Word Books, 1976.
Discusses concept of verbal inspiration.
_____. *God, Revelation and Authority, Vol. III: God Who Speaks and Shows: Fifteen Theses, Part Two.* Waco, Tx.: Word Books, 1979.
Discusses revelation in Christ and in Scriptures.
Kantzer, Kenneth. "The Authority of the Bible," in *The Word for This Century,* ed. by M. C. Tenney. New York: Oxford University Press, 1960.
Fine defense of biblical claims to revelation in answer to recent misrepresentations.
McDonald, H. D. *Theories of Revelation.* Grand Rapids: Baker Book House, 1979 reprint of 1959, 1963 eds., one volume reprint of two volumes.
Comprehensive survey of ideas of revelation from A.D. 1700-1960.
McGarvey, J. W. *Evidences of Christianity.* Nashville: Gospel Advocate, 1956 reprint of 1880 ed.
Deals with the text, authorship, authenticity, and inspiration of the New Testament scriptures. McGarvey's material is updated and condensed by Wallace Wartick in *Lessons on New Testament Evidences.* (College Press, 1980).

Morris, Leon. *I Believe in Revelation.* Grand Rapids: Wm. B. Eerdmans, 1976.

Interacts with the contemporary challenges to the evangelical view of Scripture. A fine work.

Packer, J. I. *"Fundamentalism" and the Word of God.* Grand Rapids: Wm. B. Eerdmans, 1958.

Solid, readable study on the nature of Scripture.

_____. *God Has Spoken.* Downers Grove: InterVarsity Press, 1979.

Revision of an earlier work. Discusses revelation and inspiration emphasizing that a loving God has spoken in Scripture.

Pinnock, Clark. *Biblical Revelation.* Chicago: Moody Press, 1971.

Scholarly defense of an inspired, inerrant Bible.

Sanday, William. *Inspiration: Eight Lectures on the Early History and Origin of the Doctrine of Biblical Inspiration,* 3rd ed. London: Longmans and Green, 1896.

Presents a case against verbal, plenary inspiration.

Tenney, Merrill C., ed. *The Bible: Living Word of Revelation.* Grand Rapids: Zondervan Publishing House, 1968.

Helpful essays on Biblical revelation and inspiration. The chapter by Kantzer is especially good.

Warfield, B. B. *The Inspiration and Authority of the Bible.* Philadelphia: Presbyterian and Reformed Publishing Co., 1948.

Scholarly, classical defense and explanation of plenary, verbal inspiration.

_____. "Inspiration" and "Revelation" in *The International Standard Bible Encyclopedia,* ed. by James Orr. Grand Rapids: Wm. B. Eerdmans, 1939, vol. III, 1473-1483; IV, 2573-2582.

Excellent articles.

CHRIST AND SCRIPTURE

France, R. T. *Jesus and the Old Testament.* Downers Grove, Il.: InterVarsity Press, 1971.

Extensive study on Jesus' use of the Old Testament.

Geldenhuys, Norval. *Supreme Authority.* Grand Rapids: Wm. B. Eerdmans, 1953.

Excellent study showing that Christ promised inspiration to the apostles, the apostles claimed inspiration and the early church recognized their inspiration.

Kantzer, Kenneth. "Christ and Scripture" *His* magazine reprint.

Argues that to reject biblical inspiration in the end results in rejecting Christ.

Lightner, Robert P. *The Savior and the Scriptures.* Philadelphia: Presbyterian and Reformed Publishing Co., 1966.

Author develops the doctrine of Scripture from the teaching of Christ.

Pinnock, Clark, "The Inspiration of Scripture and the Authority of Jesus Christ," in *God's Inerrant Word,* ed. by J. W. Montgomery. Minneapolis: Bethany Fellowship, Inc., 1973.

Jesus teaches a trustworthy and inerrant Bible.

Ridderbos, H. N. *The Authority of the New Testament Scriptures.* Philadelphia: Presbyterian and Reformed Publishing Co., 1963.

Develops the authority of the New Testament Scriptures from Jesus' promises of Holy Spirit inspiration to the apostles.

Stott, John R. W. *The Authority of the Bible.* Downers Grove: InterVarsity Press, 1974.

Popular booklet affirming the authority of the Bible on the basis of the authority of Jesus.

_____. "The Authority of the Bible" in *Understanding the Bible.* Glendale, Ca.: Regal Books, Gospel Light, 1972, pp. 181-205.
Clear presentation of Jesus' testimony to the inspiration of the Old and New Testaments.

Tasker, R. V. G. *The Old Testament in the New Testament.* Grand Rapids: Wm. B. Eerdmans, 1946.
Surveys Jesus' attitude toward and use of the Old Testament.

Wenham, John. *Christ and the Bible,* Downers Grove: InterVarsity Press, 1972.
Strong defense of the inspiration and truthfulness of the Bible from the authoritative teaching of Jesus.

Wilson, Robert Dick. "Jesus and the Old Testament," *Princeton Theological Review,* XXIV: (October, 1926) 632-661.
Excellent essay on this subject.

CANON OF SCRIPTURE

Archer, Gleason L. *A Survey of Old Testament Introduction,* rev. ed. Chicago: Moody Press, 1974, pp. 66-80.
Good, brief essay on the canon of the Old Tesatment.

Ferguson, Everett. "Lectures on the New Testament Canon," *The Seminary Review,* XXIV (Dec. 1978) 113-143.
Deals with the early Christian doctrine of Scripture and the canon in theological and historical perspective.

Geisler, Norman L. and William E. Nix. *A General Introduction to the Bible.* Chicago: Moody Press, 1968, pp. 127-207.
Helpful information concerning the canon of the Old Testament and New Testament.

Harris, R. Laird *Inspiration and Canonicity of the Bible,* rev. ed. Grand Rapids: Zondervan Publishing House, 1969, pp. 131-294.
Prophetic or apostolic inspiration of biblical books is the basis of canonicity.
_____. "What Books Belong in the Canon of Scriptures?" in *Can I Trust the Bible?* ed. by Howard Vos. Chicago: Moody Press, 1963, pp. 67-91.
Very good, concise essay on the canon.

McGarvey, J. W. *Evidences of Christianity.* Nashville: Gospel Advocate, 1956 reprint of 1880 ed.
Good presentation of evidence for the genuineness of the New Testament books.

Ridderbos, H. N. *Authority of the New Testament Scriptures.* Philadelphia: Presbyterian and Reformed Publishing Co., 1963.
Scholarly defense of New Testament canon. The early church did not invest the books with authority; they recognized the books which possessed apostolic authority and authorization.
_____. "Canon of the New Testament," in *Revelation and the Bible,* ed. by Carl Henry. Grand Rapids: Baker Book House, 1958, pp. 187-201.
Brief summary of the above book.

Stonehouse, Ned B. "The Authority of the New Testament," in *The Infallible Word,* 3rd rev. ed. Philadelphia: Presbyterian and Reformed Publishing Co., 1967, pp. 95-140.
Deals with the authority and canon of the New Testament.

Warfield, B. B. "The Formation of the Canon of the New Testament," in his *The Inspiration and Authority of the Bible.* Philadelphia: Presbyterian and Reformed Publishing Co., 1948, pp. 411-416.
Brief, but good.

311

Westcott, B. F. *The Bible in the Church, a Popular Account of the Collection and Reception of the Holy Scriptures in the Christian Churches,* rev. ed. Grand Rapids: Baker Book House, 1979 reprint of 1885 ed.
Extensive, historical treatment. Classic.

Young, Edward J. "The Authority of the Old Testament," in *The Infallible Word,* 3rd rev. ed. Philadelphia: Presbyterian and Reformed Publishing Co., 1967, pp. 55-91.
A defense of the canon of the Old Testament.

_____. "Canon of the Old Testament," *Revelation and the Bible,* ed. by Carl Henry. Grand Rapids: Baker Book House, 1958, pp. 153-167.
Brief summary of the previous essay.

INERRANCY OF SCRIPTURE

Beegle, Dewey. *Scripture, Tradition and Infallibility.* Grand Rapids: Wm. B. Eerdmans, 1973.
Argues for inspiration and against inerrancy. Revision of his *The Inspiration of Scripture* (Westminster, 1963).

Boice, James M., ed. *The Foundation of Biblical Authority.* Grand Rapids: Zondervan Publishing House, 1978.
Chapter by chapter response to *Biblical Authority* edited by Jack Rogers.

Geisler, Norman L., ed. *Inerrancy: The Extent of Biblical Authority.* Grand Rapids: Zondervan Publishing House, 1980.
Strong defense of inerrancy.

Haley, John W. *An Examination of the Alleged Contradictions of the Bible.* Grand Rapids: Baker Book House, 1977 reprint of 1874 ed.
One of the best works dealing with alleged errors in the Bible.

Kantzer, Kenneth. "Evangelicals and the Inerrancy Question," in *Evangelical Roots*, ed. by K. Kantzer. Nashville: Thomas Nelson Inc., 1978, pp. 83-100.
Practical guidelines for facing the issue of inerrancy today.

Lindsell, Harold. *The Battle for the Bible*. Grand Rapids: Zondervan Publishing House, 1976.
Attempts to document the view that a denial of inerrancy leads to compromise or denial of other basic Christian doctrines.

_____. *The Bible in the Balance*. Grand Rapids: Zondervan Publishiong House, 1979.
Lindsell seeks to answer those who criticized his *Battle For the Bible*.

Montgomery, John W., ed. *God's Inerrant Word*. Minneapolis: Bethany Fellowship, Inc. 1974.
Leading evangelicals defend inerrancy.

Nicole, Roger R. and J. Ramsey Michaels, eds. *Inerrancy and Common Sense*. Grand Rapids: Baker Book House, 1980.
A low-keyed, irenic defense of inerrancy.

Packer, J. I. *Beyond the Battle for the Bible*. Westchester, Il.: Cornerstone Books, 1980.
Author affirms inerrancy but urges moving beyond the battle for the Bible by emphasizing Bible reading and Bible exposition. He insists we examine our traditions and interpretations in the light of Scripture.

Rogers, Jack, ed. *Biblical Authority*. Waco, Tx.: Word Books, 1977.
A response by Fuller Seminary and friends to Lindsell's *Battle for the Bible*. Most of the authors hold the Bible is infallible in matters of faith but believe it is not infallible otherwise.

313

_____ and Donald McKim. *The Authority and Interpretation of the Bible: An Historical Approach.* San Francisco: Harper and Row, 1979.
Extensive survey of how theologians through the church's history have viewed scripture. Affirms an "infallible" Bible but denies inerrancy.
Young, Edward J. *Thy Word Is Truth.* Grand Rapids: Wm. B. Eerdmans, 1957.
Explanation and defense of inerrancy by an Old Testament scholar.

TOPICAL INDEX FOR *WHAT THE BIBLE SAYS ABOUT THE BIBLE*

As arranged in *Monser's Topical Index and Digest of the Bible* edited by Harold E. Monser with A. T. Robertson, D. R. Dungan and Others.

ALLEGORY. Gal. 4:24.

APOSTLES. Gr. *Apostolos*, "To send on a mission."

Christ Himself was the Apostle of the Father.—John 17:18; Heb. 3:1, 2.

Paul uses the term in stating various commissions.—II Cor. 8:23; Phil. 2:25; Rom. 16:7.

But the ordinary application is to the twelve.—Matthias was added in the place of Judas Iscariot. The name was given to the twelve by Jesus—Lu. 6:13. A record of the group is found in—Mt. 10:2-4; Mk. 3:14-19; Lu. 6:13-16; Acts 1:13. The first appointment embraced twelve, corresponding to the twelve tribes of Israel—Rev. 21:12, 14. Afterwards 70 were sent forth (Lu. 10:1), indicating, perhaps prospectively, the broadening out of the commission, since the Jewish conception of mankind comprised 70 nations. But the term "apostles" was not applied to the 70 in the technical sense. The development was gradual. (1) Called to be companions and followers of Jesus—Mk. 1:16-20; John 1:35-50. (2) Organized into a band of twelve—Lu. 6:13-16. (3) Instructed in the kingdom. The purpose threefold (1) That they might company with Him. (2) Witness His deeds, remember His words, and attest His resurrection as disciples. (3) That they might go into all the world as His commissioners (apostles)—Mk. 3:14; Mt. 28:19, 20. They wandered to and fro (Mt. 8:19, 20) and thus became detached from the world—John 17:16. The miracles were to prove to them the power of their leader—John 11:15. The parables were to utilize their knowledge of nature and of human nature—Mt. 13:51, 52. Half of them were in the training a trifle over 3 years. They were to become witnesses of Jesus, of His death and resurrection—Lu. 24:48; Acts 1:8. They were to preach the gospel to the world—Mt. 28:18-20; Mk. 16:15, 16; Lu. 24:45-47; Acts 2:41, 42. But they were to tarry in Jerusalem until they were endued with power from on high—Lu. 24:49. Paul was not a member of the body of twelve. He was an independent apostle on a par with them—Acts 14:4, 14. Barnabas and James, the Lord's brother, are sometimes called apostles, probably in the more general sense of the term.

Signs and qualifications of apostles.—II Cor. 12:12. Must have seen Jesus and be able to testify to what they had seen and heard—John 15:27; Acts 1:21, 22; 22:14, 15; I Cor. 9:1; 15:8. Must have been called—Mt. 10:2-4; Mk. 1:16-20; Lu. 6:13-16; Rom. 1:1; I Cor. 1:1; Gal. 1:1; I Tim. 2:7; II Tim. 1:11. Performed miracles—Mk. 16:17, 18. 20; Acts 2:43; Rom. 15:19; I Cor. 12:8-11; II Cor. 12:12. Had power to confer the gift of the holy spirit—Acts 6:6; 8:14-21; 19:6; I Tim. 4:14.

APOSTLESHIP. Acts 1:25; Rom. 1: 5; I Cor. 9:2; Gal. 2:8.

Apostolic authority, duty, faith, inspiration, knowledge, persecutions, witness.

Apostolic authority (Jesus' teaching). —Mt. 10:1, 40; 16:18, 19; 18:18, 19; 28:19, 20; Mk. 3:14, 15; 6:7; Lu. 9:1, 2; 22:28-30; John 20:23.

Apostolic inspiration (Jesus' teaching)—Mt. 10:19, 20; Lu. 21:14, 15.

By the Holy Spirit—Mk. 13:11; Lu. 12:11, 12; 24:49; John 7:39; 14: 26; 15:26; 16:7, 13-15; Acts 1:4-8.

Apostolic witness (Jesus' teaching) —Lu. 24:44-48; John 15:27; 21: 24; Acts 1:8.

Authority (Jesus' teaching)—Mt. 9:6, 8; 10:1; 16:18, 19; 18:18, 19; 21: 23-27; Lu. 19:17, 19, 22-27; John 5:25-27. See Mt. 7:28, 29; Mk. 1: 21, 22; Lu. 4:6, 31-32, 36.

All authority given to Jesus—Mt. 11: 27; 28:18; John 17:2.

BOOKS. How written.—On tablets— Is. 8:1; Hab. 2:2; Lu. 1:63. Stone —Ex. 24:12; 34:1, 4; Deut. 4:13; Job 19:24. Papyrus (roll)—Ezra 6: 12; Is. 34:4; Jer. 36:2, 4, 6, 14, 20, 21, 23, 25, 27-29, 32; Ez. 2: 9; 3:1, 2, 3; Zech. 5:1. Parchment —II Tim. 4:13. With iron pens and ink—Job 19:24; Jer. 17:1; 36:18; III John 13. Written on both sides —Ez. 2:10. Sealed—Is. 29:11; Dan. 12:4; Rev. 5:1, 2, 5, 9; 6:1, 3, 5, 7, 9, 12; 8:1. Dedicated—Lu. 1:1; Acts 1:1. Erasures possible—Ex. 32: 33; Num. 5:23.

Numerous.—Eccl. 12:12; Acts 19:19.

Divine revelation and laws written. —Ex. 17:14; 24:4, 12; 34:1, 4, 28; Deut. 4:13; 9:10, 11; 17:18; 28: 58, 61; 29:20, 21, 27; 30:10; 31:9.

Book of the Covenant.—Contained the law—Ex. 17:14; 24:7, 8; II Ki. 23:2, 3, 21, 24. Delivered to the priests and kept in the ark—Deut. 31:9-13, 24-26. To be read every seven years—Deut. 31:10, 11; Josh. 8:34, 35; II Ki. 23:2; II Chr. 34:18, 19; Neh. 8:8, 18; 9:3. Copies made —Deut. 17:18; Josh. 8:32. Lost and found—II Ki. 22:8; 23:21; II Chr. 34:14, 15, 30.

Book of the law.—Deut. 28:58, 61; 29:20, 21; 30:10; 31:26; Josh. 1: 8; 8:31, 34; 23:6; 24:26; II Ki. 14: 6; 22:8, 11; 23:24; II Chr. 17:9; 25:4; 34:14, 15; Neh. 8:1-8, 18; 9:3.

Book of Moses.—II Chr. 35:12; Neh. 13:1.

Book of Chronicles.—I Ki. 14:19; 15: 7, 23; 23:31; 16:5, 14, 20, 27; 22: 39, 45; II Ki. 1:18; 8:23; 10:34; 12:19; 13: 8, 12; 14:15, 18, 28; 15:6, 11, 15, 21, 26, 31, 36; 16: 19; 20:20; 21: 17, 25; 23:28; 24:5. Persian—Esth. 2:23; 6:1; 10:2.

Book of life.—Ps. 69:28; Dan. 7:10; 12:1; Phil. 4:3; Rev. 3:5; 13:8; 17: 8; 20:12, 15; 21:27; 22:19.

Book of remembrance.—Ps. 139: 16; Mal. 3:16.

COMMANDMENTS, the Ten Commandments. Primarily the Decalogue, or Ten Words.—Ex. 20:3-17; Deut. 5:7-21. Given orally from Sinai—Ex. 20:1; 24:3; Deut. 5:4, 22-25; 9:10; 10:4. Written in Book of Covenant—Ex. 24:4. Written on tables of stone—Ex. 24:12; 34:1, 4; Deut. 4:13; 5:22; 9:9-11; II Cor. 3:3, 7. Moses broke the first tables of stone—Ex. 32:19; Deut. 9:17;

10:2. God gave a later copy—Ex. 31:18; 34:1, 28; Deut. 10:1-5. God wrote—Ex. 24:12; 32:16; 34:1, 28; Deut. 4:13; 5:22; 9:19; 10:2, 4. Seem to fix number at ten—Ex. 34:28; Deut. 10:4. Put in the ark —Deut. 10:1-5; I Ki. 8:9; II Chr. 5:10; Heb. 9:4. Called covenant —Deut. 4:13. Words of the covenant—Ex. 34:28. Tables of the covenant—Deut. 9:9, 11; Heb. 9:4. Tables of testimony—Ex. 31:18; 32:15, 16; 34:29. Ministration of death—Rom. 7:5; II Cor. 3:7, 9. Given to Moses for the children of Israel—Ex. 25:22; 34:3; Lev. 26: 46; 27:34; Deut. 1:3.

Hints that the principles involved in these commandments had been taught before.—Gen. 26:5; I. Ex. 8:10; 9:14; II. Gen. 35:2; IV. Ex. 16:23-30; V. Gen. 9:20-27; VI. Gen. 4:9-11; 9:5, 6; VII. Gen. 20: 2-7; 26:6-11; 39:7-9; VIII. Gen. 30:33; 31:19, 30, 32.

These commandments repeated prior to the death of Jesus:

I. Ex. 20:23; 22:20; 23:13, 24, 32; 34:14-16; Lev. 11:7; Deut. 4:35, 39; 5:7; 6:4, 14; 8:19, 20; 11:26-28; 13:1-11; 17:2-7; 30:17, 18; Ju. 6:10; II Ki. 17:35-39; Is. 40:18-26; Jer. 2:11; 5:7, 12-17; 7:6; 25: 6; 35:15; Hos. 13:4; Mk. 12:29, 30; Lu. 10:27.

II. Ex. 20:23; 32:8, 19-35; 34:13-17; Lev. 19:4; 26:1; Deut. 4:16-23; 5:8-10; 16:21, 22; 27:15; 29:17-21; I Ki. 18:17-40; Jer. 16:20, 21.

III. Ex. 22:28; Lev. 18:21; 19:12; 20: 3; 21:6; 22:32; 24:10-16, 23; Deut. 5:11; 6:13; 10:20; Mt. 5:33-37; 23:16-22.

IV. Ex. 23:12; 31:13-17; 34:21; 35: 2, 3; Lev. 19:3, 30; 23:3; 26:2; Num. 15:32-36; Deut. 5:12-15; Neh. 13:15-21; Jer. 17:21-25; Ez. 20:12, 20; 44:24.

V. Ex. 21:15, 17; Lev. 19:3; 20:9; Deut. 5:16; 21:18-21; 27:16; Mt. 15:4; 19:19; Mk. 7:10; 10:19; Lu. 18:20.

VI. Ex. 21:12, 14, 20, 21; Lev. 24: 17, 21; Num. 35:16-21, 30-33; Deut. 5:17; 19:10-13; Mt. 5:21-26; 19:18; 26:52; Mk. 10:19; Lu. 18:20.

VII. Lev. 18:20; Num. 5:12-31; 20: 10; Deut. 5:18; 2:22-27; 24:1-4; Jer. 3:1; 5:7-9; 28:21-23; Mt. 5: 27-32; 19:3-9, 18; Mk. 10:19; Lu. 18:20.

VIII. Ex. 21:16; 22:1-4, 7-15; Lev. 6:2-7; 19:11, 13, 35, 36; Deut. 5: 19; 23:24, 25; 25:13-16; Amos. 8:4-11; Mic. 6:10-15; Mt. 19:18; Mk. 10:19; Lu. 18:20.

IX. Ex. 23:1, 7, 8; Lev. 19:11, 12; Deut. 5:20; 19:16-21; Mt. 19:18; Mk. 10:19; Lu. 18:20.

X. Deut. 5:21; Jer. 22:13-19; Amos 8:4-11; Mic. 2:1-3; Heb. 2:9; Lu. 12:15-21.

These commandments repeated after the death of Jesus:

I. Acts 17:23-31; Rom. 1:23-25; I Cor. Cor. 8:4-6.

II. Acts 14:11-17; 17:23-31; I Cor. 6: 9, 10; 8:4-6; 10:7, 14, 19, 20; II Cor. 6:16, 17; Gal. 5:19-21; Eph. 5:3-6; Col. 3:5; I John 5:21; Rev. 21:8; 22:15.

III. Jas. 5:12.

IV. The only commandment not repeated after the death of Jesus—Mk. 2:27. Not in force as a commandment after His death. See Mk.

2:27; Rom. 14:5, 16; Gal. 4:10, 11; Col. 2:16, 17; Heb. 8:5; 10:1, 9.
V. Eph. 6:1-3; Col. 3:20.
VI. Rom. 13:9; I John 3:15; Rev. 21: 8; 22:15.
VII. Rom. 13:9; I Cor. 6:13-18; Gal. 5:19-21; Eph. 5:3-6; Col. 3:5; I Thess. 4:4-7; Heb. 13:4; Rev. 22: 15.
VIII. Rom. 13:9; I Cor. 6:10, 11; Eph. 4:28.
IX. Rom. 13:9.
X. Rom. 7:7; 13:9; I Cor. 6:10; Eph. 5:5; Col. 3:5; I Tim. 6:9-11, 17; Heb. 13:5.

Bind on hand.—Ex. 13:9, 16; Deut. 6:8; 11:18. For frontlets—Ex. 13: 9, 16; Deut. 6:8; 11:18. Written on doorposts and gates—Deut. 6:9; 11:20.

Keeping the commandments.—Lev. 18:5; 22:31; Deut. 4:4, 6; 5:10, 29; 6:17; 8:6; 11:8, 22; 26:13, 18; 28:9; I Ki. 2:3; 3:14; 6:12; 8:58, 61; 9:4; II Ki. 23:1-24; I Chr. 29: 19; Ps. 119:1-176; I Cor. 7:19; I John 5:2, 3; Rev. 12:17; 14:12.

Blessing pronounced on those who keep the commandments.—Lev. 18:5; Deut. 4:40; 5:10, 29; 7:9-11; 26:12-19; 28:1-68; 29:10-28; 30:1-20; I Sam. 12:14, 15; I Ki. 2: 1-4; 3:14; 6:12, 13; 8:56-61; 9:3-9; Ps. 78:5-72; 119:97-104; Is. 48: 17-22; Mt. 19:17; Lu. 10:28; Rom. 10:5; Gal. 3:12.

People taught to wear a fringe or border on their garments to remind the wearers of the commandments.—Num. 15:37-41; Deut. 22:12.

Possession of the land dependent on the obedience of these commandments.—Deut. 4:40; 6:17-25; 7: 17-26; 8:1-20; 11:7-15, 22-32; 29: 22-28; 30:1-5; I Ki. 9:6-9; I Chr. 28:8; Neh. 9:13-25; Ez. 20:15-44. See Num. 13:30-33; 14:1-38; Deut. 1:21-40; 9:23.

Violation of the commandments, instances of.—The children of Israel—Num. 15:30-36; Deut. 9:11-21; Ju. 2:10,23; 3:1-8; II Ki. 17:1-17; Ps. 78:8-78; Amos 2:1-16. Of Judah—I Ki. 14:22-25; II Ki. 17:19; II Chr. 12:1-12; Of Saul—I Sam. 13:14, 15; 15:3-28; Of David—II Sam. 12:7-15; Of Solomon—I Ki. 11:1-13; Of Jeroboam—I Ki. 11: 26-33; 13:1-5, 33, 34.

Led into captivity because of violation.—Deut. 28:47-52, 62-68; 29: 25-28; 30:1-5; Ju. 3:7, 8; I Ki. 9: 6-9; 14:1-16; II Ki. 17:18, 20, 23; 18:9-12; 23:27; 24:1-4; II Chr. 7: 20; Neh. 1:8, 9; 9:26-30; Ps. 106: 34-47; Jer. 21:3-14; 22:1-30; 24: 1-10; 25:1-11; Ex. 39:23, 24.

The kingdom divided because of violation.—I Ki. 2:1-4; 9:7-9; 11:9-13, 26-39; 12:19, 20; 14:8; II Ki. 17:21; I Chr. 28:6-9; II Chr. 7:17-22; Ps. 89:29-33.

Making void through the traditions of men.—Mt. 15:1-9; Mk. 7:3-13.

Penalty for breaking the commandments.—Mt. 5:19; Jas. 2:10-13.

Death penalty for violation.—I. and II. Ex. 22:20; Lev. 17:7; Deut. 13: 1-17; 17:2-7; 30:17, 18; Acts 17: 23-31; I Cor. 6:9, 10; II Cor. 6:16, 17; Gal. 5:19-21; Rev. 21:8; 22: 15. III. Lev. 24:10, 16, 23. IV. Ex. 31:13-17; Num. 15:32-36. V. Ex. 21:15, 17; Deut. 21:18-21; Mt. 15: 4-16; Mk. 7:10-13. VI. Ex. 21:12-14; Lev. 24:17, 21; Num. 35:16-34; Deut. 19:1-13; Mt. 5:21, 22;

26:52; I John 3:15; Rev. 13:10; 21:8; 22:15. VII. Lev. 18:20; 20: 10-12; Deut. 22:22-27; Mt. 5:27-32; John 8:5; Gal. 5:19-21; Eph. 5:3-5; I Thess. 4:4-7; Heb. 13:4; Rev. 21:8; 22:15. VIII. Ex. 21:16; 22:1-5, 7-12; Amos 8:4-11; Mic. 6:10-15; I Cor. 6:10. IX. Deut. 19: 16-21; Rev. 21:8; 22:15. X. Josh. 7:20-26; I Cor. 6:10; Eph. 5:5; Col. 3:5, 6; I Tim. 6:9, 10; Jas. 5:1-6.

Knowledge of sin by the law.—Rom. 3:20; 4:15; 5:13, 20; 7:7-13; I Cor. 15:56; II Pet. 2:21.

As a law, commands are spiritual.— Mt. 5:17-40; Rom. 7:14.

The commandments summed up by Christ.—Mt. 22:35-40; Mk. 12:28-34; Lu. 10:25-37. See Lev. 19:18; Deut. 6:5; 10:12; 30:6, 16, 20; Mt. 5:43, 44; 7:12; 19:19; Lu. 6:31-35; Rom. 12:14, 20; 13:8-10; 15: 1; Gal. 5:14, 15; 6:2; Jas. 2:8.

The new commandment.—John 13: 34; 15:12, 17; I John 2:7-11; 3: 10-16, 22-24; 4:20, 21; II John 5.

Keeping Jesus' commands.—John 14:15, 21, 23; 15:10-14; I Cor. 7: 19; I John 2:3-5; 3:22-24; 5:2, 3; II John 6.

Commandments or precepts of men. —Mt. 15:9; Mk. 7:7; Col. 2:22; Tit. 1:14.

Jesus' teaching concerning commandments.—Of Moses—Mt. 19: 7-9; Mk. 10:3-12. *Ten commandments*—Mt. 5:21-37; 15:4-6; 19: 17-19; 23:16-22; Mk. 1:44; 7:8-13; 10:19, 20; 12:29, 30; Lu. 10: 27; 18:20, 21. Making void through traditions of men—Mt. 15:1-6; Mk. 7:8-13. Jesus came to fulfil—Matthew —5:17-19. Commandments summed up by Christ—Mt. 5:43-48; 7:

12; 22:35-40; Mk. 12:28-34; Lu. 6:31-38; 10:25-37. He commanded —Mt. 11:1; 14:19; 15:35; Mk. 6: 39; Lu. 9:21; John 15:14, 17. A new commandment—John 13:34; 15:12, 17. Keeping commandments—Mt. 5:19; John 14:15, 21, 23; 15:10-14.

COUNSEL OF GOD.—Ju. 18:5; 20: 18; I Sam. 14:37; Ezra 10:3; Ps. 16:7; 33:11; 73:24; 106:13; 107: 11; Ps. 1:25, 30; 19:21; Is. 5:19; 25:1; 28:29; 46:10, 11; Jer. 23: 18, 22; 32:19; 49:20; 50:45; Mic. 4:12; Lu. 7:30; Acts 2:23; 20:27; Eph. 1:11; Heb. 6:17; Rev. 3:18.

DOCTRINE. In the gospels "teaching" is the word used to express what Jesus taught, not yet formulated into specific doctrines. The apostles had the living word and the following generation the inspired utterances of apostles and spirit-filled men. Doctrine in its usual sense occurs only in the later pastoral epistles—I Tim. 1:3; 1:10; 4:6, 13; 6:3; II Tim. 3:6; Tit. 1:9; 2:7, 10. Used in a disparaging sense—Mt. 15:9; Mk. 7:7; Eph. 4:14; Col. 2: 22. Meaning instruction—Deut. 32: 2; Job 11:4; Prov. 4:2; Is. 29:24. First principles of—Heb. 6:1. False doctrine, called heresy—II Pet. 2:1.

False doctrine, to be avoided.—I Tim. 1:4; II Tim. 4:3; Rev. 2:14. Teachers of, described—Acts 20:29, II Cor. 11:13; I Tim. 6:3, 4; II Tim. 3:8; Tit. 1:11; II Pet. 2:3; Jude 4, 8.

GOD: He knows all.—Job 23:24; Ps. 39:1-6; 149:4, 5; Pr. 5:21; 15:3; Is. 40:12, 14, 26-28; 46:9, 10; Jer. 23:24; Mt. 24:36; Rom. 11:33, 34; I John 1:5. The searcher of hearts —Gen. 20:6; Deut. 32:21; I Sam.

319

16:7; I Ki. 8:39; I Chr. 28:9; II Chr. 6:30; Job 11:11; Ps. 7:9; 44:21; 139:1-16; Pr. 15:11; 17:3; 21:2; 24:12; Jer. 11:20; 17:10; Amos 4: 13; Mt. 6:4, 8, 18, 32; Lu. 16:15; Acts 1:24; 15:8; I Cor. 3:20; I Thess. 2:4; Heb. 4:13. He knows man's condition and needs—Ex. 3:7; Deut. 2:7; II Chr. 16:9; Job 34:21, 22, 25; Ps. 1:6; 11:4; 33:13-15; 66:7; 103:13, 14; Is. 29:15; 37:28; 66: 18; Jer. 32:19; Amos 9:2-4; Mt. 10:29, 30; I Cor. 8:3.

Foreknowledge.—Gen. 41:25-32; I Sam. 23:10-12; Ps. 139:15, 16; Is. 41:26; 42:9; 44:7; 45:11, 21; 46:10; 48:3, 5; Jer. 1:5; Dan. 2: 28-45; 10:14; Mt. 6:8, 32; 24:36; 25:24; Lu. 22:22; 24:27, 44; Acts 2:23; 3:18; 4:28; 15:18; Rom. 8: 29; 11:2; Gal. 1:15, 16; II Tim. 1: 9; I Pet. 1:2, 20.

His appearances to men.—To Adam —Gen. 3:8-24. To Cain—Gen. 4: 6, 7, 9-15. To Abraham—Gen. 12: 7; 17:1; 18:1-33; Ex. 6:3. To Isaac —Ex. 6:3. To Jacob—Gen. 32:30; 35:7, 9-13; 48:3; Ex. 6:3. To Moses Ex. 3:4-22; 4:1-17; 19:19-24; 24: 1-18; Deut. 34:10. To Moses and Joshua—Deut. 31:14, 15. To Solomon—I Ki. 3:5-14; 9:2-9; 11:9; II Chr. 1:7-12; 7:12-22. To Job— Job 42:5, 6. To Isaiah—Is. 6:1-8. To Ezekiel—Ez. 1:24-28; 2:1-9; 3: 1-27; 8:1-4; 43:2, 3. To Daniel— Dan. 7:9, 10. To Amos—Amos 9: 1. To John—Rev. 4:2, 3; 20:11.

Faithful who promised.—Gen. 9:16; 21:1; 28:15; Ex. 2:24; 6:4, 5; Lev. 26:44, 45; Josh. 22:4; 23:10-14; Ju. 2:1; I Sam. 12:22; II Sam. 7: 28: 23:5; I Ki. 8:56; II Ki. 13:23; Neh. 9:7, 8; Ps. 18:30; 19:9; 25:

10; 33:4; 40:10; 100:5; 132:11; Rom. 3:3, 4; 11:2, 29; 15:8; I Cor. 1:9; II Cor. 1:20; I Thess. 5:24; II Tim. 2:13; Tit. 1:2; I Pet. 4:19; Rev. 6:10; 15:3.

Our Guide.—Gen. 12:1; Ex. 13:21; 33:13-15; Deut. 32:10, 12; Neh. 9:19, 20; Ps. 5:8; 23:2, 3; 25:5, 9; 27:11; 31:3; 32:8; 48:14; 73: 24; Is. 40:11; 42:16; 55:4; Lu. 1: 79; John 10:3, 4; 16:13. As He guided the wise men to Bethlehem by the finger of light, so He makes so plain the path of duty that the wayfaring man, though a fool, shall not err therein—Is. 35:8.

GOSPEL: In prophecy.—Gen. 3:15; 12:3; 22:18; 49:10; Deut. 18:15; Job 19:25, 26; Ps. 2:7, 8; 16:8-10; 110:4; Is. 9:6, 7; 35:4-10; 41:27; 49:6; 52:7; 61:1-3; Jer. 31:31-34; Dan. 2:44; Joel 2:28-32; Mic. 4:1, 2; 5:2; Zech. 6:12, 13; Mal. 3:1-3; Lu. 24:25-27.

In preparation.—Mt. 2:1-6; 3:13-15; Lu. 2:29-32, 40, 49; 3:15-17, 21, 22; 4:1, 2; 24:44-47; John 1:14-17, 29, 34; 17:7, 8; Acts 1:6-9; 2: 22-23.

In purpose.—John 1:29; 3:16, 17; 14:12; Rom. 1:13-17; 8:18-23; 10: 4-13; Eph. 3:8-11; Phil. 2:5-11; Col. 1:19.

In progress.—Geographical—Acts 1: 8; 2:8-11; 8:5; 9:19, 20; 10:17-22; 13:2-6, 13, 14; 14:1, 6, 7; 15: 39-41; 16:1, 6, 10-12; 18:1, 18, 19, 22, 23; 28:16.

Doctrinal.—John 1:16, 17; Acts 19: 1-7; Rom. 5:1-5; 7:22; 8:11, 30; 10:8-17; 12:1, 2; 14:17-19; I Cor. 9:19-27; 13:1-8; I Pet. 2:1-5; II Pet. 1:5-7.

In fulfillment.—Mt. 11:4, 5; Lu. 7:22.

320

With—Is. Ch. 35; John 17:4; Acts 2:16-21; 10:34-44; I Cor. 15:51-57; Col. 1:3-6; Rev. 15:3, 4; 19:5-9; 21:1-4; 22:1-5, 10-14.

What is the gospel?—Before the death of Jesus.—The kingdom of heaven is at hand—Dan. 2:44; Mt. 3:2; 4:17, 23; 9:35; 10:5-7; 24:14; Mk. 1:14, 15; Lu. 4:43; 8:1; 10:9-11; 11:20; 16:16; 21:31. Jesus the Christ—Mk. 1:1; Lu. 9:26; John 1:14-17, 29, 36; 3:14-17; 5:24; 6:33-45; 17:3; 20:31. The words or sayings of Jesus—Mt. 7:24-27; 13:3-9, 18-23; Mk. 4:3-9, 14-20; 8:38; 13:31; Lu. 6:46-49; 8:21; 9:26; 11:28; 21:33; John 6:63, 68; 8:31, 32, 37, 51; 12:48-50; 14:23, 24; 17:6-8.

After the death of Christ.—The kingdom of Christ—Acts 1:3, 6; 8:12; 20:25; 28:23, 31.

Christ the Son of God, crucified and risen for sinners—The promise of the free forgiveness of sins for Christ's sake—Acts 1:8; 2:22-36; 3:13-26; 8:5, 12, 25, 35; 9:15, 20; 10:36-43; 15:7; 16:30-32; 17:2, 3, 17, 18; 22:12-15; 24:24, 25; 26:16-18; 28:23, 31; Rom. 10:8-12; I Cor. 1:17-24; 2:2; 15:1-8, 12-17; II Cor. 4:1-5; 5:18-21; Gal. 1:15, 16; 3:8; Eph. 1:12-14; 2:13-20; 3:6-8; Phil. 1:15-18; Col. 1:27, 28; I Thess. 1:5-10; I Tim. 1:15; II Tim. 1:8-14; 2:8; I Pet. 1:10-12; Rev. 1:2, 9; 6:9; 20:4.

The great commission—Mt. 28:19, 20; Mk. 16:15, 16; Lu. 24:26, 27, 44-48.

The conditions of salvation, or of entrance into Christ—Acts 2:37-42; 3:19; 8:12, 13, 36, 39; 10:44-48;

16:14, 15, 33; 22:16; Rom. 10:8-11.

The gospel must be preached: By Jesus.—Mk. 1:38, 39; Lu. 20:1; John 15:3. *To the poor and afflicted* —Is. 61:1-3; Mt. 11:5; Lu. 4:18, 19. *The gospel of the kingdom*— Mt. 4:23; 9:35; Mk. 1:14, 15; Lu. 4:43; 8:1; 16:16. *The words which He received from the Father*—John 5:34; 8:38; 12:48-50; 17:6-8, 14.

By His disciples—Is. 52:7; Nah. 1:15; John 6:44, 45; Acts 9:6; 11:19-21; 15:32-36; 22:10; Rom. 1:16; 10:8-18; I Cor. 1:18-24; II Cor. 5:18-21; Eph. 1:13; 2:13-20; Phil. 2:14-16; 4:3; Col. 1:5, 6; I Thess. 1:5-10; Heb. 2:2-4; 4:2; I Pet. 1:12, 23-25; 4:6.

To the whole world—Mt. 24:14; 26:13; 28:19, 20; Mk. 13:10; 14:9; 16:15; Col. 1:23.

By the seventy—Lu. 10:1-20.

By the apostles—Acts 5:20; 6:4, 7; 8:25.

The apostles sent out—Mt. 10:5-15; 28:19, 20; Mk. 6:7-13; 16:15; Lu. 9:2-6; 24:47-49. *By Peter*— Acts 2:14-40; 3:12-26; 4:1-4, 29-37; 10:22, 32-48; 11:1, 14; 15:7. *By Paul*—Acts 17:2-4; 18:11; 20:24; 22:14, 15; 24:24, 25; 26:15-23; 28:23; I Cor. 1:17; 2:4-6, 13; 4:15; 9:16-23; 15:1-4; II Cor. 4:1-5; Gal. 1:6-16; Eph. 6:17-20; Phil. 1:12-18; Col. 1:23-29; II Thess. 3:1; I Tim. 1:11-16. *Paul an apostle to the Gentiles*—Acts 9:15; 13:5-49; 14:5-7, 21-28; 16:6-17, 31-33; 19:1-5, 8-10, 18; 28:28-31; Rom. 1:13-15; 15:15-21; II Cor. 10:14-16; Gal. 2:2-10; 4:13-15; Eph. 3:6-8; I Thess. 2:2-16; II Thess. 2:14, 15. *By Stephen*—

321

Acts 6:8, 10, 14; 7:2-53; *By Philip* —Acts 8:4-6, 12, 13, 14, 30-40. *By Timothy*—II Tim. 4:1-5. *The gospel preached to Abraham*—Gal. 3:8.

Jesus' teaching concerning the gospel: Gospel, What is the?—The kingdom of heaven—Mt. 4:17, 23; 9:35; 10:5-7; 24:14; Lu. 4:43; 8: 1; 10:9-11; 11:20; 16:16; 21:31; Acts 1:3. The words *or* sayings of Jesus—Mt. 7:24-27; 13:3-9, 18-23; Mk. 4:3-9, 14-20; 8:38; 13:31; Lu. 6:46-49; 8:21; 9:26; 11:28; 21:33; John 6:63; 8:31, 32, 37, 51; 12:48-50; 14:23, 24; 17:6-8. Jesus is the Christ, the Son of God —Mt. 10:33; Mk. 8:38; Lu. 9:26; 12:9; John 3:14-17; 5:24; 6:33-45; 17:3; Acts 1:8.

Revealed to the apostles—Mt. 11:25; 13:11; 16:17; 19:11. By the Holy Spirit—Mt. 10:19, 20; Mk. 13:11; Lu. 12:12; 21:15; 24:49; John 14: 26; 16:13.

Man saved by the gospel—Mt. 4:4; 10: 32, 33; Lu. 9:26; 12:9; John 5:34; 6:33-45, 63; 8:31, 32, 51; 12:48-50; 15:3; 17:6-8, 14, 17, 20.

Parable of the sower—Mt. 13:3-9, 18-23; Mk. 4:3-9, 14-20; Lu. 8:5-15.

Must be preached—Lu. 16:16. Preached to the poor—Mt. 11:5; Lu. 4:18, 19. To the whole world— Mt. 24:14; 26:13; 28:19, 20; Mk. 13:10; 14:9; 16:15, 16; Lu. 24:46, 47; Acts 1:8. Apostles sent out— Mt. 10:1-15; 28:19, 20; Mk. 6:7-13; 16:15, 16; Lu. 9:1-6; 24:47-49. Seventy sent out—Lu. 10:1-20.

Must be heard—Mt. 7:24, 25; 10:14; 13:13-23; Mk. 4:12; Lu. 6:47; 8: 21; 10:16; 11:28; John 5:24, 25; 6:45; 8:43, 47; 9:27; 14:23, 24.

Must be believed—Mk. 16:16; Lu. 8: 12, 13; John 3:14-16, 36; 5:24; 6:29, 40, 47; 8:24; 11:25, 26; 17: 20.

Must be obeyed—Mt. 7:16-27; 12: 50; 28:19, 20; Mk. 16:15, 16; Lu. 6:46-49; 8:21; 24:46, 47.

HOLY SPIRIT. The Spirit of God in the Old Testament: *Ruach*—Ps. 51:11, 12; 139:7; 143:10; Is. 40: 7-13; 59:19, 21; Ez. 36:27; 37:14; Mic. 2:7; Hag. 2:5; Zech. 4:6; 7: 12.

Directs the movements of the prophets.—I Ki. 16:12; II Ki. 2:16; Is. 48: 16; 63:11-14; Ez. 3:12, 14, 25; 8: 3; 11:1; 37:1; 43:5.

The Spirit creative.—Gen. 1:2; 2:7; Job 26:13; 33:4; Ps. 104:30.

Personality of the Holy Spirit.—John 14:17, 26; 15:26; 16:7-13; Rom. 8:26; I Cor. 2:10; 12:11.

By whom sent.—John 14:16, 26; 15: 26; 16:7; Acts 2:23.

Will not come to dwell in the world until after the death of Jesus.— John 7:38, 39; 15:26; 16:7; Acts 1:4, 8; 2:33.

To whom promised.—Joel 2:28-32; Lu. 11:13. The apostles—John 14: 17; 15:26; Acts 1:4, 8; 2:4, 33. Disciples—John 14:17; Acts 2:38; Rom. 8:4-17; I Cor. 3:16, 17; II Cor. 3:3; I Thess. 4:7, 8; I John 3:23, 24; 4:13. Sons of God—Lu. 11:13; Rom. 8:14-17; Gal. 4:6, 29. Believers—John 7:39; Acts 10:44; 15: 7-9; Eph. 1:13; Heb. 6:4. Those that obey—Acts 5:32.

Baptism of the Holy Spirit.—Is. 32: 15; 44:3; Joel 2:28-32; Ez. 39:29; Mt. 3:11; Mk. 1:8; Lu. 3:16; John 1:33; Acts 1:5, 8; 2:4, 33; 4:8, 31; 10:45; 11:15; I Cor. 12:13.

Filled with the Holy Spirit.—Lu. 1:

15; Acts 2:4; 4:8, 31; 6:3, 5; 7:55; 11:24; 13:9, 52; Eph. 5:18.

The Holy Spirit poured out.—Is. 32:15; 44:3; Ez. 39:29; Joel 2:28, 29; Zech. 12:10; Acts 2:17, 33; 10: 45; 11:15, 16.

The Holy Spirit conferred by the laying on of the apostles' hands.—Acts 6:6; 8:14-21; 19:6; I Tim. 4:14.

Gifts of the Spirit.—Acts 2:38; 10: 46; 19:6; Rom. 12:6-8; I Cor. 2:4-6; 12:4-11; Eph. 4:7, 8; II Tim. 1: 6; Heb. 2:4.

Conception of Jesus by the Holy Spirit.—Mt. 1:18-20; Lu. 1:35.

Jesus anointed and led by the Holy Spirit.—Is. 11:2; 42:1; 61:1; Mt. 3:16; 4:1; 12:28; Mk. 1:10, 12; Lu. 3:22; 4:1, 14, 18; John 1:32, 33; 3:34; Acts 1:2; 4:27; 5:32; 10:38; Heb. 1:9; 9:14.

How was the Holy Spirit given?—Without mediation—See "Baptism of the Holy Spirit" and "The Holy Spirit poured out." With mediation —Through laying on of hands of the apostles—Acts 8:17-19; 19:6. Given in answer to prayer—Lu. 11:13; Acts 8:15. Received by the hearing of faith—Gal. 3:2, 3, 14. Given to those who obey gospel commands —Acts 2:38; Eph. 1:13.

Christians are temples of the Holy Spirit.—John 14:17; Rom. 8:9-17; I Cor. 3:16, 17; 6:19; Eph. 2:21, 22; 3:16, 17; II Tim. 1:14.

Communion of the Holy Spirit.—II Cor. 3:6-18; 11:4; 12:18; 13:14; Phil. 2:1; Col. 1:8.

Inspires.—Num. 12:6, 8; II Ki. 17: 13; Neh. 9:20-30; Is. 59:21; Zech. 7:12; Mt. 10:20; Mk. 13:11; Lu. 1:70; 12:11, 12; Acts 3:18; 4:8; 11:28; 20:23; 21:10, 11; Rom. 1:

1:2; 3:21; 16:26; I Cor. 2:4, 9-14, 7:40; 12:3; Eph. 3:5, 6; II Tim. 3: 16; Heb. 1:1; 3:7, 8; 9:8; 10:15, 16; I Pet. 1:10-12; II Pet. 1:21; Rev. 2:7; 22:6.

Instances of inspiration: Noah—I Pet. 3:18-20. Joseph—Gen. 41:38. Bezalel—Ex. 31:3; 35:31. Seventy elders—Num. 11:16, 17, 25, 26-29. Joshua—Num. 27:18; Deut. 34:9. Balaam—Num. 24:2. The Judges: *Gideon*—Ju. 6:34. *Othniel* —Ju. 3:10. *Jephthah*—Num. 11: 29. *Samson*—Ju. 13:25; 14:6, 19; 15:14; 16:28. Saul—I Sam. 10:6, 13; 11:6; 16:13, 14; 19:23, 24. Messengers of Saul—I Sam. 19:20, 21. David—II Sam. 23:2; I Chr. 28:11, 12; Mk. 12:36; Acts 1:16. Amasai —I Chr. 12:18. Azariah—II Chr. 15:1; Ez. 2:1-4; 11:5, 24. Elijah— II Ki. 1:9-15; 2:15. See Lu. 1:15-17. Elisha—II Ki. 1:9-15; 2:15-22. Micaiah—I Ki. 22:14, 23, 28; II Chr. 18:23, 27. Jahaziel—II Chr. 20:14. Zechariah—II Chr. 24:20. Micah —3:8. Isaiah—Is. 59:21; Acts 28: 25. Ezekiel—Ez. 2:2. Elizabeth— Lu. 1:41. John the Baptist—Lu. 1: 15; Zacharias—Lu. 1:67. Simeon —Lu. 2:25-27. Apostles—Mt. 10: 20; Mk. 13:11. John 20:22; Acts 2: 4; 4:8; 9:17; Rev. 1:10, 11. Agabus —Acts 11:28; 21:10, 11. Stephen —Acts 7:55. Disciples at Tyre—Acts 21:4.

Reveals.—Mk. 12:36; Lu. 2:26; I Cor. 2:10, 11; Eph. 3:5; I Tim. 4:1; I Pet. 1:12; Rev. 2:7, 11, 29; 14:13.

Teaches or guides into all truth.— Neh. 9:20; Is. 40:13, 14; Mk. 12: 36; 13:11; Lu. 2:26, 27; 12:12; 24: 49; John 12:16; 14:26; 16:13, 14; Acts 13:2-4; 15:28; 16:6-10; Rom.

8:26; I Cor. 2:13; 12:8; Eph. 1:16, 17; I John 2:20, 27.

Confirms the word.—Lu. 24:49; Acts 1:4, 8; 2:38; 19:11, 12; Rom. 15: 18, 19; I Cor. 2:4; II Cor. 6:6; 12: 12; I Thess. 1:5; Heb. 2:2.

Comforts the Christian.—John 14: 16, 17, 26; 15:26; 16:7, 8; Acts 9: 31; Rom. 5:5; 8:26; 14:17.

Begotten or "born of" the Spirit.— Lu. 8:11; John 1:12, 13; 3:3-8; 6: 63; I Cor. 4:15; Gal. 4:19; Philemon 10; Jas. 1:18; I Pet. 1:23.

Convinces the world of sin.—Gen. 3:6; John 6:44, 45; 16:7-9; Acts 7:51, 52; Gal. 5:16-23; Eph. 6:17.

Commissions.—Acts 13:2-4; 20:28.

Baptism in the name of the Father, Son, and Holy Spirit.—Mt. 28:19.

Invites to salvation.—Rev. 22:17.

Makes intercession.—Rom. 8:26; Eph. 2:18; 6:18; Jude 20.

Sanctifies.—Rom. 15:16; I Cor. 6: 11; II Thess. 2:13; I Pet. 1:2.

Bears witness.—John 15:26; 16:14; Acts 5:32; Rom. 8:15, 16; 9:1; I Cor. 12:3; II Cor. 6:6; Gal. 4:6; Heb. 10:15; I John 3:24; 4:13; 5:6-8.

Earnest of the Spirit.—Rom. 8:23; II Cor. 1:22; 5:5; Eph. 1:14; 4:30; Rev. 2:7.

Sealed by the Spirit.—II Cor. 1:22; Eph. 1:13; 4:30.

Sin against the Holy Spirit.—Acts 8:18-23; I John 5:16. Blasphemy— Mt. 12:31, 32; Mk. 3:29; Lu. 12: 10. Resisting—Is. 63:10; Acts 5:1-3, 9; 7:51, 52. Grieving—Is. 63: 10; Eph. 4:30; Heb. 10:29. Quenching—I Thess. 5:19.

Unity of the Spirit.—I Cor. 12:13; Eph. 4:3-6.

Fruits of the Spirit.—John 15:2; Rom. 8:23; Gal. 5:22, 23.

Walking in.—Rom. 8:4; II Cor. 12: 18; Gal. 5:16.

The word the sword of the spirit.— Eph. 6:17.

Jesus' teaching concerning the Holy Spirit.—John 20:22. Anointing of Jesus—Lu. 4:18-21. Baptism in the name of the Father, Son, and Holy Spirit—Mt. 28:19. Baptism of the Holy Spirit—Lu. 24:49; Acts 1:5, 8. Born of the Spirit—John 3:5-8. Gifts of the Spirit—Mk. 16:17, 18. Given by God to disciples—John 3:34; 14:16, 17. *Not given until Jesus was glorified*—John 7:38, 39; 16:7. *Sent in name of Jesus*—John 14:26. *Sent by Jesus from the Father* —John 15:26; 16:7. Inspiration of —Mt. 10:20; Mk. 12:36; 13:11; Lu. 12:11, 12; John 14:26; 16:13. Sin against—Mt. 12:32. *Blasphemy* —Mk. 3:39; Lu. 12:10. Work of —John 16:8-14.

INSPIRATION. Job 32:8; II Tim. 3: 16.

INSPIRED. II Tim. 3:16.

INSTRUCTION, or, **TEACHING,** and **TEACHERS: Importance.**— Valued as one's life—Pr. 4:13; 6: 23. Die without—Job 4:21; 36:12; Pr. 5:23. Gives freedom—John 8: 32. Better than gold—Pr. 8:10; I Cor. 14:6. Wisdom is knowledge of God and the way of life—Ps. 34: 11-14; Pr. 1:7; 8:32-35; 23:15-18; John 7:17; 17:3; 20:31.

Who instruct?—God—Deut. 4:36; Job 35:11; 36:22; Ps. 71:17; 90: 12; 94:10, 12. He taught Moses— Ex. 4:12, 15. Ordinances—Ps. 119: 108. Statutes—Ps. 119:93, 102, 171. The good way—I Ki. 8:36; II Chr. 6:27; Ps. 25:8, 12; 27:11; 32:

324

8; 86:11; Is. 2:3; 8:11; 48:17; Mic. 4:2. War—II Sam. 22:35; Ps. 18: 34; 144:1. How to live—Tit. 2:12.

The Holy Spirit.—Neh. 9:20; Is. 44: 3, 4; Joel 2:28, 29; Zech. 12:10; Mt. 10:19, 20; Lu. 12:12; John 14: 26; 16:13; Acts 2:4, 11, 17, 18, 33, 36; 4:8; 6:10; 10:19, 20; I John 2:27.

Jesus called teacher.—Mt. 8:19; 9: 11; 10:24, 25; 12:38; 17:24; 19: 16; 22:16, 24, 36; 26:18; Mk. 4: 38; 5:35; 9:17, 38; 10:17, 20, 35; 12:14, 19, 32; 13:1; 14:14; Lu. 3: 12; 6:40; 7:40; 8:49; 9:38; 10:25; 11:45; 12:13; 18:18; 19:39; 20: 21, 28, 39; 21:7; 22:11; John 1: 38; 3:2; 8:4; 11:28; 13:13, 14; 20: 16. He taught with authority—Mt. 7:29; Mk. 1:38, 39; Lu. 4:32. Sitting down—Mt. 5:1; Lu. 5:3; John 4:6. Claims to teach God's words only —John 3:11-13; 5:19; 8:28. By apostles—Acts 4:2, 18; 5:21, 25, 28, 42; Eph. 4:20, 21; II John 9, 10. Still teaching—Acts 1:1.

Moses.—Ex. 18:20; 24:12; Deut. 4: 1, 5, 14; 5:31.

Priests.—Lev. 10:11; Deut. 24:8; 33: 10; II Chr. 35:3; Ezra 7:10, 25.

Princes.—II Chr. 17:7, 9.

Judges.—Deut. 17:10, 11; I Sam. 12: 23.

Sages.—Job 4:3; Dan. 11:33.

Scribes.—Ezra 7:6, 10; Neh. 8:1-3; Mt. 7:29; 13:52; 23:22; Mk. 1:22; 9:11; 12:35.

Apostles.—Their commission.—Mt. 28:20. Their practice—Acts 2:42; 4:2; 5:21, 28, 42; 11:26; 15:35; 18:11; 20:20; I Cor. 4:17; Col. 1: 28; 3:16.

Pharisees.—Jews—Mt. 16:6, 11, 12; 23:2, 3; Mk. 8:15-21; Lu. 12:1.

Christians.—Acts 15:1, 5.

Evangelists.—I Tim. 4:11; 6:2; II Tim. 4:2.

False teaching.—Prophets—I Ki. 13: 11-18; 22:5, 6, 10-12, 19-23; Jer. 14:13-16; 23:31, 32; 28:8, 9, 21-23; Zech. 10:2. Idolaters taught abomination—Deut. 20:18. Teachers—I Tim. 1:7; II Tim. 2:7, 8; 4: 3, 4; Tit. 1:9, 10. For money—Mic. 3:11; Tit. 1:11. Judaizers—II Cor. 11:13-15; Gal. 1:6-9.

What was taught.—Arts—Gen. 4:21, 22; Ez. 17:17; Deut. 31:19, 22; II Sam. 1:18; I Chr. 25:7, 8; Dan. 1: 4. Jehovah is the one God and is to be loved—Deut. 6:4-7; Ps. 25:4, 5, 9; 34:11. The Law—Deut. 6:1; 31:9-13; Josh. 8:32-35; II Ki. 23: 2; Ezra 7:10; Neh. 8:1-3, 8, 9; Ps. 119:12, 26, 64, 68, 124, 135; I Tim. 1:7. Jesus Christ or the gospel— Acts 4:2; 5:20, 21, 28, 40-42; 14: 21; 15:35; 18:11; 20:24; 28:23; I Cor. 4:17; I Tim. 1:10; 2:7; II Tim. 1:11; Tit. 1:9; 2:7, 12; Heb. 5:12; 8:11; I John 2:27; II John 9:10.

Who were taught?—All Israel—Ex. 4:12; Lev. 10:11; Deut. 17:11; 24: 8; 33:10; I Ki. 8:36; II Chr. 6:27; Jer. 6:8; Ez. 44:23. Children—Ex. 12:26, 27; 13:8, 14; Deut. 4:10; Rom. 2:20. All nations—Is. 2:3, 4; 42:4; 60:3; Mic. 4:2; Zech. 2:10, 11; Mt. 28:19, 20. Christians—Lu. 1:3, 4; Acts 2:42; 18:25, 26; I Cor. 14:26; Col. 1:28; 2:7; 3:16.

Methods of instruction.—Miracle. Neh. 9:14; Ps. 119:4, 15, 27, 40, 45, 56, 63, 69, 78, 87, 93, 94, 100, 104, 110, 128, 134, 141, 159, 168, 173; Is. 28:10, 13; 29:13; Jer. 35: 18; Dan. 9:5; Mk. 10:5; Heb. 9:

325

19. Ez. 12:22. Revelation—Deut. 29:29; I Sam. 3:7, 19-21; Is. 22:14; Dan. 2:19, 22, 28, 29, 30, 47; Mt. 11:25, 27; 16:17; Lu. 10:21, 22; I Cor. 2:10; 14: 6, 26:30; II Cor. 12:1, 7; Gal. 1:12; 2:2; 3:23; Eph. 1:17; 3:3, 5; I Pet. 1:12; Rev. 1:1.

LAW: Adamic.—Broad permission with but one prohibition—Gen. 2: 16, 17; 3:2, 3.

The law given to Noah.—To abstain from eating blood, from murder, to multiply and replenish the earth—Gen. 9:4-7.

The Law of Moses.—Was added because of transgression—Rom. 5:20, 21; Gal. 3:19; I Tim. 1:8-10. Given by Jehovah, through Moses, at Sinai —Ex. 19:11, 20; 20:1-17; Deut. 5:1-5, 27, 28; John 1:17; 7:19.

The law of ordinances given.—Ex. Chs. 21-23.

Given through the ministration of angels.—Acts 7:53; Gal. 3:19; Heb. 2:2.

Called.—Law of Moses—Ezra 7:6; Neh. 8:1; Heb. 10:28. Fiery law— Deut. 33:2. Letter—Rom. 2:29; II Cor. 3:6. Word spoken by angels —Heb. 2:2. Ministration of death —II Cor. 3:7. Ministration of condemnation—II Cor. 3:9; Gal. 3:10-13. See Deut. 27:26; 29:21; Heb. 12:18-21; Jas. 2:10-13. Living oracles—Acts 7:38; Rom. 3:2. Royal law—Jas. 2:8. Book of the law—Deut. 29:21; 30:10; 31:26; Josh. 1:8; 8:34; II Ki. 22:8; II Chr. 34:14, 15. Book of Moses— II Chr. 25:4; 35:12. Book of the covenant—Ex. 24:7; II Chr. 34:30.

The law given to the children of Israel.—Lev. 26:46; 27:34; Deut. 4:5; 29:1.

Gentiles did not have the decalogue. —Rom. 2:11-16; 9:1-5; I Cor. 9: 21; Gal. 3:2-14, 19.

References to the law.—Moses cites the law—Deut. 5:1-21. He relates the circumstances connected with the giving of the law—Deut. 10:1-5; 33:1-4. Moses wrote the law in the book of the covenant and delivered it to the priests—Deut. 31: 9-13, 24-29. He orders that it be put by the side of the ark—Deut. 31:26-29. Tables of the law put into the ark—Ex. 25:16, 21, 22; Deut. 10: 5; I Ki. 8:9, 21; II Chr. 5:10; 6:11; Heb. 9:1-4. Written on stones— Deut. 27:2, 3. Upon gates and doorposts—Deut. 6:9; 11:20. Carried in frontlets between the eyes and bound on the hands—Ex. 13:9; Deut. 6:8. Read every seven years —Deut. 31:9-10. By Joshua—Josh. 8:34.

Children of Israel required.—To know the law—Ex. 18:16. To keep the law—Deut. 4:5-9. Not to add to or diminish—Deut. 4:2. To teach it to their children—Deut. 4:9-10; 6:6; 11:18-19. Lay it up in their hearts— Deut. 6:6; 11:18. To obey it— Deut. 4:40; 5:32-33; 6:17; 7:11; 10:12-13; 27:1; 30:10-14; Josh. 1:7; I Ki. 2:3-4.

The law rightly used.—Is a royal law —Lev. 19:18; Jas. 2:8. Is a revealer of sin—Rom. 3:20; 4:15; 7:7-8. It is holy and good—Rom. 7:12, 16. Is magnified and made honorable— Is. 42:21. Is a tutor to bring us to Christ—Gal. 3:24. A shadow of good things to come—Col. 2:14, 17; Heb. 8:5; 9:23; 10:1-9.

The law violated.—Is a fiery law—Deut. 33:2; Heb. 12:18-20. Is a ministration of condemnation and death—II Cor. 3:7-9; Gal. 3:10-13. See Deut. 27:26; 29:21; Heb. 12:18-21; Jas. 2:10-13. Is an administration of guilt and judgment—John 5:45; Rom. 2:12; 3:19, 20.

The law interpreted by.—Priests and Levites—Lev. 10:11; Deut. 33:10; II Chr. 35:2-3; Neh. 8:7; Mal. 2:7. Scribes—Ezra 7:10; Mt. 7:29; 13:52; Ch. 23. Apostles—Acts 13:15-16; 17:1-3; 18:4. Jesus—Mt. 5:17-48; 22:35-40; Mk. 12:28-34; Lu. 10:25-37.

Facts concerning.—Read responsively at Ebal and Gerizim—Deut. 27:12-26; Josh. 8:33-35. Discovered by Hilkiah in the temple—II Ki. 22:8; 23:2. Read before Joshiah the king with effect—II Ki. 22:10-20. Reformation instituted—II Ki. Ch. 23. Read by Ezra on the return from Babylon—Neh. Ch. 8. Read in the synagogues every sabbath—Acts 13:14-15; 15:21; II Cor. 3:14. Following after the law the Jews rejected Christ—Rom. 9:31-33. Christ accused of breaking it—John 19:7 (Lev. 24:16).

Inherent defects of the law as respects salvation.—Could not make perfect—Heb. 7:11, 18, 19; 9:9, 10; 10:1, 2. Could not justify—Acts 13:38, 39; Rom. 3:20, 27, 28; Gal. 2:16; 3:10-12; 5:4. Could not give peace of conscience—Heb. 9:9; 10:1, 2. Righteousness could not come by the law—Rom. 3:21; 4:15; 5:13; 7:7; 9:30-32; Gal. 2:21; 3:21; Phil. 3:6. Has no grace for man—John 1:17. Could not give life—

Rom. 4:15; 7:9-13; II Cor. 3:6-13; Gal. 2:19; 3:21.

Christ fulfils.—Mt. 5:17; Mk. 1:15; Lu. 24:44-47; Acts 17:3; Rom. 10:4; Gal. 4:4-6; Eph. 1:9, 10.

Christ sums up.—Mt. 22:35-40; Mk. 12:28-34; Lu. 10:25-37. See Lev. 19:18; Deut. 6:5; 10:12; 30:6, 16, 20; Mt. 5:43, 44; 7:12; 19:19; Lu. 6:31-35; Rom. 12:14, 20; 13:8, 10; 15:1; Gal. 5:14, 15; 6:2; Jas. 2:8.

Temporary character of.—Rom. 7:1-6; II Cor. 3:7-14; Col. 2:14; Gal. 3:23-25; 4:1-5.

References.—Ps. 19:7; 119:70, 97, 109; Is. 8:20; Lu. 16:16, 17; John 7:51; I Cor. 6:1; I Tim. 1:7.

LAWGIVER. God the—Is. 33:22. Referred to—Gen. 49:10; Num. 21:18; Deut. 33:21; Ps. 60:7; 108:8.

MIRACLES. From *mirari*, to wonder. Generally sign of divinity. *Dunamis*, Power.

Purpose of miracles.—To produce belief.—Ex. 4:5-9; John 2:23; 4:48; 11:42; 20:30, 31. To reveal God—Ex. 7:5; 16:12; I Ki. 18:23, 24. To show glory of God—Ex. 16:7; John 11:42. To show works of God—Num. 16:28-30; Josh. 3:10; John 9:3. To act as credentials—Ex. 4:1-5; Mt. 11:4; Mk. 2:9-12; 16:20; Lu. 7:21, 22; John 2:11; 4:48; 5:36; 11:4, 40-42; 14:11; 15:24. To put difference between—Ex. 11:7; I Ki. 18:23, 24. To confirm the worker—Mk. 16:20; Heb. 2:3, 4. To produce fear toward God—I Sam. 12:17, 18; Dan. 6:20-27; Jonah 1:14-16. To produce obedience—Ex. 16:4, 5; 19:4, 5; Deut. 11:1-2; 29:2-9; Ps. 78:10-34. To aid in propagation of gospel—Acts 2:1-4; 3:6-16; 5:5, 12-14; 8:5-8; Rom. 15:18, 19. Miracles of Jesus wrought to confirm His claims about Himself—John 5:36; 10:25, 37ff.; 14:11; 15:24. Examples of confession of Jesus—Mt. 9:36; 14:14; Mk. 3:10; Lu. 9:11; John 6:2.

To teach spiritual lessons.—Lu. 5: 10.

Miracles foretold.—Birth of Isaac—Gen. 17:19; 18:10-14. Smiting Egypt—Ex. 3:20; 7:17-19; 8:2-23; 9:2-5; 10:4-6. Driving out nations —Ex. 34:10-11. Downfall of Jeroboam—I Ki. 14:7-11. Virgin birth —Is. 7:14; Lu. 1:31. Birth of John —Lu. 1:13. Life and character of Jesus—Is. Ch. 53. Introduction of the gospel accompanied by miracles —Is. 61:1, 2; Joel 2:28-32; Acts 2:17.

Miracles of Old Testament.—Creation—Gen. 1:1-27. Translation of Enoch—Gen. 5:24. The flood—Gen. Ch. 6. Destruction of Sodom, etc.—Gen. 19:24. Lot's wife—Gen. 19:26. Burning bush—Ex. 3:3. Change of Moses' rod into serpent —Ex. 7:8-10. Ten plagues—Ex. Chs. 7-12. Crossing Red Sea—Ex. 14:21, 22. Bitter waters sweetened —Ex. 15:25. Manna—Ex. 16:13-36. Water from smitten rock—Ex. 17:5-8; Num. 20:7-13. Pillar of cloud and fire—Ex. 14:19, 24; 33: 9. Moses' shining face—Ex. 34:29-35; II Cor. 3:7. Sacrificial fire from heaven—Gen. 15:17; Lev. 9:24; I Ki. 18:38; I Chr. 21:26; II Chr. 7:1. Strange fire and results—Lev. 10: 1, 2. Miriam's leprosy—Num. 12: 10-15. Earth swallows Korah *et al.*

—Num. 16:31, 32. Budding of Aaron's rod—Num. 17:8. Brazen serpent—Num. 21:9; John 3:14, 15. Speaking of Balaam's ass—Num. 22:28. Crossing Jordan by Israel—Josh. 3:14-17. Fall of walls of Jericho—Josh. 6:6-20. Stopping of sun and moon—Josh. 10:12-14. Dew on Gideon's fleece—Ju. 6:37-40. Dagon's fall before ark—I Sam. 5:1-12. Smiting of men of Beth-shemesh—I Sam. 6:19. Uzzah's death—II Sam. 6:6, 7. Withering of Jeroboam's hand—I Ki. 13:4-6. Widow's cruse—I Ki. 17:12-16. Raising of her son—I Ki. 17:17-23. Answer to Elijah's prayers—I Ki. Chs. 17, 18. Feeding of Elijah by ravens—I Ki. 17:4-6. Destruction of captains by fire—II Ki. 1:9-12. Dividing Jordan by Elijah and Elisha —II Ki. 2:8-14. Elijah's ascension to heaven—II Ki. 2:11. Healing of waters of Jericho—II Ki. 2:20-22. Destruction of young men by bears —II Ki. 2:24. Water for Jehoshaphat—II Ki. 3:16-20. Widow's oil —II Ki. 4:2-7. Shunammite's child —II Ki. 4:16-37. Curing deadly pottage—II Ki. 4:38-41. Multiplication of bread—II Ki. 4:42-44. Cure of Naaman's leprosy—II Ki. 5:10-14. Gehazi's leprosy—II Ki. 5:26, 27. Floating of axehead—II Ki. 6:5-7. Foretelling Benhadad's plans—II Ki. 6:8-13. Smiting Syrian army—II Ki. 6:18-20. Revival of dead by touch with Elisha's bones—II Ki. 13:21. Destruction of Sennacherib's army —II Ki. 19:35. Uzziah's leprosy—II Chr. 26:16-21. Delivery of three children from fiery furnace—Dan.

3:19-27. Daniel in lions' den—Dan. 6:16-23. Preservation of Jonah—Jonah 2:1-10.

Miracles of New Testament.—Miracles an evidence of Christ's divinity—Mt. 11:20-23; Mk. 2:5-12; John 2:11, 23; 3:2, 11; 4:48-53; 9:4; 10:37, 38; 11:45, 46; 14:11, 12; 20:30, 31; Acts 2:22. Miracles of the tongues, Pentecost—Acts 2:3. Cornelius—Acts 10:46. John's disciples—Acts 19:6. Corinthians—I Cor. 12:10. Miracles of Peter: *At beautiful door*—Acts 3:6, 7. *Ananias and Sapphira*—Acts 5:5-10. *Peter's shadow*—Acts 5:15, 16. *Aeneas*—Acts 9:34. *Tabitha*—Acts 9:40. Miracles of Stephen—Acts 6:8. Miracles of Philip: Acts 8:6, 7, 13. Miracles of Paul: *Blinding of Elymas*—Acts 13:11. *Healing of cripple*—Acts 14:10. *Casting out of demons and healing sick*—Acts Chs. 16, 19, 20. *Restoration of Eutychus*—Acts 20:10. *Viper on hand*—Acts 28:3. *Father of Publius*—Acts 28:8, 9. Disciples work miracles: *The seventy*—Lu. 10:17-20. One forbidden by apostles—Mk. 9:38. Corinthians—I Cor. 12:8-10.

Miracles were wrought: By power of God—Ex. 4:1-5; 8:19; John 3:2; Acts 14:3; 15:12; 19:11. By power of Christ—Mt. 10:1; Mk. 3:13-15; 6:7. By power of Holy Spirit—Mt. 12:28; Acts 2:2-4; Rom. 15:18, 19; I Cor. 12:4-11. In the name of Christ—Mk. 9:38, 39; 16:17; Acts 3:16; 4:30. Through faith of the agent in God—Lack of faith is the reason for failure—But few instances—Mt. 17:20; 21:21; John 14:10-12.

Effect on spectators.—Old Testament: Children of Israel—Ex. 4:30, 31; 14:31; Num. 17:1-13; Deut. 1:31-33; 10:21; II Chr. 7:3; I Ki. 18:39; Ps. 78:42-56. Pharaoh—Ex. 10:16, 17; 12:31, 32. Servants of Pharaoh—Ex. 10:7. Egyptians—Ex. 12:33; I Sam. 6:6, 7. Rahab and Canaanites—Josh. 2:9-11; 5:1. Gideon—Ju. 6:17-22, 36-40. Philistines—I Sam. 4:8; 5:2-5. Naaman—II Ki. 5:14, 15. Nebuchadrezzar—Dan. 2:47; 3:28; 4:2, 3. Darius—Dan. 6:20-27.

New Testament disciples.—Fig-tree—Mt. 21:20. Jesus walks on sea—Mk. 6:45-51. Draft of fishes—Lu. 5:8, 9. Miracle of wine—John 2:9, 11. Destroying temple—John 2:19-22. The multitude—Mt. 15:31; Lu. 4:36; 5:26; 8:35-37; John 7:31; 11:45, 48; Acts 2:6-12; 3:10, 11; 8:6.

Pretended miracles.—Egyptian magicians—Ex. 7:11, 22; 8:7. False prophets and religion—Deut. 13:1-3. Witch of Endor—I Sam. 28:7-14. False prophets—Mt. 7:22; 24:24. False Christs—Mt. 24:24. Deceive the ungodly—II Thess. 2:9-12; Rev. 13:14; 16:14; 19:20.

MOUTH, as a means of communication.—Prophets—Ex. 4:16; Num. 23:5, 16; II Chr. 36:21; Jer. 36:18; Ez. 3:26, 27; Acts 1:16; 3:18, 21.

The mouth of Jesus.—Mt. 5:2; Lu. 1:64; 4:22; 11:54; 22:71; John 19:29; I Pet. 2:22; Rev. 1:16; 19:15.

The mouth of God.—Deut. 8:3; II Sam. 22:9; Job 22:22; Is. 45:23; Lam. 3:38; Mt. 4:4.

MYSTERY OF GODLINESS OR OF GOD'S PLAN. That the Gentiles

should hear the gospel and be saved.—Rom. 11:1-36; Eph. 1:3-11; Col. 1:25-29; 4:3, 4; I Tim. 3:16.

This mystery hidden from men before the advent of Jesus.—Is. 60: 2, 3; Mt. 11:25; 13:34, 35; Lu. 8: 16-18; 10:24; 12:2, 3; John 8:56; 15:21; Rom. 11:1-36; 16:25, 26; I Cor. 1:18-21; 2:7-9; II Cor. 3:13-16; 4:3-5; Eph. 3:4-9; Col. 1:26, 27; Heb. 9:8; 11:13, 39, 40; I Pet. 1:10-12.

Having eyes that see not and ears that hear not.—Is. 6:9, 10; Jer. 5:21; Ez. 12:2; Mt. 13:14-17; Mk. 4:11, 12; Lu. 8:10; John 12:37-41; Acts 28:23-28.

This mystery revealed to the apostles. —Mt. 10:26; 11:25; 13:11, 16; 16: 16, 17; Mk. 4:11, 12, 22-25; Lu. 8:10, 16-18; 12:2, 3; I Cor. 4:1; II Cor. 4:5-7; Eph. 1:9, 10.

Revealed by the Spirit.—John 14:26; 16:13; I Cor. 2:9-16; Eph. 3:2-11.

This mystery made manifest through the death of Christ and the preaching of the gospel.—Lu. 12:2, 3; Rom. 11:1-36; 16:25, 26; I Cor. 1:18-28; 2:4-16; II Cor. 3:12-18; Eph. 6:19; Col. 1:25-29; 2:2, 3; 4:3, 4; I Tim. 3:9, 16; II Tim. 1:9-11; Heb. 9:8; I Pet. 1:12; I John 2:20, 27.

OBEDIENCE. A fundamental law. —Deut. 13:1-4; Rom. 5:19; 6:16; Phil. 2:12.

Life depends on obedience.—God's instructions to Adam—Gen. 2:16-17. To Israel through Moses—Lev. 18:5; Deut. 8:1-3. Through Joshua —Josh. 5:6; Rom. 5:18-19.

Faith is assured by obedience.—Acts 6:7; 5:31-32; Rom. 1:5; 5:19; 6:

17-18; II Cor. 7:15; Heb. 5:8-9; 11: 7-8; I Pet. 1:22.

Christ an example of.—Mt. 3:14-15; John 15:10; Phil. 2:5-11; Heb. 5:8.

Can obey but one God.—Deut. 4:1-4; I Ki. 18:21; Lu. 16:13; Acts 5: 29; Gal. 1:6-9.

Knowing depends on obedience.— John 7:17; 13:34-35; II Cor. 9:12-13; II Thess. 1:8; I John 1:3-6; 3: 23-24; 5:2-3.

Fulfillment of promises depends on obedience.—Old Testament—Deut. 11:8-9, 26-28; 32:46-47; 28:1-14; Jer. 38:20; Zech. 3:7. New Testament—Mt. 19:17; Lu. 11:28; John 10:27-28; 14:15-16, 23; Acts 2:38-39; 3:19-20; Jas. 1:25; Rev. 22:14.

Obedience must be from the heart.— Deut. 11:13; Mk. 12:33; Rom. 10: 8-10; 6:17.

Obedience better than sacrifice.—I Sam. 15:22; Ps. 50:8-15; 69:31; Pr. 15:8; 28:9; Is. 1:12-17; Jer. 6: 20; Hos. 6:6; Amos 5:22; Mt. 9: 13; 21:19; Mk. 12:33.

Obedience must be rendered to masters.—Eph. 6:5; Col. 3:22; Tit. 2:9.

By children to parents.—Eph. 6:1; Col. 3:20. By Disciples—Tit. 3:1-2.

General fruits of obedience.—Gen. 18:19; Lev. 26:3-13; Num. 14:24; Deut. 7:9, 12-15; 15:4; 28:1-15; Josh. 1:8; 14:6-14; I Ki. 2:3-4; II Ki. 21:8; I Chr. 22:13; 28:7-8; II Chr. 26:5; 27:6; Job 36:11; Is. 1: 19; Jer. 7:3-7; 11:1-5; 22:16; Mal. 3:10-12. New Testament—Mt. 5: 19; 7:24; 12:50; 25:20-23; Mk. 3: 35; Lu. 6:46-48; 8:21; 11:28; 12: 37-38; John 12:26; 13:17; 14:23;

15:10, 14; Jas. 1:25; I John 2:17; 3:24; Rev. 22:7.

Examples of obedience.—Noah—Gen. 6:22. Abram—Gen. 12:1-4; 22:3, 12; Heb. 11:8. Jacob—Gen. 35:1-4. Moses and Aaron—Ex. 7: 6; 40:16-33. Israelites—Ex. 12:28; 24:7; 39:42-43; Num. 9:20-23. Caleb and Joshua—Num. 14:24; 32:12; Josh. 10:40; 11:15. Elijah —I Ki. 17:5. David—I Ki. 11:34. Hezekiah—II Ki. 18:6-7. Josiah—II Ki. 22:2. Jehoshaphat—II Chr. 17:3-6. The three Hebrews—Dan. Ch. 3. Cornelius—Acts 10:33. Paul —Acts 26:16-20. Disciples—Rom. 6:17.

ORDINANCES (authoritative and established rites).

Ordinances of Israel.—Ex. 15:25; Num. 15:15, 16; Ps. 122:4. The passover—Ex. 12:14, 25, 43; 13: 8-10; Num. 9:14; II Chr. 35:13. Trumpet blowing—Lev. 23:24; Num. 10:1-11; Ps. 81:3-5. Concerning building a house for Jehovah—II Chr. 2:4. Ordinance of mourning —II Chr. 35:25. Putting away false gods—Josh. 24:23-25. Jehovah's ordinances are compulsory—Lev. 18:4-5; II Chr. 33:8.

The first covenant had ordinances.—Num. 9:3, 14; Lev. 18:4-5; Heb. 9:1-5.

These ordinances imposed for a time.—Jer. 31:31-34; Heb. 9:10.

Ordinances blotted out.—Eph. 2:14-16; Col. 2:14-15. Unduly depended upon—Is. 1:10-14; Mic. 6:6-8.

Folly of turning back to Jewish ordinances.—Gal. 5:1-14; 6:12-15; Eph. 2:14-22; Col. 2:20-23; 3:1-4; Heb. 7:11-19.

Ordinances of David.—Concerning the courses of priests and Levites—II Chr. 8:14. Concerning going to battle—I Sam. 30:22-25.

Teaching on ordinances.—Ps. 19: 9; 119:13, 30, 39, 43, 62, 91, 102, 106, 149, 156, 160, 164, 175.

Ordinances of the Jews.—Concerning the altar—Ez. 43:18; 46:14. Failure to keep ordinances—Ez. 11: 9-12; Mal. 3:13-15.

Walketh faithfully in the ordinances.—Neh. 12:28-33; Is. 58:2; Lu. 1:6.

Christian ordinances.—Baptism—Mt. 3:15; 28:19-20; Mk. 16:16; Acts 2:38-39; Rom. 6:3-6. The Lord's Supper—Mt. 26:26-29; Mk. 14:22-25; Lu. 22:14-20; I Cor. 11:23-26.

Civil ordinances.—Must submit—Rom. 13:2; I Pet. 2:13.

Ordinances of the heavens.—Job 38: 33; Ps. 8:3-4; 19:1-4; Jer. 31:35-36; 33:25.

PARCHMENT. II Tim. 4:13.

PAUL'S LETTERS.—They divide into four groups:

(1) The two to the Thessalonians written in winter of 53-54 A.D. (2) The two Corinthian letters, the Galatian and Roman, 58-59 A.D. (3) Colossians, Philemon, Ephesians, and Philippians, 63 A.D. (4) The two Timothys and Titus, his last letters, 66 A.D.

The style of Paul's letters.—(1) **Variety:** Logical—Rom. 4:12-21. Legal —Rom. 2:11-29; 13:1-10. Didactic —I Cor. 10:21; II Cor. 9:6-14. Laconic—Rom. 12:9-18; 14:5-9; Eph. 4:26-32. Elastic—I Cor. 9:19 -23. Corrective—I Cor. 4:18-21; II Cor. 10:1-11; 13:1-10. Persuasive —I Cor. 4:14-17; Phil. 2:1-16.

331

Imaginative—Rom. 8:18-39. (2) **Intensity.**—I Cor. 15:54-58; II Cor. 11:16-29; Gal. 4:12-20. (3) **Hopefulness.**—Rom. 8:20-25; 16:20; II Cor. 4:16-18; Phil. 1:19-26; II Tim. 4:18; I Thess. 4:13-18. (4) **Tact.**—The letter to Philemon—II Cor. 8:9-10. (5) **Compactness.**—II Cor. 6:3-10; Eph. 1:3-14; 4:11-16; Col. 1:9-23; I Thess. 5:4-18. (6) **Strength.**—I Cor. 4:7-13; I Tim. 6:3-10; II Tim. 4:1-8. (7) **Comparison.**—Rom. 7:9-23; I Cor. 10:6-12.

POETRY, BIBLICAL. Writing characterized by imaginative conception and versified form of expression.

Poetical books: Job, Pslams, Proverbs, Song of Solomon, Lamentations.

Prophetic literature, largely poetic in substance if not in form.

Poems in prose, in the Old Testament: Song of Lamech—Gen. 4:23, 24. Curse of Noah—Gen. 9:25-27. Oracle of Jacob and Esau—Gen. 25:23. Blessing of Isaac—Gen. 27:27-29, 39, 40. Blessing of Jacob—Gen. 49:2-27. Song of Miriam—Ex. 15:1-18. From the "Wars of Jehovah"—Num. 21:14, 15. The Song of the Well—Num. 21:17, 18. From the "Sayings of those who speak in proverbs"—Num. 21:37, 30. The Oracles of Balaam—Num. 23:7-10; 18:24; 24:3-9; 15:24. The Song of Moses—Deut. 32:1-43. The Blessing of Moses—Deut. 33:2-29. From the "Book of Jashar"—Josh. 10:12, 13. The Song of Deborah—Ju. 5:2-31. Samson's riddle and its answer—Ju. 14:14, 18. Samson's boast—Ju. 15:16.

The Song of Hannah—I Sam. 2:1-10. The Praise of David—I Sam. 18:7; 21:11; 29:5. David's Lament over Saul and Jonathan—II Sam. 1:19-27. David's Lament over Abner—II Sam. 3:33, 34. David's Psalm of Praise—II Sam. 22:2-51. David's Last Words—II Sam. 23:1-7. David's thanksgiving—I Chr. 16:8-36 (cf. Ps. 105:1-15). Hezekiah's thanksgiving—Is. 38:9-20. Jonah's prayer—Jonah 2:2-9. The prayer of Habakkuk—Hab. 3:2-19.

In the New Testament: The Magnificat—Lu. 1:46-55. The Benedictus—Lu. 1:68-79. The angel's Song (Gloria in Excelsis)—Lu. 2:14. The Nunc Dimittis—Lu. 2:29-32. From Cleanthes' Hymn—Acts 17:28. Spiritual Sight—I Cor. 2:9. Early liturgical fragment—I Tim. 3:16.

Kinds of Poetry in the Bible: Lyric, The Psalms. Elegiac, The Lament (Dirge)—II Sam. 1:19-27; 3:33, 34. Gnomic (Didactic), Proverbs, Special Type, The Riddle—Pr. 30:15, 16; Ju. 14:14, 18. Dramatic: In strict sense absent. Quasi-dramatic: Job, Song of Songs.

Versification: Chief feature parallelism, i.e., the expression of a thought in repeated similar or contrasted forms. (1) Synonymous: Repetition in varied expression. Duplicate—Ps. 21:1, 2; Job 8:5. Triplicate—Num. 6:24-26; cf. Mt. 7:7, 8. (2) Antithetical, Contrasted expressions—Ps. 1:6; Pr. 1:7; 22:29; 27:10; Mt. 8:20. (3) Progressive—Ps. 23:1; Pr. 25:8. (4) Chiastic (Introverted)—Pr. 23:15, 16. (5) Synthetic—Ps. 25:12. (6) Climactic—Ps. 121:3, 4. (7) Comparative—Ps. 42:1; Pr. 15:16.

332

Rhythm: Made by accent rather than length of syllable.

Metre: Unit, the accented syllable; Prevalent measures, 3-3 Accents, 4-4 Accents, 2-2 Accents.

Strophes. Marked by refrain—Ps. 42 and 43; 107.

Acrostics: Poems with artistic arrangement of initials.

Alphabetic peoms—Ps. 25, 24; Lam. Chs. 1, 2, 3, 4. Poem of 22 stanzas, each stanza consisting of 8 verses with the same initials—Ps. 119.

Artificial acrostic, incorporating name of author in initials of lines (Pedaiah in the Heb. text)—Ps. 25.

PRECEPT. Col. 2:22. Jehovah, Of—Ps. 19:8; 103:18; 119:4-173; Jer. 35:18; Dan. 9:5. Precept upon precept—Is. 28:10, 13.

PROMISES. *Promissum,* from *promittere,* to send, or put forward. Commands involved in promises—Ex. 19:5-8; 23:20-23; II Cor. 7:1; Gal. 3:21, 22; Heb. 3:14-19.

Promises founded upon five pillars. —(1) God's justice—Gen. 18:25; Job 8:3-7; Is. 9:7. (2) God's goodness—Deut. 11:31-32; Is. 49:15, 16; Heb. 6:10. (3) God's truth—Num. 23:19; Ps. 102:24-28; Mal. 3:6; Heb. 1:10-12. (4) God's power —II Chr. 20:6, 7; 25:7-9; Dan. 3: 17; 6:20-22; Mt. 9:27-30; Acts 20: 32; Rom. 4:20, 22; 11:23; 14:4; I Cor. 10:13; II Cor. 9:8-11; Eph. 3:20; Phil. 3:20, 21; II Tim. 1:12; Heb. 2:18; 7:25; Jude 24, 25. (5) God's oath—Deut. 7:8; Ps. 89:3, 4; 105:9; Jer. 11:6; Heb. 6:13-20.

Promises dealing with Old Testament covenants.—From Creation to Israel: Food—Gen. 1:27-29. Enmity of seeds—Gen. 3:15. Cain—Gen. 4:11-15. Flood—Gen. 6:17, 18. Noah's protection—Gen. 9:1-3. Bow in heavens—Gen. 9:11-17. Abraham's departure—Gen. 12:1-3. Separates from Lot—Gen. 13: 14-17. Vision of bondage—Gen. 15:5-14. Name changed—Gen. 17: 1-8. Concerning Sodom—Gen. 18: 26-33. Offering of Isaac—Gen. 22: 15-18. Covenant with Isaac—Gen. 26:3, 4. Covenant with Jacob—Gen. 28:13, 14. Covenant through Moses—Ex. 6:2-8.

Promises to Israel.—Contents of promise: The blessing—Deut. 28:1-12. The fulfilment—Ex. 15:1-13; I Ki. 8:55, 56; Ps. 77:8-15; 105:42-45. In answer to Solomon's request —I Ki. 8:22-26; 9:3-5; II Chr. 1:9-12. While in captivity—Neh. 1:8-11; 2:4-8; Jer. 32:42-44; 33:14-22. Messianic—Gen. 3:15; 12:3; 22:18; 26:4; 28:14; 49:10; Deut. 18:15; Ps. 2:6-8; 110:1, 4; Is. 9:7; 42:1-4; 53:10, 11; 55:3-5; 60:1-3; 61:1, 2; Dan. 2:44; 9:25f.; Mic. 5: 2; Zech. 9:9; 13:1; Mal. 3:1-3; John 1:41; 4:25. *Cf.* John 1:45. Prophecy concerning Jesus—Gen. 3:15.

Promises confirmed in Christ.—Mt. 1:22, 23; 2:5, 6; Lu. 1:54, 55; 1: 68-75; Acts 3:22-26; Rom. 1:2-3; 15:8, 9; Gal. 3:8-16.

Promises to Old Testament saints. —In sorrow—Ps. 50:14, 15; 55: 22; 91:1-7; Is. 43:2. In affliction—II Ki. 14:26, 27; Job 33:29, 30; Ps. 9:9, 10; 12:5; 18:27; Is. 51:21-23; Mic. 4:6; Nah. 1:12, 13. To widows and orphans—Ex. 22:22-24; Deut. 10:17, 18; Pr. 15:25; Jer. 49:11.

To worshippers—Ex. 20:24; Ps. 77:8-13; Is. 40:31. To the liberal—Ps. 41:1-3; 112:9; Pr. 3:9, 10; 11: 25; 22:9; 28:27; Eccl. 11:1; Is. 58: 10-12; Mal. 3:10. To the meek—Ps. 10:17; 22:26; 25:9; 37:11; 149: 4; Pr. 29:23; Is. 29:19. To the poor—Ex. 22:27; Ps. 12:5; 35:10; 69: 33; 72:2, 12-14; 109:31; Pr. 22: 22, 23; Is. 41:17. To the penitent—Lev. 26:40-42; Deut. 4:29-31; II Chr. 7:14; 30:9; Ps. 34:18; Is. 1:18, 19; 55:7. To the obedient—Ex. 15:26; 19:5, 6; Deut. 4:40; 12: 28; Ps. 1:1-3; 25:10; 103:17, 18; Pr. 1:33; Is. 1:19; Ez. 18:19. To seekers—Deut. 4:29; I Chr. 28:9; Ps. 34:10; 145:18; Is. 55:6, 7. To those who fear God—Ps. 34:7; 103: 11-14, 17; 112:1, 2; 115:12, 13; 128:1-4; 145:19; Pr. 19:23; Eccl. 7:16-18; 8:12.

Declarations dealing with the New Testament.—Concerning new covenant—Is. 55:3-5; Jer. 31:31-34; Gal. 4:24-28; Heb. 8:8-12; 12:24; 13:20. Declarations of Christ—Mt. 5:3-12; 10:39-42; 11:28-30; 16: 18, 19; 16:27; 18:19; 21:21, 22; Lu. 6:35-38; 11:9-13; 12:8, 31; 18:22, 29, 30; 21:14, 15; John 6: 35-40, 51; 7:17; 10:9, 16, 28; 11: 25, 26; 12:26, 32, 46; 14:3, 12, 21, 23; 15:7-10, 16; 16:22, 23.

Concerning the Holy Spirit.—Ez. 36: 26-28; Joel 2:28, 29; John 7:38, 39; 15:26; 16:13; 20:22, 23; Acts 1:8, 16; 2:33, 38; 5:32; Gal. 4:6; 6:8.

Concerning the kingdom.—II Sam. 7:11-17; Ps. 89:3-5, etc.; 145:11-13; Dan. 2:44; Ob. 21; Mt. 13:43;

16:18f.; Lu. 1:32f.; 22:29, 30; Acts 1:6-8; II Pet. 1:11.

Concerning the gospel.—Is. 61:1-3; 62:1, 2; Mt. 4:23; 26:13; 28:19, 20; Mk. 16:13; Lu. 24:47.

Concerning sinners.—Mk. 16:16; Lu. 19:10; 24:47; Acts 2:38, 39; 3:19, 20; 5:31; 16:31.

Concerning the Church.—Mt. 16:18; Eph. 3:6, 10; 5:26, 27; Heb. 2:12; Rev. 2:7, 10, 11, 17, 26-29; 3:5, 12, 20-22.

Promises token of participation with God.—John 14:2, 3; I Cor. 15:48, 49; II Cor. 4:14; Heb. 3:12-14; II Pet. 1:3-4; Rev. 21:7.

General promises.—Rom. 9:8; II Cor. 1:20; 6:6-18; Gal. 3:22, 29; Eph. 3:6; I Tim. 4:8; Titus 1:2; Heb. 10: 23; 11:13, 33; Jas. 1:12; II Pet. 3: 13; I John 2:25.

PROPHECY: Nature of prophecy. It is one person's speaking for another.—Illustrated by Aaron speaking for Moses—Ex. 7:1, 2; *cf.* 4:16. Especially it is man's speaking for God—Deut. 18:18; II Chr. 36:15, 16; Is. 45:21; Jer. 20:7-9; 23:22; Ez. 3:17-19; Dan. 9:22; Amos 3:7, 8; Jonah 1:2; Hag. 1:13.

Source of prophecy.—Not the prophet's private interpretation of the times, but given of God—Num. 12:6; I Ki. 22:14; Jer. 19:14; Amos 3:8; 7: 15; Lu. 1:67; II Pet. 1:20, 21.

Delivery of prophecy.—To the masses—Jer. 19:14; Ez. 33:31; Amos 5:1; 7:10; Hag. 2:2-4. To individuals—I Ki. 20:13, 22, 39-42; Amos 7:14-17; Hag. 2:21-23. Committed to writing—Ex. 17:14; Is. 8:1, 2, 16; 30:8; Jer. 30:2; 36:1-4, 17, 18, 32;

334

45:1; 51:60; Dan. 12:4, 9; Rev. 1:11, 19; 21:5.

Material of prophecy.—Prediction— Gen. 41:25; 49:1; Deut. 18:22; Num. 24:16, 17; I Ki. 11:29, 39; Is. 42:9; Jer. 28:9; Dan. 2:45; Rev. 1:1, 19; 22:6. Warnings—Ex. 3:18; Deut. 18:19; Is. 58:1; Jer. 1:16, 17; 26:2-6; Ez. 33:7-9. Religious instruction—Deut. 31:19, 21, 22; Is. 1:18; 2:3; Jer. 32:33. Moral exhortation—Is. 1:2-6, 16, 17; 3:10, 11; Jer. 25:4-6; Hos. 4:1-14; 6:5. Political or practical advice—II Sam. 7:5; 2:25; I Ki. 1:11-14; II Ki. 6:12, 21, 22; 14:25; Is. 7:3, 4; 37:21, 33; Jer. 27:1-15. Promotion of an enterprise—Ez. 6:14; Hag. 1:2-11. Interpretation of current events— Joel 1:2; 2:27; Hag. 1:5, 6, 9-11; 2:15-19. Revealing hidden things —Gen. 40:8; II Ki. 6:12; 7:1, 2; Is. 48:6; Dan. 2:19, 22, 23; 8:16-25; Mt. 26:68. Blessings—Gen. 9:26, 27; 27:27-29, 40; 49:3-27; Num. 23:9, 20-24; 24:7-9, 17-19; Lu. 2:29-32. Promises—II Sam. 7:8-17; Is. 2:2-4; Jer. 2:1, 2, 4; Hos. 4:1; Joel 2:31, 32; 3:18-21; Amos 3:1; Hag. 2:6-9; Zech. 13:1; Mal. 3:1. Threats and judgment—I Ki. 13:21, 22; II Sam. 12:10-12; Is. 1: 20, 24-31. Doom of cities and nations: *Babylon*—Is. 13:1-22; 21:1-10; Jer. 25:12-14. *Assyria*—Is. 14: 24-27. *Damascus*—Is. 17:1; Jer. 49:23-27; Amos 1:3-5; Zech. 9:1. *Philistia*—Is. 14:29-31; Jer. 47:1-7. *Arabia*—Is. 21:13-17. *Egypt*—Is. 19:1-22; 20:3, 4; Jer. 46:13-26; Ex. 29:1-16, 19, 20; 30:4, 6; 32: 32. *Moab*—Is. 15:1; 16:14; Jer. 48: 1-42. *Ammon*—Jer. 49:1-6; Ez.

21:28-32; 25:2-11; Amos 1:13-15; Zeph. 2:8, 9. *Edom*—Is. 21:11, 12; Jer. 49:7-22; Ez. 25:12-14; 35:1-15; Amos 1:11, 12; Ob. 1-21. *Tyre*— Is. 23:1-18; Jer. 25:22; 47:4; Ez. 26:2; 28:24; Amos 1:9, 10; Zech. 9:2-4. *Jerusalem*—Is. 22:1-14; Jer. 26:18; 9:11; Mic. 3:12. *Judah*— Jer. 1:15-18; 4:16; 7:30-34; 13:9-14, 19; 20:4, 5; 21:4-10; Ez. 8:17, 18; Hos. 5:10; 6:4; Amos 2:4-5.

Characteristics of prophecy.—Usually fragmentary or limited in scope— I Cor. 13:9; Heb. 1:1. Connected with the times of utterance—*e.g.*, Gen. 3:14-19; I Sam. 13:13, 14; Is. 7:10-17; and very often. Usually conditional, expressed—Is. 55:6, 7. Or unexpressed—*e.g.*, Jonah 3:5-10. For general principle, see Jer. 18:1-12. Conditions based on Jehovah's character—Joel 2:12-14; Jonah 4:2, 11. Some are unconditional, mostly messianic utterances —*e.g.*, II Sam. 7:14-16; Is. 55:3; Acts 13:34. Often for posterity— Deut. 18:18, 19; 31:19, 24-29; I Cor. 10:11; I Pet. 1:10-12. Rarely dates future events—*e.g.*, II Chr. 36:21; Jer. 25:11; 29:10; *cf.* Dan. 9:2. Exceeds other gifts in value— I Cor. 14:1-5.

Form of prophecy.—Public addresses —I Sam. 12:6-17; Is. 1:4-20; Jonah 3:4. Object lessons—I Ki. 18:38; Is. 8:1-4; Jer. 27:1-8; Ez. 37:15-23; Hos. 3:1-5. Historical illustrations —Ju. 6:7-10; Ez. 17:11-16; Hos. 11:1-4; Nah. 3:8; Hag. 2:5; Zech. 1:5, 6; Mt. 24:37, 38; II Pet. 2:5. Poetry (the following and many other prophecies have poetic form in the original language)—Gen. 9:

335

25-27; 49:2-27; Ps. 2:7-9; 110:4-7; Is. 52:13—53:12; 61:1-9. Dramatic composition—e.g., Ps. 24:7-10; 91:1-16; Is. 21:6-11; 63:1-6. Allegory or parable—e.g., Is. 5:1-7; Ez. 17:1-24; 20:49; 24:3-14; Zech. 1:8-11, 18, 21; 2:1-5; 3:1-5; 4:2-14; Gal. 4:21-31.

Fulfilment of prophecy.—Many fulfilled in short time—Gen. 40:12-14, 18-22; 41:25-36, 47-56; Josh. 6: 26; I Sam. 13:32; I Ki. 16:34; 20: 13-21; II Ki. 2:10-14; 14:25; 15: 12; 23:16; Acts 11:28; 21:11, 27-36. Many fulfilled in Christ. Some to be fulfilled after Christ's ascension —Acts 3:21. Others to be fulfilled at the end of the world—Dan. 12: 2; Mt. 24:30, 31, 40, 41; 25:31-46; Jas. 5:28, 29; I Cor. 15:22-25; I Thess. 4:14-17; II Thess. 1:9, 10; II Pet. 3:10-13; Rev. 20:11. Fulfilments a confirmation of prophecy —I Sam. 2:34; cf. 4:11; I Ki. 13: 3-6; 18:37-38; II Ki. 7:1-18; 19: 32-37; Jer. 28:15-17.

Christ in prophecy.—As seed of the woman—Gen. 3:15. As Abraham's Seed—Gen. 22:17; Gal. 3:8, 16. As David's Seed—II Sam. 7:12-16; Ps. 89:35-37; Mt. 22:42-45. As King—I Chr. 17:12, 14; Ps. 2:6; 45:6; 110:1, 2; Is. 9:7; 16:5; 55: 3, 4; Jer. 30:9; Ez. 37:24; Dan. 7: 14. As Priest—Ps. 110:4; Ez. 21: 26, 27; Zech. 3:5, 8; 6:12, 13. As Prophet—Deut. 18:15-19. As Shepherd—Is. 40:11; Ez. 24:23, 24; 37: 24. As Judge—Is. 11:3, 4; 16:5; Ps. 110:6; Mic. 4:3. As Servant of Jehovah—Is. 52:13; 49:5, 6; 53: 11. As a Sufferer—Is. 52:14, 15; 53:3-12; Zech. 13:7. As Son of

God—II Sam. 7:14; Ps. 2:7. As a Redeemer—Job 19:25; Is. 59:20. As the Anointed—Ps. 2:2; Is. 61: 1. As the Branch—Is. 11:1-5; Jer. 23:5; 33:15; Zech. 3:8; 6:12, 13. **Man in prophecy.**—Gen. 1:26-30; Job 8:20; Ps. 8:4-8; 144:3, 4; Heb. 2:5-18.

Church in prophecy.—As Jehovah's people—Ps. 47:9; 87:5, 6; 110:3; Jer. 31:33, 34; Dan. 7:27; Hos. 2: 23; Mic. 4:2-5; Zech. 13:9; 2:11. As a kingdom—Ps. 145:13; Is. 9:7; Dan. 2:45; 4:3; 7:27. As the redeemed—Ps. 107:2; Is. 35:9, 10; 62:12; 51:11.

World in prophecy.—Nations in unity under Jehovah—Ps. 22:27; 67:7; 82:8; Is. 19:23; 2:2-4; 56:6-8; Mic. 4:1-2. World's blessing—Gen. 22: 18; Is. 11:9; Jer. 3:19; 4:21; Acts 3:25; Gal. 3:8, 16, 29. World's conquest—Ps. 2:8, 9; 65:2; 110:5, 6; Is. 66:18, 19; Jer. 3:17; 16:19. World judged—Ps. 58:11; 82:8; 110:6; Is. 66:23, 24; Jer. 25:31; Joel 3:2, 12-15; Mic. 4:3; Mt. 25: 31, 32. World's salvation—Is. 45: 22; 49:6; 52:10. New heavens and new earth—Is. 65:17; 66:22; Rom. 8:21, 22; II Pet. 3:13; Rev. 21:1, 2.

PROPHETS: Are God's messengers. —I Sam. 8:7-9; I Ki. 13:1, 3, 9; II Ki. 17:13, 23; 20:4, 5; II Chr. 36: 15-21; Is. 6:8-11; 48:16; Jer. 7: 13, 25; 11:7; 25:3, 4; 26:5; 32: 33; Ez. 2:4; 3:4-11, 17-21, 27; Dan. 9:1, 6-10; Hos. 12:10; Amos 7:14, 15; Zech. 7:12; Heb. 1:1; Rev. 10: 11.

Are inspired by Jehovah.—I Sam. 9:6; II Ki. 3:12; Is. 50:4, 5; Jer. 20: 9; Amos 3:7, 8; Zech. 7:7; Lu. 1:

336

1:70; Acts 3:18; Rom. 1:1, 2; Jas. 5:10; I Pet. 1:10, 11; II Pet. 1:21; Rev. 4:1; 10:7; 22:6.

Methods of Jehovah in communication to them: By voice.—To Moses —Ex. 6:13, 29; 7:2; 19:3-5; 25: 22; 33:11; Lev. 1:1; Num. 1:1; 7: 89; 9:8; 12:8; Deut. 5:5, 31; 18: 18; 34:9, 10; Josh. 3:7. To Joshua —Josh. 3:7; 4:14. To Balaam— Num. 22:18-20, 38; 23:5-12, 16, 20, 26; 24:15, 16. To Samuel— I Sam. 3:4-14, 21; 9:15; 15:16, 19-21. To David—II Sam. 23:2. To Elijah—I Ki. 22:14, 28. To Isaiah —Is. 6:8, 9; 51:15, 16. To Jeremiah —II Chr. 36:12, 15; Jer. 1:1-10; 13:1-3; 16:1; 18:1; 24:4-10; 26:1, 2; 27:1, 2; 29:30; 33:1, 2; 34:1, 2; 42:4, 7; Dan. 9:2. To Ezekiel— Ez. 3:10, 11, 22, 27.

By dreams and visions—Gen. 41:15-40; Num. 12:6; I Chr. 17:15; II Chr. 26:5; Job 4:12-16; 33:14-17; Is. 6:1-9; Ez. Chs. 1-3, 8-10; Dan. 2:19; 7:13, 15; 8:1, 15-27; 10:7-9; Hos. 12:10; Joel 2:28.

By angels.—To Moses—Gal. 3:19; Heb. 2:2. See Heb. 3:2-5. To Balaam—Num. 22:35. To Gad—I Chr. 21:18, 20, 30. To Daniel— Dan. 7:13-28; 8:15-19. To John —Rev. 1:1; 17:1; 19:9, 10; 21:9; 22:1-9, 16.

By the Holy Spirit.—Neh. 9:20, 30; Joel 2:28; Zech. 7:12; Mt. 22:43; Acts 7:51, 52; Heb. 3:7-11; 10:15-17; I Pet. 1:10, 11; II Pet. 1:21; Rev. 1:10.

Instances of inspiration of the Holy Spirit.—Noah—I Pet. 3:18-20. Joseph—Gen. 41:38. Bezalel—Ex. 31:2, 3; 35:31. Seventy elders—

Num. 11:16, 17, 25, 26-29. Balaam—Num. 24:2. The judges: Othniel—Ju. 3:10. Gideon—Ju. 6:34. Jephthah—Ju. 11:29. Samson—Ju. 13:25; 14:6, 19; 15:14; 16:28. Saul—I Sam. 10:6, 13; 11: 6; 16:13, 14; 19:23, 24. Messengers of Saul—I Sam. 19:20, 21. David—I Sam. 16:13; II Sam. 23: 2; I Chr. 28:11, 12; Mk. 12:36; Acts 1:16. Azariah—II Chr. 15:1. Ezekiel—Ez. 2:1-4; 11:5, 24. Micaiah—I Ki. 22:14, 23, 28; II Chr. 18: 23, 27. Jahaziel—II Chr. 20:14. Zechariah—II Chr. 24:20. Micah— Mic. 3:8. Isaiah—Acts 28:25. Elisabeth—Lu. 1:41. John the Baptist —Lu. 1:15. Zacharias—Lu. 1:67. Simeon—Lu. 2:25-27. Apostles— Mt. 10:20; Mk. 13:11; John 20:22; Acts 2:4; 4:8; 9:17; Rev. 1:10, 11. Agabus—Acts 11:28; 21:10, 11. Stephen—Acts 7:55. Disciples at Tyre—Acts 21:4.

By the gift of knowledge and wisdom. I Chr. 28:19; Job 32:8; Jer. 11:18; Dan. 1:17-20; 2:21, 23; 4:8, 9; 5: 11-14; 9:22. See I Ki. 3:12, 28.

By permission of the divine name.— Ex. 3:13, 14; Deut. 18:18, 19; II Chr. 33:18; Ez. 3:11; Jas. 5:10.

Christ came in fulfilment of prophecy.—II Sam. 7:12; Mic. 5:2 (Mt. 2:5; John 7:42); Lu. 1:70.

Christ appealed to Moses and the prophets as if they were inspired to show that He came to fulfil their predictions.—Lu. 24:27, 44, 45; John 1:45; 5:45, 46. See John 13:18; 17:12.

The apostles appealed to Moses and the prophets as if they were inspired.—Acts 1:16, 20; 2:25-35;

3:18, 22, 23; 7:37 (Deut. 18:15);
8:28-35; 10:43; 13:29, 33-41; 17:
2, 3; 24:14, 15; 26:22, 23; 28:23-
27; Rom. 1:1-4; 3:21; 15:8; 16:
25, 26.

Prophets worked miracles as their endorsement.—Moses—Ex. 4:1-9; 7:9; 8:16-19; Num. 16:28-33. Elijah—I Ki. 18:30-39. Elisha—II Ki. 5:3, 8, 14. Daniel—Dan. 3:19-28; 4:2.

They taught the people through emblems.—Is. 20:2-4, Jer. 19:1, 10, 11; 27:1-11; 43:8-10; 51:63; Ez. 4:1-13; 5:1-4; 7:23; 9:4-6; 12:3-7; 21:6, 7; 24:1-24; Hos. 1:2-9.

Wickedness destroys prophetic vision.—I Sam. 28:6; Lam. 2:9; Ez. 7:26-27.

Must deliver God's message faithfully.—Num. 22:8, 18, 19, 38; 23: 5, 11, 12, 17, 26; 24:12, 13; I Sam. 3:16, 17; II Sam. 7:17; I Ki. 22:13-14; Is. 21:10; Jer. 6:27; 23: 28; 26:2, 12; Ez. 3:10-21; 11:25; 13:10-14; Mic. 2:6, 7.

Jehovah supports His faithful prophets.—Ex. 4:10-12; Jer. 1:6-19; 15:19-21; Ez. 2:6; 3:8-9.

False prophets described and denounced.—Deut. 18:20; I Ki. 13: 11-25; Is. 9:15; Jer. 6:13-15; 14: 13-16; 23:9-40; 27:14-18; 28:15-17; 29:8-9; Lam. 2:14; Ez. 13:4-7, 22; 21:29; 22:25-28; Mic. 2:11; Mt. 24:11; Lu. 6:26; II Pet. 2:1; I John 4:1. Adulterous—Jer. 23: 14; 29:21-23. Covetous—Mic. 3: 11. Drunken—Is. 28:7.

The people are warned against them.—Deut. 13:1-3; Jer. 23:16; 27:14-17; 29:8; Mt. 7:15; 24:5, 23-26; Mk. 13:6, 21-23; Lu. 21:8.

Punishment of false prophets.—Deut. 18:20; I Ki. 13:11-25; 18:22-40; 22:24-25; Jer. 13:13-14; 14:15; 20:6; 23:13, 15, 30-32; 28:15-17; 29:15-32; Ez. 13:2, 3, 8, 9; Mic. 3:5-7; Zech. 13:3-6. Punishment of their followers—Jer. 14:16; Ez. 13:15-16; 14:10-11.

Maltreatment of God's prophets.—I Ki. 19:10; II Chr. 36:16; Neh. 9: 26; Jer. 2:30; Mt. 5:12; 23:29-38; Lu. 11:47-51; Rom. 11:3; I Thess. 2:14-16; Rev. 18:24. God avenges wrongs done to His prophets—Deut. 32:43; II Ki. 9:7; I Chr. 16: 21, 22; Mt. 23:35-38; Lu. 11:47-51.

List of prophets in their order according to Old Testament.—Enoch—Gen. 5:21-24; Jude 14, 15. Noah—Gen. 9:25-27; II Pet. 2:5. Jacob—Gen. 49:1. Moses—Deut. 18:18; Acts 3:22; 7:37. Aaron—Ex. 7:1. Balaam—Num. 22:20, 38; II Pet. 2:16. The prophet sent to Israel—Ju. 6:8, 9. The prophet sent to Eli—I Sam. 2:27. Samuel—I Sam. 3: 20-21; Acts 3:24; 13:20; Heb. 11: 32-34. David—Ps. 22:1, 16, 18; Acts 1:16; 2:25-31; 4:25, 26. Nathan—II Sam. 7:2-3; 12:1-7. Gad—II Sam. 24:11-14. Ahijah—I Ki. 11:29-32. The prophet of Judah—I Ki. 13:1-10. Iddo—II Chr. 9:29. Shemaiah—I Ki. 12:21-24; II Chr. 12:5. Azariah—II Chr. 15:2-7. Hanani—II Chr. 16:7-10. Jehu—I Ki. 16:1, 7, 12. Elijah—I Ki. 17:1; 18:1-2; 19:1-8; Rom. 11:2-4. Elisha—I Ki. 19:16, 19-21; II Ki. 5:1-14; Lu. 4:27. Micaiah—I Ki. 22:7-9. Joel—Joel 1:1. Jonah—II Ki. 14:25; Mt. 12:39-41. Amos

—Amos 1:1; 7:14, 15. Hosea— 1:1. Isaiah—II Ki. 19:2; Lu. 4:17. Micah—Mic. 1:1. Nahum—Nah. 1:1. Zephaniah—Zeph. 1:1. Jeremiah—Jer. 1:1-2. Habakkuk— Hab. 1:1. Obadiah—Ob. 1, 2. Ezekiel—Ez. 1:3. Daniel—Dan. 2: 14-16. Haggai—Ezra 5:1; Hag. 1:1. Zechariah—Ezra 5:1; Zech. 1:1. Malachi—Mal. 1:1.

New Testament prophets.—Zacharias —Lu. 1:67-79. John the Baptist— John 1:6, 29-31. Jesus—Mt. 6:14- 21. (See His prophecies throughout the gospels.) Agabus—Acts 11: 28; 21:10. Paul—I Tim. 4:1. Peter —II Pet. 1:1-2; 3:3. John—Rev. 1:1-3.

Customs and habits.—Were anointed —I Ki. 19:16. Attached to king's household—II Sam. 24:11; II Chr. 29:25; 35:15. Had servants—I Ki. 19:3; II Ki. 3:11; 4:12. Presents offered—I Sam. 9:7, 8; I Ki. 14:3; II Ki. 4:42. Presents refused— Num. 22:18; II Ki. 5:5, 16. Frequently married men—II Ki. 4:1; Ez. 24:18; Hos. 1:2, 3. Often led a wandering life—I Ki. 18:10-12; 19:3, 8, 15; II Ki. 4:10. Wore coarse mantle—Zech. 13:4; Mt. 3:4. **Were sent to reprove and to call to repentance.**—II Ki. 17:13; II Chr. 24:18, 19; Is. 62:6; Jer. 6:17; 7: 3-7, 25; 11:7; 18:11; 25:4, 5; Ez. 3:17-21; 18:30-32; 33:7-9. To denounce the weakness of kings:

THE PROPHETS AND THEIR BOOKS IN THEIR ORDER

Name	Place of Ministry	Date B.C.	Historical Connection
Joel	Israel and Nineveh	About 830-810	In reign of Joash of Judah.
Jonah	Judah	About 800	In reign of Jehoahash of Israel.
Amos	Israel	About 760	In reign of Jeroboam II.
Hosea	Israel	About 750-725	From reign of Jeroboam II to that of Hezekiah.
Isaiah	Jerusalem	About 740-695	From death of Uzziah to reign of Manasseh.
Micah	Judah	About 735-700	From reign of Jotham to that of Hezekiah.
Nahum	Probably Judah	About 640-610	In reign of Assurbanipal or later.
Zephaniah	Judah	About 630	In reign of Josiah.
Jeremiah	Judah and Egypt	About 628-585	From reign of Josiah till after the commencement of Babylon exile.
Habakkuk	Judah	About 609-600	In reign of Jehoiakim.
Obadiah	Judah or Babylonia	About 585 (?)	Shortly after destruction of Jerusalem.
Daniel	Babylon and Persia	About 602-534	During the exile.
Ezekiel	Chaldea	About 593-571	Among Jewish exiles.
Haggai	Judea	About 520	In reign of Darius Hystaspes.
Zechariah	Judea	About 520-480	During rebuilding of temple and afterwards.
Malachi	Judea	About 433	Contemporary with Nehemiah.

Samuel to Saul—I Sam. 15:10-23. *Nathan to David*—II Sam. 12:7-14. *Elijah to Ahab and Jezebel*—I Ki. 18:17, 18; 21:17-29. To predict the downfall of nations—Is. Chs. 13-23; Jer. Chs. 46-51.

PROPHETESSES.—Miriam—Ex. 15: 20. Deborah—Ju. 4:4. Huldah—II Ki. 22:14. Anna—Lu. 2:36. See Joel 2:28; Acts 2:17-21.

PROVERBS. Several words may be translated "Proverb." "Taunting proverb" against the Chaldean—Hab. 2:6. "Dark speeches"—Num. 12: 8. "Riddle"—Ju. 14:12-19; Ez. 17: 2. "Hard questions"—I Ki. 10:1; II Chr. 9:1. "Dark sayings"—Ps. 49: 4; 78:2; Pr. 1:6. "Dark sentences" —Dan. 8:23. Translated "byword" in Ps. 44:14; 69:11. Called "Parable" when extended—Num. 23:7, 18; 24:3, 15, 20, 21, 23; Job 27: 1; 29:1; Ps. 49:4; 78:2; Pr. 26:7, 9; Ez. 17:2; 20:49; 24:3; Mic. 2: 4; Hab. 2:6.

Samples of proverbs.—Num. 21:27-30. Some proverbs prohibited—Ez. 12:23; 18:2, 3. A new proverb— Ez. 16:44. Translated parable in— Ez. 17:2; 20:49; 24:3.

Solomon spake 3,000.—I Ki. 4:32; Pr. 1:1, 6; 10:1; 25:1; Eccl. 12:9.

How a proverb arose.—I Sam. 10: 12. Ancients used proverbs—I Sam. 24:13.

A reproach to be a proverb.—Deut. 28:37; I Ki. 9:7; II Chr. 7:20.

Jesus used.—John 16:25, 29. Peter also—II Pet. 2:22.

SCRIBES: Originally writers, secretaries.—Ez. Ch. 9.

Writers.—I Chr. 24:6; Jer. 8:8; Ezra 4:8, 9, 17, 23; Esth. 3:12; Ez. 9: 11.

Secretaries.—To kings—II Sam. 8: 17; 20:25; I Ki. 4:3; II Ki. 12:10; 18:18; 19:2; I Chr. 18:16; 24:6; 27:32. To prophets—Jer. 36:27, 32.

Treasurers.—Neh. 13:13; II Ki. 12: 10; II Chr. 24:11.

Families noted for furnishing scribes. —I Chr. 2:55; Ju. 5:14—I Chr. 24: 6; II Chr. 34:13.

Notaries.—In court—Jer. 32:11, 12; I Chr. 24:6.

Keepers of muster rolls.—Ju. 5:14; II Ki. 25:19; II Chr. 26:11; Jer. 52:25.

Teachers of the law.—II Chr. 34: 18-21; Neh. 8:4-6; Ezra 7:6; Jer. 8:8; Mt. 23:2; 2:4; 17:10; 7:29; 13:52; Mk. 12:35.

Members of the council which opposed Jesus.—Mt. 2:4; 20:18; Lu. 22:66; Mt. 21:15; Mk. 8:31; 11: 18; Lu. 19:47; 22:2; 23:10; John 8:3.

Charge Jesus with blasphemy.—Mt. 9:3; Mk. 2:6-7; Lu. 5:21.

Conspire against Jesus.—Mt. 26:3; 27:41; Mk. 14:1; Lu. 22:6.

Reproved by Jesus.—Mt. 5:20; 15:1-9; 23:1-36; Mk. 2:16, 17; 3:22-30; Lu. 11:38-54; Lu. Ch. 20.

Persecuted disciples.—Acts 4:5, 18, 21; 6:12; 23:6-10.

Manner of teaching contrasted with that of Jesus.—Mt. 7:29; Mk. 1:22.

Characteristics of.—Garb and egotism—Mk. 12:38, 39. Various works —Mt. 23:1-7. Reputed wisdom—I Cor. 1:19, 20. Hypocrisy—Mt. 23: 13-15.

SCRIPTURES. Searching of, commended—Deut. 17:19; Josh. 1:8;

John 5:39. Cannot be broken—John 10:35. Given by inspiration from God—Acts 1:18; II Tim. 3:16; Heb. 1:1; 3:7; 10:15; II Pet. 1:20, 21. Given through prophets—Lu. 16:31; Rom. 3:2; Heb. 1:1. Fulfilled in Christ—Mt. 5:17; Lu. 24: 27; John 19:24; Acts 13:29. Expounded by Christ—Mt. 4:4; 26: 54; Lu. 4:19-21; 24:26, 27, 32; John 7:42. By Peter—Acts 2:16-36; 3:17-24. By Stephen—Acts 7:51-53. By Philip—Acts 8:25-35.

TESTIMONY. Ex. 31:18; 32:15; Ps. 25:10; Mt. 10:18. Apostles, Of—Acts 22:18; II Thess. 1:10; II Tim. 1:8. Bind up—Is. 8:16. Cleave unto Ps. 119:31. Conscience, Of—II Cor. 1:12. Consider thy—Ps. 119:95. Delight, My—Ps. 119:24. Good—I Tim. 3:7. God, Of—I Cor. 2:1. Jesus, Of—Rev. 1:2; 19:10. Love thy—Ps. 119:119. Nations, Unto —Mt. 24:14. Our Lord, Of—II Tim. 1:8. Shake off dust for a—Mk. 6:11. Sure—Ps. 93:5. Wonderful —Ps. 119:129.

TRADITION. II Thess. 3:6. Elders, Of the—Mt. 15:2-6; Mk. 7:3-13. Fathers, Of—Gal. 1:14. Hold fast —I Cor. 11:2; II Thess. 2:15. Men, Of—Col. 2:8.

TRUTH. In Old Testament usually means faithfulness, permanence, fidelity, sincerity, trustworthiness, honesty, justice, and reality.

God's faithfulness to covenant promises.—His stability and sincerity—Gen. 24:27; 32:10; Ex. 34:6; II Sam. 2:6; Ps. 25:5, 10; 30:9; 31: 5; 40:10, 11; 43:3; 57:3, 10; 69: 13; 71:22; 86:11, 15; 89:14; 91: 4; 96:13; 108:4; 11:7, 8; 115:1;

117:2; 132:11; 138:2; 146:6; Is. 25:1; 38:19; 61:8; 65:16; Dan. 4: 37. See Rev. 15:3.

Trustworthiness in man.—I Ki. 17: 24; Pr. 8:7; I Cor. 13:6; Eph. 4: 14, 15; III John 3. Honesty—Gen. 42:16; Pr. 12:17; Eph. 4:15, 25; John 8:44; I Tim. 2:7; II John 3. Justice—Ex. 18:21; Pr. 20:28; Rom. 2:2; Rev. 16:7. See Rev. 15: 3. Justice of Messianic king—Ps. 45:4; Is. 16:5; 42:3.

God requires truth in character.—Ps. 51:6; Jer. 4:2; Zech. 8:16, 19; Eph. 4:15, 25; 6:14; I John 3:18.

Collective system of statements which conform to reality.—Law is truth—Ps. 119:142, 151, 160; Dan. 9:13; Mal. 2:6-8; Rom. 2:20. Words of truth—Pr. 22:19-21. Word of truth—Ps. 119:43; Eph. 1:13; Col. 1:5; II Tim. 2:15; Jas. 1:18.

Gospel such a collective system.—John 8:31, 32; Rom. 1:18; II Cor. 13:6; Gal. 2:5; I Tim. 2:7; II Tim. 4:4; Tit. 11:14; Jas. 3:14; II Pet. 1:12; 2:2; I John 3:19; II John 2; III John 3, 4, 8, 12. Knowledge of the truth—Col. 1:5; I Tim. 2:4; 4: 3; II Tim. 2:15, 25; 3:7; Tit. 1:1; I John 2:21. Heard—Col. 1:5, 6. Believed—II Thess. 2:10, 12, 13; I Tim. 4:3. Obeyed—Gal. 5:7; I Pet. 1:22.

Truth disregarded.—Is. 59:4, 14,15; Jer. 7:28; 9:3, 5; I Tim. 6:5.

Man must serve God in truth (= Sincerity)—Josh. 24:14; I Sam. 12: 24; I Ki. 2:4; 3:6; II Ki. 20:3; Ps. 15:2; 26:3; 86:11; 145:18; Is. 38: 3; John 4:23; II John 4.

Exhortation to truth.—Pr. 3:3; 22:

21; 23:23; I Cor. 5:8; 13:6; I John 3:18.

Reality.—Deut. 13:14; Ju. 9:15; Pr. 12:17; Is. 43:9; Dan. 7:16; Mk. 5: 33; John 8:40, 45, 46; 16:7; Acts 26:25; Rom. 9:1; Gal. 4:16; Eph. 4:15, 25; Phil. 4:8; I Thess. 2:13; I Tim. 2:7; I John 2:21, 27; 3:18, 19; Ii John 1, 3.

Welfare.—State of society in which justice and honesty prevail—II Ki. 20:19; Esth. 9:30; Ps. 85:10; Zech. 8:16, 19.

Jesus the expression of the divine life. The highest expression of truth.— John 1:14; 8:31-36; 14:6; 18:37, 38; Eph. 4:15, 21.

Spirit of truth.—John 14:17; 15:26; I John 4:16.

Witness unto the truth.—John 5:33; 18:37; III John 12.

Church a pillar and ground of truth. —I Tim. 3:15.

Of a truth.—I Sam. 21:5; II Ki. 19: 17; Job 9:2; Is. 37:18; Jer. 26:15; Dan. 2:47; Mt. 14:33; Lu. 4:25; 9:27; 12:44; 21:3; 22:59; John 7: 40; Acts 4:27; 10:34.

VISIONS: Of.—Abraham—Gen. 15: 1-17. Jacob—46:2-5. Moses—Ex. 3:3, 4; 33:11, 18-23. Aaron and Miriam—Num. 12:6; Balaam— Num. 24:6, 16. Samuel—I Sam. 3:10-15. Nathan—II Sam. 7:4-17; I Chr. 17:3-15. Micaiah—I Ki. 22:19-22; II Chr. 18:18-21. Iddo —II Chr. 9:29. Eliphaz-Job 4: 12-17. Isaiah—II Chr. 32:32; Is. 1: 1; 2:1; 6:1-8; 21:2; 22:1-5. Jeremiah—Jer. 1:11-13; 23:16; 24:1-8. Ezekiel—Ez. 1:1; 2:8-10; 8:4-18; 11:24; Chs. 40, 41, 42, 43. Nebuchadrezzar—Dan. Ch. 4. Belshazzar—Dan. 5:5. Daniel—Dan.

1:17; 2:19; 7:1, 7, 13, 15; 8:1, 2; 13:17, 26, 27; 9:21-24; 10:1, 7, 8, 14, 16. Hosea—Hos. 12:10. Obadiah—Ob. 1; Mic. 3:6, 7; Nah. 1:1. Habakkuk—1:1; 2:2, 3. Zechariah—Zech. 1:7, 8; Chs. 2-6. Zacharias—Lu. 1:11-22. Christ— Mt. 17:2-7. Peter—Mt. 17:2; Acts 10:10-17; 11:5-10; 12:7-11. James —Mt. 17:2. John—Mt. 17:2; Rev. 1:4-22. Stephen—Acts 7:55, 56. Ananias—Acts 9:10. Cornelius— Acts 10:3-6. Paul—Acts 9:3; 16: 9, 10; 18:9; 22:6; 23:11; 26:13-19; 27:23; II Cor. 12:1-4; Ps. 89: 19. Of God—Gen. 12:7; 17:1; 18: 1; 26:2, 24; 35:9; Num. 24:4; Job 7:14, 15; Is. 1:1; Acts 2:17; II Cor. 12:1. No vision of Jehovah—I Sam. 3:1; Pr. 29:18; Lam. 2:9; Ez. 7:26; Mic. 3:6.

As a book that is sealed.—Is. 29:11.

False.—Ez. 12:24; 13:7, 23; Lam. 2:14.

Lying.—Jer. 14:14; 23:16; 29:8-9.

Their own.—Jer. 23:16.

Ashamed of.—Zech. 13:4; Mic. 3:7.

Fulfilment of.—Ez. 12:22, 23, 24, 27, 28. Young men shall see visions— Joel 2:28; Acts 2:17.

For multitude.—Ez. 7:13.

Of peace.—Ez. 13:16. Grievous—Is. 21:2.

Of night.—Job 4:13; 20:8; Is. 29:7.

Heavenly.—Acts 26:19.

Figurative.—Job 7:14; 20:8; 33:15; Is. 22:1; 29:7. Err in—Is. 28:7.

Valley of.—Is. 22:1, 5. Saw horses in—Rev. 9:17.

VOICE: Of God.—Gen. 3:8, 10; Deut. 5:25, 26; 18:16; II Sam. 22: 14; Ps. 29:3-9; 46:6; 81:11; 95:7; 106:25. Delegating Moses—Ex. 3:

342

4. Giving the law—Ex. 19:19; 20: 1, 18; Num. 7:89; Deut. 4:12, 33, 36; 5:24-26. To Ezekiel—Ez. 1:24; 10:5. His majesty—Job 37:4; Ps. 18:13; 29:4; 68:33; Jer. 25:30; Joel 2:11. Heard at baptism of Jesus—Mt. 3:17; Mk. 1:11; Lu. 3: 22. Disciples thought it thundered —John 12:28. Transfiguration— Mt. 17:5; Mk. 9:7; Lu. 9:35; II Pet. 1:17, 18. Hearken to the voice of God—Ex. 5:2; 15:26; 23:21, 22; Num. 14:22; Deut. 8:20; 9:23; 13: 18; 15:5; 26:14, 17; 28:1, 2, 15, 45, 62; Josh. 5:6; 22:2; 24:24; Ju. 2:2, 20; 6:10; I Sam. 12:14, 15. Obey the voice of God—Gen. 22: 18; 26:5; Deut. 13:4; 27:10; 30: 2, 8, 10, 20; I Sam. 15:19, 20, 22; 28:18; II Ki. 18:12; Jer. 3:13, 25. **Voices of Men.**—Gen. 3:17; 16:2; 21:12, 16, 17; 27:22; 30:6; Ex. 3: 18; 4:1, 8, 9; 18:19, 24; 23:21; 24:3; Num. 20:16; 21:3; Deut. 1: 45; 21:18, 20; 26:7; 33:7; Josh. 10:14; Ju. 13:9; 18:3, 25; 20:13; I Sam. 1:13; 2:25; 8:7, 9, 19, 22; 12:1; 15:24; 19:6; 24:16; 25:35; 26:17; 28:21, 23; II Sam. 12:18; 13:14; 22:7; I Ki. 17:22; II Ki. 4:31; 7:10; 10:6; 19:22; Job 3:7, 18; 4:16; 9:16; 38:34; Ps. 3:4; 5: 2, 3; 18:6; 44:16; 58:5; 74:23; 77:1; 116:1; 119:149; 130:2; 141: 1; 142:1; Pr. 5:13; Eccl. 5:6; Song of Sol. 2:8; 5:2; 8:13; John 3:8; 10:4; 12:30; Acts 9:7; 22:14; I Cor. 14:8; I Thess. 4:16; II Pet. 2: 16. Of adjuration—Lev. 5:1. Birds —Eccl. 12:4; Song of Sol. 2:12, 14. Charmers—Ps. 58:5. Cities— Is. 42:11. Floods—Ps. 93:3. Fools —Eccl. 5:3; Pr. 10:10, 14; 14:16;

18:6, 7; 29:11. Heaven—Ps. 19:3. Groaning—Ps. 102:5. Joy—Job 3: 7; Ps. 42:4; 118:15. Lion—Job 4: 10; Is. 31:4. Melody—Ps. 98:5; Is. 51:3. Praise—Ps. 42:4; 66:8. Prayer —Ps. 66:19. Singing—Ex. 32:18; II Sam. 19:35; I Chr. 15:16; II Chr. 5:13. Supplication—Ps. 28:2, 6; 31.22; 86:6; 130:2; 142:1. Thanksgiving—Ps. 26:7. Thunder—Job 37: 4, 5; 40:9; Ps. 18:13; 77:18; 104: 7. Triumph—Ps. 47:1. Tumult—Is. 66:6. Weeping—II Sam. 15:23; 19: 4; Job 2:12; 30:31. See Ju. 2:4; Ruth 1:9. Wilderness—Is. 42:11. One crying in the wilderness—Is. 40:3, 6; Mt. 3:3; Mk. 1:3; Lu. 3: 4; John 1:23. Wisdom—Pr. 1:20; 8:1, 4, 32; 5:13. Words, Of—Deut. 1:34; 5:28; I Sam. 15:1; Job 33: 8; 34:16; Ps. 103:20.

Lifting up the voice.—Gen. 29:11; 39:15, 18; Num. 14:1; Ju. 2:4; 9: 7; Ruth 1:9, 14; I Sam. 30:4; II Sam. 3:32; 13:36; I Chr. 15:16; II Chr. 5:13; Job 2:12; Pr. 2:3; Is. 24:14; 40:9; 42:2; 52:8; 58:1.

Loud voice.—Gen. 39:14; Deut. 27: 14; I Sam. 28:12; II Sam. 19:4; I Ki. 8:55; II Ki. 18:28; Ezra 3:12; 10:12; Neh. 9:4; Pr. 27:14; Is. 36: 13.

WORD OF GOD. Any expression of God's mind or will.

Names of.—Oracles of God—Rom. 3:2. Word of faith—Rom. 10:8. Word of the gospel—Acts 15:7. Word of Reconciliation—II Cor. 5: 19. Word of truth—Eph. 1:13.

Word of Life.—Phil. 2:16. Word of Christ—Mk. 10:24; Lu. 24:8, 44; Rom. 10:17; Col. 3:16; I Thess. 4: 15. In prayer—Mk. 14:39. In temple

343

—John 8:20. Sword of Spirit—Eph. 6:17. Word of promise—Rom. 9:6-9; I Tim. 4:5. Hearing of word—Lu. 11:28; Jas. 1:22. The word—Acts 10:36. Hence "Word" is a name of Christ—John 1:1; I John 1:1; Rev. 19:13. Jesus, the full self-expression of the God-head, is the Living Word—John 1:1-5, 14.

Character of.—Everlasting—Ps. 119: 89, Is. 40:8; Mt. 24:35; Mk. 13: 31; Lu. 21:33; I Pet. 1:23, 25. Not bound—II Tim. 2:9. Good—Is. 39: 8. Pure—Pr. 30:5. John 15:3. Worlds framed—Heb. 11:3; II Pet. 3:5. Powerful—Jer. 23:29; Lu. 4: 32; Acts 20:32; Heb. 4:12; Jas. 1: 21. Source of strength—I John 2: 14. Commanding—II Chr. 30:12; 35:6; Neh. 1:8. Wise—II Tim. 3: 15.

Supreme authority of.—Deut. 4:1-10; 12:32; Josh. 1:8; Ps. 33:6; Pr. 30:5, 6; Mk. 4:24; Lu. 8:12; John 12:48-50; Heb. 1:1-3; 2:1-4; Rev. 1:1-3; 20:12; 22:18, 19.

Direct words of.—Alpha and Omega —Is. 44:6; 48:12; Rev. 1:8; 21: 6. Word of—II Chr. 11:4; Jer. 30: 4. To angel—I Ki. 13:18. Man of Judah—I Ki. 13:1.

Functions of word of God.—Give life —John 6:63; I Pet. 1:23. Sanctifies —John 17:17. Gives hope—Ps. 119:74, 81, 114, 116; 130:5. Comforts—Ps. 119:82, 105.

Word of Jehovah is tried.—II Sam. 22:31; Ps. 18:30; Pr. 30:5. Despised —Num. 15:31; Is. 5:24. Rejected —Ex. 9:21; I Sam. 15:26; II Chr. 34:21; Ps. 119:158; Jer. 8:9. Feared —Ex. 9:20; Ps. 119:161; Is. 66: 5. Loved—Num. 22:18; I Sam. 3:

1; Job 23:12; Ps. 119:140. Received—Acts 2:41; 11:1; I Thess. 3:13. Obeyed—Ps. 119:67, 134; Acts 20:35; II Cor. 4:2; Tit. 2:5. Praised—Ps. 56:4, 10; 119:162. To be studied—Ps. 119:148; II Tim. 2:15.

Word revealed. To Abraham—Gen. 15:1, 4; Jacob—I Ki. 18:31; Ps. 147:19; Is. 9:8. Joseph—Ps. 105: 19. To judges—*Joshua*—Josh. 3: 9; *Samuel*—I Sam. 8:10; 9:27; 15: 1, 10. To kings—*David*—I Chr. 22: 8; II Chr. 6:17; *Solomon*—I Ki. 6: 11; *Jehu*—I Ki. 16:1, 7, 12; II Ki. 15:12; *Jehoiakim*—Jer. 26:1. To the people of Israel through the prophets—Is. 1:10; 28:14; 39:5; 66:5; Jer. 2:4, 31; 7:2; 9:20; 10: 1; 17:20; 19:3; 21:11; 22:29; 29: 20, 30; 31:10; 34:4. To prophets— I Ki. 13:20, 26, 32; Ezra 9:4; Zech. 7:7, 12. *Amos*—Amos 3:1; 7:16; 8:11. *Elijah*—I Ki. 17:2, 8; 18:1; 19:9; 21:17, 28. *Elisha*—II Ki. 3: 12; 7:1. *Ezekiel*—Ez. 1:3; 3:16; 7: 1; 11:14; 12:1, 8, 17, 26; 13:1, 2; 14:2, 12; 15:1; 16:1, 35; 17:1, 11; 18:1; 20:2, 45, 47; 21:1, 8, 18; 22:1, 17, 23; 23:1; 24:1, 15, 20; 25:1, 3; 26:1; 27:1; 28:1, 11, 20; 29:1, 17; 30:1, 20; 31:1; 32:1, 17; 33:1, 23; 34:1, 7, 9; 35:1; 36:1, 4, 16; 37:4, 15; 38:1. *Gad*—II Sam. 24:11. *Haggai*—Hag. 1:1, 3; 2:1, 5, 10, 20. *Hosea*—Hos. 1:1, 2; 4:1. *Isaiah*—II Ki. 20:4, 16, 19; Is. 16:13; 24:3; 37:22; 38:4. *Jeremiah*—Jer. 1:2, 4, 11, 13; 2:1; 13: 1, 3, 8; 14:1; 16:1; 18:1; 24:4; 25: 3; 27:1; 28:12; 32:6, 26; 33:1, 19, 23; 34:12; 35:12; 36:4, 6, 8, 27; 37:6, 17; 38:21; 39:15; 42:7, 15;

43:8; 44:24, 26; 46:1, 13; 47:1; 49:34; 50:1; Dan. 9:2. *Joel*—Joel 1:1. *Jonah*—Jonah 1:1; 3:1, 3. *Malachi*—Mal. 1:1. *Micah*—Mic. 1:1; 4:2. *Micaiah*—I Ki. 22:19, 22; II Chr. 18:18. *Moses*—Ex. 4:28, 30; 10:1; 19:7; 24:3, 4; 35:1; Num. 11:24; 36:5; Deut. 5:5; 34: 5; Neh. 1:8. *Nathan*—I Chr. 17:3. *Shemaiah*—I Ki. 12:22, 24. *Zechariah*—Zech. 1:1, 7; 4:6; 6:9; 7:1, 4, 8; 8:1, 18; 9:1; 11:11; 12:1. To priests—*Zacharias*—Lu. 1:20. To apostles—*John*—Lu. 3:2.

Fulfilment of.—I Ki. 2:27; 13:2, 5, 9, 17; 14:18; 16:12, 34; 17:5, 16; 22: 38; II Ki. 1:17; 4:44; 7:16; 9:25, 26, 36; 10:10; 14:25; 15:12; 23: 16; 24:2; I Chr. 10:13; 11:3, 10; 12:23; 15:15; II Chr. 36:21, 22; Ezra 1:1; Ps. 103:20; 119:65, 76, 107, 154, 169, 170; 148:8; Jer. 13:2; 32:8; Lam. 2:17; Mt. 26:75; Mk. 14:72; Lu. 22:6; Col. 1:25; I John 2:22; Rev. 17:17. Commands —Num. 3:16, 51.

Spreading of.—Ps. 147:15, 18. Of gospel—Acts 6:7; 11:19; 12:24; 13:5, 7, 44, 46, 48, 49; 14:3, 25; 15:7, 35, 36; 16:6, 32; 17:11, 13; 18:11; 19:10, 20; 20:32; 22:22; Rom. 9:6; 10:17; I Cor. 14:36; I Thess. 1:8.

Ministry of the word of God.—Acts 4:29, 31; 8:4, 25; II Cor. 2:17; I Thess. 4:15; II Thess. 3:1; Heb. 13: 7. Eternal life—Mt. 4:4.

Martyrs for.—Rev. 6:9; 20:4.

Word of God sought for.—I Ki. 22: 5; II Chr. 18:4; Jer. 17:15.

Followers of.—Num. 24:4, 16; I Chr. 25:5; II Chr. 29:15; Acts 4:4; 6:2; 8:14; I John 2:14.

Judgments for all despising the word of God.—Lev. 26:14-40; Deut. 28: 15-68; II Ki. 22:13; II Chr. 36:15, 16; Pr. 1:24-32; Is. 55:11, 12; 56: 4; Rom. 3:11, 12, 16; II Thess. 1: 7-9.

Prophecies concerning.—Is. 2:3; 28: 13; 40:8; Jer. 6:10; Amos 8:11, 12; Mic. 4:2; Zech. 4:6, 8.

Index of Scriptures

Old Testament
Genesis

1:1	33, 35, 36
1:1—2:3	156
1:11	41
1:25	41
1:26	38
1:26, 27	37
1:27	28
2:2	22
2:2, 3	36, 37
2:3	36
2:4	69, 156
2:4—3:24	156
2:8, 9	38
2:12-18	157
2:21, 22	28
2:23	30
2:24	28, 31
3:15	157
3:24	39
4:1	130
4:2-8	43
4:9, 10	36
5:1	69
5:2	29
5:2—6:8	154
6:9	155
6:9-29	155
11:27	159
11:27—25:11	158
12:1	159
12:1-4	47, 161
12:1—25:11	161
12:4	160
16:1-16	161
16:2	161
16:12	163
18:17, 8	164
18:23-32	165
21:13	162
22:2	165
25:8—35:29	170

Genesis

25:19—35:29	158
25:21—28:29	171
25:23	171
26:1	168
26:1-8	157
26:2, 3	168
26:2, 24	168
26:3, 4	169
26:17, 18	169
26:24	170
28:10—31:55	171
28:12-15	172
32:2 & 32:22-32	173
35:11, 12	174
36	158
37:2—50:36	158
50:19, 20	176
50:20	177

Exodus

14:1	2
20:2-4	153
23:20	26

Deuteronomy

31:11, 12	152
31:24-27	151

Joshua

11:15	152

Judges

3:4	152

II Samuel

1:17ff.	11
7:11-13	54

I Kings

22:19	14

Job

1:5	205
1:8	213, 214
1:21	207
2:4	207
2:7	207
2:8	207
2:10	207
2:13	208
3:1—31:4	204
3:3a-11	209
3:20-21	209
3:23	209
4:4f.	209
4:7	209
4:7-8	60
4:18, 19	209
5:3	209
5:7-27	209
5:7, 8, 17, 18	209
5:13	20
6:2, 3b	209
6:6b	210
6:8	210
6:12	210
7:2, 6	210
7:11-21	210
8:1	210
8:4	210
8:8-10	211
8:11b-13	211
8:20	210
9:2b-3	211
9:24	211
11:3a	211
11:11	212
11:13b-14	212
31:35	213
31:40b	213
32:1—37:24	204, 212
38:1—42:6	204
39:30	213

Job

40:1-5	214
42:5	221
42:5, 6	217
42:6	214
42:7-17	204
45:9	145

Psalms

8	38
8:4	37
8:6-8	38
19	146
22	23, 48
22:22-25	49
22:26-31	49
51	19
102	34, 35
102:24, 25	34

Isaiah

1:5, 6	178
2:1-5	9
6:1	14
6:5	178
6:7	179
6:8	179
7:3	23
7:14	64
8:3, 4	23
8:8	23
8:18	22
20:9	180
40:31	200
42:2, 3	59
45:9	145, 146
52:2ff.	59
52:14, 15	59
66:1-2	34

Jeremiah

1:4a	191
1:4	2

Jeremiah

1:4-10	191
1:4-19	191
1:6	180
1:8, 9	12
1:10	192
1:11, 12	193
1:11-12	194
1:13-16	193
1:14-16	195
1:17-19	193
2:7-8	187
2:9	188
4:3	12
4:16-18	201
5:29	188
7:1-4	12
13:1-27	198
13:12-14	195
15:18	51
18:1-12	196
18:11	196
19:1, 2 & 10, 11	198
20:7	51
20:9	51
20:14, 18	51
24:1-10	198
27:1—28:17	199
30:6	200
30:12-13	200
31:3-6	200
31:33	55
36:2	190
36:2, 32	190
36:32	189, 190
Chps. 46-50	193

Ezekiel

1:3	181
1:1, 26, 28	14
2:2, 3	181

Daniel

7:9	14

Hosea

2:5	14
3:1	13
10:12	13

Joel

2:12, 13	149
2:24, 26	150
2:28, 29	149

Amos

1:3, 6, 9, 15	4
2:1, 4, 6	4
3:4b	180
5:24	202
7:1	183, 184
7:1-9	185
7:2, 3	185
7:4-9	185
7:14	180
9:1	183

Obadiah

Verse 3	183
Verse 21	184

Micah

4:1-5	9

Nahum

1:1	182
2:13	182

Habakkuk

2:4	188

Malachi

3:1	26

New Testament
Matthew

1:1	67, 68, 69, 70
1:1; 1:2-17	67
1:2-17	68, 69
1:18	68
1:22f	20
2:15	2
2:17	20
3:7, 10	201
5:17	70, 187
11:10	26
19:3-5	28
21:43 . . . (quoted without reference)	71
21:43	70
24:3	53

Mark

1:1 . . . . (quoted without reference)	72
1:2b-3	73
1:2-8	73
1:9—10:52	74
10:1	87

Luke

1:1-4 . . . (quoted without reference)	75
1:1-4	79, 84
1:4	81, 85
1:32, 33	55
8:2, 3	86
10:21	200
22:25-27	140
24:13-27	58
24:32-34	201
24:45-48	150

John

1:1	57
1:1, 3	33
1:1, 14	5
1:10	32
1:14	101

John

1:14, 16	222
2:1-11	99
4:46-54	99
5:1-15	100
5:39, 40	223
6:1-15	100
6:15	102
6:16-21	100
6:22-59	102
6:50	103
6:51	103
8:56	47
9:1-12	100
9:2	60, 218
11:17-44	100
13:1—20:29	101
19:26, 27	78
19:36	56
20:30	98
20:30, 31	91, 96, 97
20:31	101
21:24	91, 102, 103
21:25	76

Acts

1:1	78
1:7	53
2:17-21, 36	150
7:2	47
7:4	107
7:5	61
7:48, 50	34
7:50	32
7:58—8:1	132
7:59, 60	133
14:15	36
14:15-17	32
15	122
16:3	134
17:24	36
17:24-29	32

Acts

22:14, 15	129
23:1	132
26:20	133

Romans

1:2	18, 19, 42
1:20	32, 36
3:4	19
4:12-17	32
4:19-21	164
6:23	60
7:15, 24	132
8:3	146
9:14-18	145
9:19	145
10:18	146
16:22	119

I Corinthians

2:9, 10	127
2:12, 13	127
2:13, 16	139
2:16	127
7:40	127
10:3, 4	57
10:13	208
11:2	80
Chps. 12-40	127
14:37	128, 139
14:38	128
15:3	80
15:9, 10	135
15:38	41
15:38-45	32, 40
15:44-49	42
16:21	119

II Corinthians

1:23	140
2:3, 4	140
5:11-20	141
8:9	57

Galatians

1:1	123
1:6	122
1:11, 12	123
1:11-17	122
1:15, 16	131
1:20	121, 122, 123
2:1, 2	124
2:3-5	134
2:14	135, 140
3:21, 22	147
3:28	144
3:29	54
6:11	119

Ephesians

Chps. 1-2	136
3:2, 7	136

Colossians

1:2	118
1:16	33
1:16, 17	32
4:16	117
4:18	119

I Thessalonians

2:13	124
4:1-7	124, 125
4:3	124
4:9	125
5:27	125

II Thessalonians

2:15	80, 126
3:3-15	126
3:17	119

I Timothy

1:2	118
2:14, 15	139
5:21	139
6:9	60

II Timothy

3:15 42
3:15, 16 . . . . 17f.
3:16 . . . . 1, 201

Philemon

Vss. 8-14 142
Vss. 15-20 143
Vss. 18, 19 121
Vs. 19 120

Hebrews

1:1 . . . . 1, 5
1:1, 2 . . . . 2f.
1:2, 10 32
1:10 35
2:6, 7 . . . . 32, 38
2:11-13 23
4:4 22
4:9, 10 32
4:11 . . . . 36, 37
4:12, 13 5
5:7f. 49
9:7-8 . . . . 19f.
11:3 32
11:4 . . . . 32, 43
11:17, 19 166

I Peter

I Peter 52
1:3-12 45
1:10 49
1:10-11 1
1:10-12 . . . . 45, 46, 60, 139
1:11 . . . . 56, 57, 58
1:12 . . . . 62, 63
4:15, 16 61

II Peter

1:20-21 45
1:21 . . . . 1, 50, 139
3:5 . . . . 32, 33

I John

1:1, 3 91

I John

1:2 92
1:3 . . . . 103, 104
1:4 . . . . 92, 105
1:5 . . . . 92, 105
1:5—2:6 106
1:6—2:2 106
2:1 . . . . 92, 105, 106
2:1, 18, 28 108
2:3-6 106
2:7-8 92
2:7, 8 106
2:7—2:17 106
2:11 110
2:11-15 112
2:12-14 . . . . 92, 106, 107, 110,
111, 112
2:13 109
2:15 110
2:18—2:27 106
2:21 . . . . 92, 106
2:26 . . . . 92, 106
3:11, 12 44
3:12 . . . . 32, 42
4:8-10 215
5:13 . . . . 92, 103, 104
5:21 108

II John

Vs. 1 113
Vss. 5, 6 . . . . 93, 114
Vs. 7 114
Vs. 12 93
Vs. 13 114

III John

Vss. 1, 9, 13 93
Vs. 9 115

Revelation

4:1-3 14
4:11 32
22:1-3 39
22:2, 3, 7, 14 32
22:14 39

351